CoffeeScript Application Development Cookbook

Over 90 hands-on recipes to help you develop engaging applications using CoffeeScript

Mike Hatfield

BIRMINGHAM - MUMBAI

CoffeeScript Application Development Cookbook

First published: March 2015

Production reference: 1260315

Published by Packt Publishing Ltd.
Livery Place
35 Livery Street
Birmingham B3 2PB, UK.

ISBN 978-1-78328-969-1

www.packtpub.com

Cover image by Jason Hatfield (theproductions@hotmail.com)

Credits

Author
Mike Hatfield

Reviewers
Becker

Paul Jensen

Alexey Smirnov

Commissioning Editor
Martin Bell

Acquisition Editor
Rebecca Youé

Content Development Editor
Ajinkya Paranjape

Technical Editors
Mrunal M. Chavan

Dennis John

Tanmayee Patil

Shiny Poojary

Copy Editors
Karuna Narayanan

Adithi Shetty

Project Coordinator
Harshal Ved

Proofreaders
Simran Bhogal

Maria Gould

Paul Hindle

Indexer
Monica Ajmera Mehta

Graphics
Abhinash Sahu

Production Coordinator
Conidon Miranda

Cover Work
Conidon Miranda

About the Author

Mike Hatfield has over 25 years of experience in developing custom business solutions for a variety of clients and industries. With a focus on the ever-expanding Web, Mike has crafted hundreds of web-based applications while spending the last couple of years developing business solutions for the mobile web.

He is the chief technology officer at Nicom IT Solutions Inc., a large independent IT consulting firm based in Halifax, Canada. As the CTO, Mike remains on the lookout for emerging trends in the development industry to identify new opportunities for his clients.

With his wife, Tracy, and their three children, Chris, Jason, and Jennifer, he lives a quiet suburban life while continually learning new technologies and satisfying his love of horror movies.

As a first-time author, my wife's support has played an integral part in helping me see this book through to the end. Thank you Tracy, I could not have done it without you.

About the Reviewers

Becker is a software engineer with expertise in the Ruby ecosystem. Passionate about building products people love from the ground up, he can usually be found working with a small team at a local start-up doing what he does best: writing code and making espresso! Always open to learning new tools and technologies, Becker has become particularly enamored with CoffeeScript based on its intuitive and clean structure and ease of use. In his mind, CoffeeScript and Ruby are a perfect pairing for happy development! Becker lives with his family in Seattle, Washington.

He has also a worked on *CoffeeScript Application Development, Packt Publishing* (https://www.packtpub.com/web-development/coffeescript-application-development).

Paul Jensen is the founder of Anephenix. He is also the lead developer of the SocketStream web framework and the creator of Dashku, a real-time dashboard application.

Alexey Smirnov works as a software engineer in a cloud computing start-up company, iRONYUN. He is broadly interested in web frameworks as well as iOS application development. In his spare time, he builds websites for nonprofit organizations. Alexey got his master's degree in computer science from Stony Brook University, USA.

www.PacktPub.com

Support files, eBooks, discount offers, and more

For support files and downloads related to your book, please visit www.PacktPub.com.

Did you know that Packt offers eBook versions of every book published, with PDF and ePub files available? You can upgrade to the eBook version at www.PacktPub.com and as a print book customer, you are entitled to a discount on the eBook copy. Get in touch with us at service@packtpub.com for more details.

At www.PacktPub.com, you can also read a collection of free technical articles, sign up for a range of free newsletters and receive exclusive discounts and offers on Packt books and eBooks.

https://www2.packtpub.com/books/subscription/packtlib

Do you need instant solutions to your IT questions? PacktLib is Packt's online digital book library. Here, you can search, access, and read Packt's entire library of books.

Why Subscribe?

▶ Fully searchable across every book published by Packt

▶ Copy and paste, print, and bookmark content

▶ On demand and accessible via a web browser

Free Access for Packt account holders

If you have an account with Packt at www.PacktPub.com, you can use this to access PacktLib today and view 9 entirely free books. Simply use your login credentials for immediate access.

Table of Contents

Preface

In my nearly 20 years of developing custom software solutions, nothing has had as great an impact on our industry or society as the Internet. Today, it would be difficult to imagine a world without HTML, CSS, and JavaScript. When I developed my first web-based application using JavaScript with Netscape Navigator in the mid 1990s, little did I know that we were in the early days of a software revolution.

Skip ahead nearly two decades and JavaScript has become one of the most widely supported programming languages in the world. Unfortunately, little has changed with JavaScript in this time and it is plagued with gotchas that can make developing a pure JavaScript system challenging. Enter CoffeeScript.

CoffeeScript provides us with a better approach to develop our applications that not only helps us to avoid these pitfalls, but also allows us to be more productive while still being able to take advantage of the large JavaScript ecosystem.

This book is a practical guide, filled with many step-by-step examples of using CoffeeScript for all aspects of building our software.

We will begin by looking at the fundamentals and getting our tools ready to be productive CoffeeScript developers. Next, we will use CoffeeScript to create our application layers, including the user interface, database, and backend services layer. After that, we will investigate various options to test and host our applications. Finally, we will look at ways CoffeeScript can be used by the DevOps to help automate their day-to-day tasks.

What this book covers

Chapter 1, Getting Ready, introduces CoffeeScript and lays the foundation to use CoffeeScript to develop all aspects of modern cloud-based applications.

Chapter 2, Starting with the Basics, covers using CoffeeScript with strings, numbers, dates, arrays, and classes.

Chapter 3, Creating Client Applications, demonstrates using CoffeeScript with various UI libraries and frameworks, including jQuery, Backbone, Angular, and Socket.IO.

Chapter 4, Using Kendo UI for Desktop and Mobile Applications, demonstrates how to use CoffeeScript with Telerik's open source Kendo UI Core framework to create both desktop and mobile applications.

Chapter 5, Going Native with Cordova, demonstrates how to use Apache Cordova with CoffeeScript to create native applications that can access native device features such as camera, geolocation, and contacts and be deployed to physical hardware.

Chapter 6, Working with Databases, covers various database technologies, including SQLite, Redis, MongoDB, and CouchDB, and how CoffeeScript can be used with each technology to perform create, read, update, and delete operations.

Chapter 7, Building Application Services, dives into the aspects of building the backend services needed by our application with a look at building RESTful services, working with Base64 encoding, and using domain name services to do DNS and reverse DNS lookups.

Chapter 8, Using External Services, examines ways to use existing services to send text messages and e-mails, use the Amazon cloud storage, and transfer files via FTP.

Chapter 9, Testing Our Applications, is dedicated to using CoffeeScript to test our applications using test frameworks such as Jasmine, Mocha, and Zombie as well as creating mocks using Persona.

Chapter 10, Hosting Our Web Applications, explains how to prepare your application for deployment using Grunt, and how to deploy to popular cloud hosting solutions such as Heroku and Windows Azure.

Chapter 11, Scripting for DevOps, examines ways that CoffeeScript can be used to help with day-to-day operation tasks such as working with files and directories, CSV and fixed-width data files, generating PDF files, and formatting data for output.

What you need for this book

To use the code in this book, you will need a code editor of your choice, a web browser, and an Internet connection to download Node packages and other libraries or frameworks.

Who this book is for

If you enjoy developing applications that can be run on desktop, tablet, and mobile devices without needing to learn platform-specific languages, this is the book for you.

Conventions

In this book, you will find a number of styles of text that distinguish between different kinds of information. Here are some examples of these styles, and an explanation of their meaning.

Code words in text, database table names, folder names, filenames, file extensions, pathnames, dummy URLs, user input, and Twitter handles are shown as follows: "In this example we will demonstrate the use of `spawn()` to execute a CoffeeScript statement."

A block of code is set as follows:

```
var multiply = function(a, b) {
  return a * b;
};
```

When we wish to draw your attention to a particular part of a code block, the relevant lines or items are set in bold:

```
if value % 2 is 0 then console.log 'Value is even'
```

Any command-line input or output is written as follows:

```
coffee -c -m counting.coffee
```

New terms and **important words** are shown in bold. Words that you see on the screen, in menus or dialog boxes for example, appear in the text like this: "Click on the **Tools** menu and select the **Extensions and Updates** menu option."

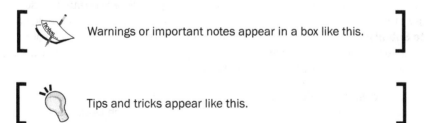

> Warnings or important notes appear in a box like this.

> Tips and tricks appear like this.

Reader feedback

Feedback from our readers is always welcome. Let us know what you think about this book—what you liked or may have disliked. Reader feedback is important for us to develop titles that you really get the most out of.

To send us general feedback, simply send an e-mail to `feedback@packtpub.com`, and mention the book title via the subject of your message.

If there is a topic that you have expertise in and you are interested in either writing or contributing to a book, see our author guide on `www.packtpub.com/authors`.

Customer support

Now that you are the proud owner of a Packt book, we have a number of things to help you to get the most from your purchase.

Downloading the example code

You can download the example code files for all Packt books you have purchased from your account at `http://www.packtpub.com`. If you purchased this book elsewhere, you can visit `http://www.packtpub.com/support` and register to have the files e-mailed directly to you.

Errata

Although we have taken every care to ensure the accuracy of our content, mistakes do happen. If you find a mistake in one of our books—maybe a mistake in the text or the code—we would be grateful if you would report this to us. By doing so, you can save other readers from frustration and help us improve subsequent versions of this book. If you find any errata, please report them by visiting `http://www.packtpub.com/submit-errata`, selecting your book, clicking on the **Errata Submission Form** link, and entering the details of your errata. Once your errata are verified, your submission will be accepted and the errata will be uploaded on our website, or added to any list of existing errata, under the Errata section of that title.

To view the previously submitted errata, go to `https://www.packtpub.com/books/content/support` and enter the name of the book in the search field. The required information will appear under the **Errata** section.

Piracy

Piracy of copyright material on the Internet is an ongoing problem across all media. At Packt, we take the protection of our copyright and licenses very seriously. If you come across any illegal copies of our works, in any form, on the Internet, please provide us with the location address or website name immediately so that we can pursue a remedy.

Please contact us at copyright@packtpub.com with a link to the suspected pirated material.

We appreciate your help in protecting our authors, and our ability to bring you valuable content.

Questions

You can contact us at questions@packtpub.com if you are having a problem with any aspect of the book, and we will do our best to address it.

1
Getting Ready

In this chapter, we will cover the following topics:

- ▶ Configuring your environment and tools
- ▶ Configuring Sublime Text
- ▶ Configuring Visual Studio
- ▶ A quick dive into CoffeeScript
- ▶ Debugging CoffeeScript using source maps
- ▶ Debugging CoffeeScript with Node Inspector

Introduction

We are living in a time where JavaScript is becoming the most widely-used programming language in the world, even though it is not a language without its faults.

With its rise in popularity, JavaScript has become a legitimate option to develop all aspects of modern applications, applications that comprise a rich HTML/CSS/JavaScript client that communicates with backend services via AJAX. These applications can be run on desktops and mobile platforms as websites, mobile web, or hybrid applications using a native wrapper such as Apache Cordova / Adobe PhoneGap.

Node.js has helped JavaScript reach well beyond the boundaries of the web browser and into our operating systems themselves.

 You might be surprised to know that Microsoft Windows has shipped with a JavaScript execution engine called **Windows Script Host** since Windows 98.

JavaScript, though very successful, can be a difficult language to work with. JavaScript was designed by Brendan Eich in a mere 10 days in 1995 while working at Netscape. As a result, some might claim that JavaScript is not as well rounded as some other languages, a point well illustrated by Douglas Crockford in his book titled *JavaScript: The Good Parts, O'Reilly Media*.

These pitfalls found in the JavaScript language led Jeremy Ashkenas to create CoffeeScript, a language that attempts to expose the good parts of JavaScript in a simple way. CoffeeScript compiles into JavaScript and helps us avoid the bad parts of JavaScript.

There are many reasons to use CoffeeScript as your development language of choice. Some of these reasons include:

- CoffeeScript helps protect us from the bad parts of JavaScript by creating function closures that isolate our code from the global namespace by reducing the curly braces and semicolon clutter and by helping tame JavaScript's notorious `this` keyword
- CoffeeScript helps us be more productive by providing features such as list comprehensions, classes with inheritance, and many others
- Properly written CoffeeScript also helps us write code that is more readable and can be more easily maintained

As Jeremy Ashkenas says:

> *"CoffeeScript is just JavaScript."*

We can use CoffeeScript when working with the large ecosystem of JavaScript libraries and frameworks on all aspects of our applications, including those listed in the following table:

Part	Some options
User interfaces	UI frameworks including jQuery, Backbone.js, AngularJS, and Kendo UI
Databases	Node.js drivers to access SQLite, Redis, MongoDB, and CouchDB
Internal/external services	Node.js with **Node Package Manager** (**NPM**) packages to create internal services and interfacing with external services
Testing	Unit and end-to-end testing with Jasmine, Qunit, integration testing with Zombie, and mocking with Persona
Hosting	Easy API and application hosting with Heroku and Windows Azure
Tooling	Create scripts to automate routine tasks and using Grunt

We will look at each of these in depth throughout this book.

Configuring your environment and tools

One significant aspect to being a productive CoffeeScript developer is having a proper development environment. This environment typically consists of the following:

- ▸ Node.js and the NPM
- ▸ CoffeeScript
- ▸ Code editor
- ▸ Debugger

In this recipe, we will look at installing and configuring the base components and tools necessary to develop CoffeeScript applications.

Getting ready

In this section, we will install the software necessary to develop applications with CoffeeScript.

One of the appealing aspects of developing applications using CoffeeScript is that it is well supported on Mac, Windows, and Linux machines. To get started, you need only a PC and an Internet connection.

How to do it...

CoffeeScript runs on top of Node.js—the event-driven, non-blocking I/O platform built on Chrome's JavaScript runtime. If you do not have Node.js installed, you can download an installation package for your Mac OS X, Linux, and Windows machines from the start page of the Node.js website (`http://nodejs.org/`).

To begin, install Node.js using an official prebuilt installer; it will also install the NPM.

Next, we will use NPM to install CoffeeScript. Open a terminal or command window and enter the following command:

```
npm install -g coffee-script
```

This will install the necessary files needed to work with CoffeeScript, including the `coffee` command that provides an interactive **Read Evaluate Print Loop** (**REPL**)—a command to execute CoffeeScript files and a compiler to generate JavaScript.

It is important to use the `-g` option when installing CoffeeScript, as this installs the CoffeeScript package as a global NPM module. This will add the necessary commands to our path.

On some Windows machines, you might need to add the NPM binary directory to your path. You can do this by editing the environment variables and appending `;%APPDATA%\npm` to the end of the system's `PATH` variable.

Configuring Sublime Text

What you use to edit code can be a very personal choice, as you, like countless others, might use the tools dictated by your team or manager. Fortunately, most popular editing tools either support CoffeeScript out of the box or can be easily extended by installing add-ons, packages, or extensions.

In this recipe, we will look at adding CoffeeScript support to Sublime Text and Visual Studio.

Getting ready

This section assumes that you have Sublime Text or Visual Studio installed.

Sublime Text is a very popular text editor that is geared to working with code and projects. You can download a fully functional evaluation version from `http://www.sublimetext.com`. If you find it useful and decide to continue to use it, you will be encouraged to purchase a license, but there is currently no enforced time limit.

How to do it...

Sublime Text does not support CoffeeScript out of the box. Thankfully, a package manager exists for Sublime Text; this package manager provides access to hundreds of extension packages, including ones that provide helpful and productive tools to work with CoffeeScript.

Sublime Text does not come with this package manager, but it can be easily added by following the instructions on the Package Control website at `https://sublime.wbond.net/installation`.

With Package Control installed, you can easily install the CoffeeScript packages that are available using the **Package Control** option under the **Preferences** menu. Select the **Install Package** option.

You can also access this command by pressing *Ctrl + Shift + P*, and in the command list that appears, start typing `install`. This will help you find the `Install Package` command quickly.

To install the CoffeeScript package, open the **Install Package** window and enter `CoffeeScript`. This will display the CoffeeScript-related packages. We will use the **Better CoffeeScript** package:

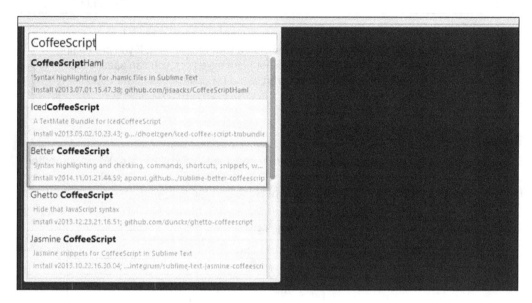

As you can see, the CoffeeScript package includes syntax highlighting, commands, shortcuts, snippets, and compilation.

How it works...

In this section, we will explain the different keyboard shortcuts and code snippets available with the Better CoffeeScript package for Sublime.

Commands

You can run the desired command by entering the command into the Sublime command pallet or by pressing the related keyboard shortcut. Remember to press *Ctrl + Shift + P* to display the command pallet window. Some useful CoffeeScript commands include the following:

Command	Keyboard shortcut	Description
`Coffee: Check Syntax`	*Alt + Shift + S*	This checks the syntax of the file you are editing or the currently selected code. The result will display in the status bar at the bottom.
`Coffee: Compile File`	*Alt + Shift + C*	This compiles the file being edited into JavaScript.
`Coffee: Run Script`	*Alt + Shift + R*	This executes the selected code and displays a buffer of the output.

 The keyboard shortcuts are associated with the file type. If you are editing a new CoffeeScript file that has not been saved yet, you can specify the file type by choosing **CoffeeScript** in the list of file types in the bottom-left corner of the screen.

Snippets

Snippets allow you to use short tokens that are recognized by Sublime Text. When you enter the code and press the *Tab* key, Sublime Text will automatically expand the snippet into the full form. Some useful CoffeeScript code snippets include the following:

Token	Expands to
`log [Tab]`	`console.log`

`cla`	`class Name`
	`    constructor: (arguments) ->`
	`        # ...`

`forin`	`for i in array` `    # ...`
`if`	`if condition` `    # ...`

`ifel`	`if condition`
	`    # ...`
	`else`
	`    # ...`

`swi`	`switch object`
	`    when value`
	`        # ...`

Token	Expands to

`try`	`try`
	`    #  ...`
	`catch e`
	`    #  ...`

 The snippets are associated with the file type. If you are editing a new CoffeeScript file that has not been saved yet, you can specify the file type by selecting **CoffeeScript** in the list of file types in the bottom-left corner of the screen.

Configuring Visual Studio

In this recipe, we will demonstrate how to add CoffeeScript support to Visual Studio.

Getting ready

If you are on the Windows platform, you can use Microsoft's Visual Studio software. You can download Microsoft's free Express edition (Express 2013 for Web) from `http://www.microsoft.com/express`.

How to do it...

If you are a Visual Studio user, Version 2010 and above can work quite effectively with CoffeeScript through the use of Visual Studio extensions.

If you are doing any form of web development with Visual Studio, the Web Essentials extension is a must-have.

To install Web Essentials, perform the following steps:

1. Launch Visual Studio.
2. Click on the **Tools** menu and select the **Extensions and Updates** menu option. This will display the **Extensions and Updates** window (shown in the next screenshot).
3. Select **Online** in the tree on the left-hand side to display the most popular downloads.
4. Select **Web Essentials 2012** from the list of available packages and then click on the **Download** button. This will download the package and install it automatically.
5. Once the installation is finished, restart Visual Studio by clicking on the **Restart Now** button.

You will likely find **Web Essentials 2012** ranked highly in the list of **Most Popular** packages. If you do not see it, you can search for Web Essentials using the **Search** box in the top-right corner of the window.

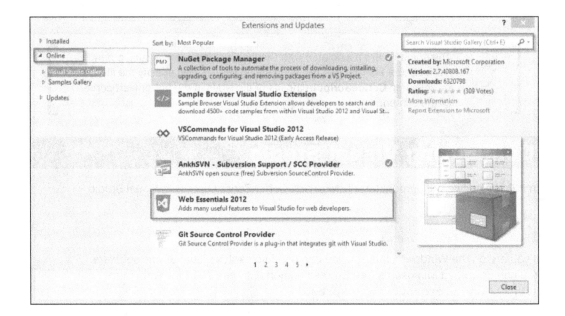

Once installed, the Web Essentials package provides many web development productivity features, including CSS helpers, tools to work with Less CSS, enhancements to work with JavaScript, and, of course, a set of CoffeeScript helpers.

To add a new CoffeeScript file to your project, you can navigate to **File | New Item** or press *Ctrl + Shift + A*. This will display the **Add New Item** dialog, as seen in the following screenshot. Under the **Web** templates, you will see a new **CoffeeScript File** option. Select this option and give it a filename, as shown here:

When we have our CoffeeScript file open, Web Essentials will display the file in a split-screen editor. We can edit our code in the left-hand pane, while Web Essentials displays a live preview of the JavaScript code that will be generated for us.

The Web Essentials CoffeeScript compiler will create two JavaScript files each time we save our CoffeeScript file: a basic JavaScript file and a minified version. For example, if we save a CoffeeScript file named `employee.coffee`, the compiler will create `employee.js` and `employee.min.js` files.

> Though I have only described two editors to work with CoffeeScript files, there are CoffeeScript packages and plugins for most popular text editors, including Emacs, Vim, TextMate, and WebMatrix.

A quick dive into CoffeeScript

In this recipe, we will take a quick look at the CoffeeScript language and command line.

How to do it...

CoffeeScript is a highly expressive programming language that does away with much of the ceremony required by JavaScript. It uses whitespace to define blocks of code and provides shortcuts for many of the programming constructs found in JavaScript.

For example, we can declare variables and functions without the `var` keyword:

```
firstName = 'Mike'
```

We can define functions using the following syntax:

```
multiply = (a, b) ->
  a * b
```

Here, we defined a function named `multiply`. It takes two arguments, `a` and `b`. Inside the function, we multiplied the two values. Note that there is no `return` statement. CoffeeScript will always return the value of the last expression that is evaluated inside a function.

The preceding function is equivalent to the following JavaScript snippet:

```
var multiply = function(a, b) {
  return a * b;
};
```

It's worth noting that the CoffeeScript code is only 28 characters long, whereas the JavaScript code is 50 characters long; that's 44 percent less code.

We can call our `multiply` function in the following way:

```
result = multiply 4, 7
```

In CoffeeScript, using parenthesis is optional when calling a function with parameters, as you can see in our function call. However, note that parenthesis are required when executing a function without parameters, as shown in the following example:

```
displayGreeting = ->
  console.log 'Hello, world!'

displayGreeting()
```

In this example, we must call the `displayGreeting()` function with parenthesis.

You might also wish to use parenthesis to make your code more readable. Just because they are optional, it doesn't mean you should sacrifice the readability of your code to save a couple of keystrokes. For example, in the following code, we used parenthesis even though they are not required:

```
$('div.menu-item').removeClass 'selected'
```

Like functions, we can define JavaScript literal objects without the need for curly braces, as seen in the following `employee` object:

```
employee =
  firstName: 'Mike'
  lastName: 'Hatfield'
  salesYtd: 13204.65
```

Notice that in our object definition, we also did not need to use a comma to separate our properties.

CoffeeScript supports the common `if` conditional as well as an `unless` conditional inspired by the Ruby language. Like Ruby, CoffeeScript also provides English keywords for logical operations such as `is`, `isnt`, `or`, and `and`. The following example demonstrates the use of these keywords:

```
isEven = (value) ->
  if value % 2 is 0
    'is'
  else
    'is not'

console.log '3 ' + isEven(3) + ' even'
```

In the preceding code, we have an `if` statement to determine whether a value is even or not. If the value is even, the remainder of `value % 2` will be 0. We used the `is` keyword to make this determination.

JavaScript has a nasty behavior when determining equality between two values. In other languages, the double equal sign is used, such as `value == 0`. In JavaScript, the double equal operator will use type coercion when making this determination. This means that `0 == '0'`; in fact, `0 == ''` is also true.

CoffeeScript avoids this using JavaScript's triple equals (`===`) operator. This evaluation compares value and type such that `0 === '0'` will be false.

We can use `if` and `unless` as expression modifiers as well. They allow us to tack `if` and `unless` at the end of a statement to make simple one-liners.

For example, we can so something like the following:

```
console.log 'Value is even' if value % 2 is 0
```

Alternatively, we can have something like this:

```
console.log 'Value is odd' unless value % 2 is 0
```

We can also use the `if...then` combination for a one-liner `if` statement, as shown in the following code:

```
if value % 2 is 0 then console.log 'Value is even'
```

CoffeeScript has a `switch` control statement that performs certain actions based on a list of possible values. The following lines of code show a simple `switch` statement with four branching conditions:

```
switch task
  when 1
    console.log 'Case 1'
  when 2
    console.log 'Case 2'
  when 3, 4, 5
    console.log 'Case 3, 4, 5'
  else
    console.log 'Default case'
```

In this sample, if the value of a task is 1, case 1 will be displayed. If the value of a task is 3, 4, or 5, then case 3, 4, or 5 is displayed, respectively. If there are no matching values, we can use an optional `else` condition to handle any exceptions.

If your `switch` statements have short operations, you can turn them into one-liners, as shown in the following code:

```
switch value
  when 1 then console.log 'Case 1'
  when 2 then console.log 'Case 2'
  when 3, 4, 5 then console.log 'Case 3, 4, 5'
  else console.log 'Default case'
```

CoffeeScript has a number of other productive shortcuts that we will cover in depth in *Chapter 2, Starting with the Basics*.

CoffeeScript provides a number of syntactic shortcuts to help us be more productive while writing more expressive code. Some people have claimed that this can sometimes make our applications more difficult to read, which will, in turn, make our code less maintainable. The key to highly readable and maintainable code is to use a consistent style when coding. I recommend that you follow the guidance provided by Polar in their CoffeeScript style guide at `http://github.com/polarmobile/coffeescript-style-guide`.

There's more...

With CoffeeScript installed, you can use the `coffee` command-line utility to execute CoffeeScript files, compile CoffeeScript files into JavaScript, or run an interactive CoffeeScript command shell.

In this section, we will look at the various options available when using the CoffeeScript command-line utility.

We can see a list of available commands by executing the following command in a command or terminal window:

```
coffee --help
```

This will produce the following output:

```
Usage: coffee [options] path/to/script.coffee -- [args]

If called without options, `coffee` will run your script.

  -b, --bare          compile without a top-level function wrapper
  -c, --compile       compile to JavaScript and save as .js files
  -e, --eval          pass a string from the command line as input
  -h, --help          display this help message
  -i, --interactive   run an interactive CoffeeScript REPL
  -j, --join          concatenate the source CoffeeScript before compiling
  -m, --map           generate source map and save as .js.map files
  -n, --nodes         print out the parse tree that the parser produces
      --nodejs        pass options directly to the "node" binary
      --no-header     suppress the "Generated by" header
  -o, --output        set the output directory for compiled JavaScript
  -p, --print         print out the compiled JavaScript
  -s, --stdio         listen for and compile scripts over stdio
  -l, --literate      treat stdio as literate style coffee-script
  -t, --tokens        print out the tokens that the lexer/rewriter produce
  -v, --version       display the version number
  -w, --watch         watch scripts for changes and rerun commands
```

As you can see, the `coffee` command-line utility provides a number of options. Of these, the most common ones include the following:

Option	Argument	Example	Description
None	None	`coffee`	This launches the REPL-interactive shell.
None	Filename	`coffee sample.coffee`	This command will execute the CoffeeScript file.
`-c, --compile`	Filename	`coffee -c sample.coffee`	This command will compile the CoffeeScript file into a JavaScript file with the same base name,; `sample.js`, as in our example.
`-i, --interactive`		`coffee -i`	This command will also launch the REPL-interactive shell.
`-m, --map`	Filename	`coffee--m sample.coffee`	This command generates a source map with the same base name, `sample.js.map`, as in our example.
`-p, --print`	Filename	`coffee -p sample.coffee`	This command will display the compiled output or compile errors to the terminal window.
`-v, --version`	None	`coffee -v`	This command will display the correct version of CoffeeScript.
`-w, --watch`	Filename	`coffee -w -c sample.coffee`	This command will watch for file changes, and with each change, the requested action will be performed. In our example, our `sample.coffee` file will be compiled each time we save it.

The CoffeeScript REPL

As we have been, CoffeeScript has an interactive shell that allows us to execute CoffeeScript commands. In this section, we will learn how to use the REPL shell. The REPL shell can be an excellent way to get familiar with CoffeeScript.

To launch the CoffeeScript REPL, open a command window and execute the `coffee` command.

This will start the interactive shell and display the following prompt:

```
02:47:22 ~$ coffee
coffee>
```

In the `coffee>` prompt, we can assign values to variables, create functions, and evaluate results.

When we enter an expression and press the return key, it is immediately evaluated and the value is displayed.

For example, if we enter the expression `x = 4` and press return, we would see what is shown in the following screenshot:

```
03:04:05 ~$ coffee
coffee> x = 4
4
coffee>
```

This did two things. First, it created a new variable named `x` and assigned the value of `4` to it. Second, it displayed the result of the command.

Next, enter `timesSeven = (value) -> value * 7` and press return:

```
coffee> timesSeven = (value) -> value * 7
[Function]
coffee>
```

You can see that the result of this line was the creation of a new function named `timesSeven()`.

We can call our new function now:

```
coffee> timesSeven 35
245
coffee>
```

By default, the REPL shell will evaluate each expression when you press the return key. What if we want to create a function or expression that spans multiple lines? We can enter the REPL multiline mode by pressing *Ctrl + V*. This will change our `coffee>` prompt to a `------>` prompt. This allows us to enter an expression that spans multiple lines, such as the following function:

```
------> isEvenOrOdd = (value) ->
.......     if value % 2 is 0
.......       'even'
.......     else
.......       'odd'
.......
```

When we are finished with our multiline expression, press *Ctrl + V* again to have the expression evaluated. We can then call our new function:

```
[Function]
coffee> isEvenOrOdd 45
'odd'
coffee> isEvenOrOdd 54
'even'
coffee>
```

The CoffeeScript REPL offers some handy helpers such as expression history and tab completion.

Pressing the up arrow key on your keyboard will circulate through the expressions we previously entered.

Using the *Tab* key will autocomplete our function or variable name. For example, with the `isEvenOrOdd()` function, we can enter `isEven` and press *Tab* to have the REPL complete the function name for us.

Debugging CoffeeScript using source maps

If you have spent any time in the JavaScript community, you would have, no doubt, seen some discussions or rants regarding the weak debugging story for CoffeeScript. In fact, this is often a top argument some give for not using CoffeeScript at all. In this recipe, we will examine how to debug our CoffeeScript application using source maps.

Getting ready

The problem in debugging CoffeeScript stems from the fact that CoffeeScript compiles into JavaScript which is what the browser executes. If an error arises, the line that has caused the error sometimes cannot be traced back to the CoffeeScript source file very easily. Also, the error message is sometimes confusing, making troubleshooting that much more difficult.

Recent developments in the web development community have helped improve the debugging experience for CoffeeScript by making use of a concept known as a **source map**. In this section, we will demonstrate how to generate and use source maps to help make our CoffeeScript debugging easier.

To use source maps, you need only a base installation of CoffeeScript.

How to do it...

You can generate a source map for your CoffeeScript code using the -m option on the CoffeeScript command:

```
coffee -m -c employee.coffee
```

How it works...

Source maps provide information used by browsers such as Google Chrome that tell the browser how to map a line from the compiled JavaScript code back to its origin in the CoffeeScript file.

Source maps allow you to place breakpoints in your CoffeeScript file and analyze variables and execute functions in your CoffeeScript module. This creates a JavaScript file called employee.js and a source map called employee.js.map.

If you look at the last line of the generated employee.js file, you will see the reference to the source map:

```
//# sourceMappingURL=employee.js.map
```

Google Chrome uses this JavaScript comment to load the source map.

The following screenshot demonstrates an active breakpoint and console in Goggle Chrome:

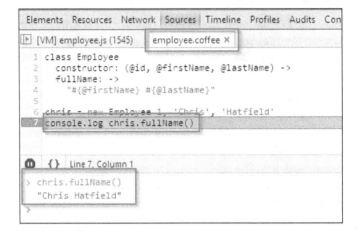

Debugging CoffeeScript using Node Inspector

Source maps and Chrome's developer tools can help troubleshoot our CoffeeScript that is destined for the Web. In this recipe, we will demonstrate how to debug CoffeeScript that is designed to run on the server.

Getting ready

Begin by installing the Node Inspector NPM module with the following command:

```
npm install -g node-inspector
```

How to do it...

To use Node Inspector, we will use the `coffee` command to compile the CoffeeScript code we wish to debug and generate the source map.

In our example, we will use the following simple source code in a file named `counting.coffee`:

```
for i in [1..10]
  if i % 2 is 0
    console.log "#{i} is even!"
  else
    console.log "#{i} is odd!"
```

To use Node Inspector, we will compile our file and use the source map parameter with the following command:

```
coffee -c -m counting.coffee
```

Next, we will launch Node Inspector with the following command:

```
node-debug counting.js
```

How it works...

When we run Node Inspector, it does two things.

First, it launches the Node debugger. This is a debugging service that allows us to step through code, hit line breaks, and evaluate variables. This is a built-in service that comes with Node. Second, it launches an HTTP handler and opens a browser that allows us to use Chrome's built-in debugging tools to use break points, step over and into code, and evaluate variables.

Node Inspector works well using source maps. This allows us to see our native CoffeeScript code and is an effective tool to debug server-side code.

The following screenshot displays our Chrome window with an active break point. In the local variables tool window on the right-hand side, you can see that the current value of i is 2:

The highlighted line in the preceding screenshot depicts the log message.

2
Starting with the Basics

In this chapter, we will cover the following recipes:

- ▶ Working with strings
- ▶ Working with numbers
- ▶ Working with dates and times
- ▶ Working with arrays
- ▶ Working with classes
- ▶ Dealing with the this keyword

Introduction

In this chapter, you will learn how to use CoffeeScript when performing common programming tasks with primitive types, collections, and classes.

We will wrap up the chapter by looking at how to deal with this in the context of classes and functions binding with instantiated objects.

Working with strings

In this section, we will look at the various aspects of working with strings or text-based data.

String interpolation

In this section, we will demonstrate the CoffeeScript feature of string interpolation.

Getting ready

In JavaScript, creating strings that include variable values involves concatenating the various pieces together. Consider the following example:

```
var lineCount = countLinesInFile('application.log');
var message = "The file has a total of " + lineCount + " lines";
console.log(message);
```

This can get pretty messy and CoffeeScript provides an elegant solution to avoid this called string interpolation.

How to do it...

CoffeeScript provides the ability to perform string interpolation by using double quoted strings containing one or more #{} delimiters.

The preceding example can be written as follows:

```
lineCount = countLinesInFile 'application.log'
message = "The file has a total of #{lineCount} lines"
console.log message
```

This not only requires less typing, but it can also be easier to read.

How it works...

String interpolation will evaluate the expression inside the delimiter and its placeholder is replaced by the expression's result.

Consider the following simple expression:

```
console.log "Simple expressions are evaluated: 5 x 6 = #{ 5 * 6 }"
```

The output of the preceding expression will be as follows:

```
Simple expressions are evaluated: 5 x 6 = 30
```

String interpolation can also evaluate complex expressions as follows:

```
num = 23
console.log "num is #{ if num % 2 is 0 then 'even' else 'odd' }."
```

The output of the preceding expression will be as follows:

```
num is odd.
```

In the two previous examples, we evaluated expressions inside the string for demonstration only. It is generally discouraged and it is almost always better to separate that logic into its own method. When in doubt, pull it out.

There's more...

String interpolation works by evaluating the expression inside the #{} delimiter and having JavaScript coerce the value into a string. We can control this on our own objects by creating a toString() function that will be used by the coercion mechanism. By default, coercion for an Object will display [object Object].

In the following example, we create an Employee class with a toString() function to override the default coercion value:

```
class Employee
  constructor: (@firstName, @lastName, @empNum) ->
  toString: ->
    return "#{@firstName} #{@lastName} (No: #{@empNum})"
```

We can now use an Employee instance with string interpolation and receive a more valuable result:

```
employee = new Employee('Tracy', 'Ouellette', 876)
console.log "Employee Info: #{employee}"
```

Its output will be:

```
Employee Info: Tracy Ouellette (No: 876)
```

Wrapping text

When working with text, you may need to wrap a long piece of text over a number of lines in order to not exceed the maximum width.

In this section, we will see how to accomplish this using a **regular expression**.

 Regular expressions are patterns to be matched against strings and can be used to perform pattern matching, string manipulations, or testing. Regular expressions have been highly optimized and perform better than other string manipulations.

How to do it...

In the following steps, we create a `wrapText()` function that uses a regular expression to split a piece of text at a specified maximum length:

1. Define the function as follows:

   ```
   wrapText = (text, maxLineWidth = 80, lineEnding = '\n') ->
   ```

2. Create a regular expression instance:

   ```
   regex = RegExp \
     ".{1,#{maxLineWidth}}(\\s|$)|\\S+?(\\s|$)", 'g'
   ```

3. Extract matching segments in `text`, join them with `lineEnding`, and return the result:

   ```
   text.match(regex).join lineEnding
   ```

How it works...

The `wrapText()` function takes a text parameter that represents the text data to be processed and a second optional `maxLineWidth` parameter representing the desired maximum width. The maximum width parameter will default to 80 characters if no value is passed. There is another optional parameter allowing you to specify the line ending, which defaults to a new line character.

We create a regular expression instance using the `RegExp()` constructor function passing a string interpolated value representing our expression and a modifier.

If we break the regular expression down into its basic blocks, we are requesting segments containing 1 to `maxLineWidth` characters `{1, maxLineWidth}`, separating each by a whitespace character or the end of the line `(\s|$)`. We also provide an additional rule to handle scenarios where there are no whitespace characters within 1 to `maxLineWidth`, which will break at the next available whitespace character `\S+?(\\s|$)`.

We use the `String.match()` function, which takes a regular expression and returns the segment or segments that match the expression. By default, only the first match is returned, which is not what we want in this case. We use the **g** (global) modifier when we create our `RegExp` instance, which will return all matching segments as an array.

Our function ends by calling the `Array.join()` function, which will join all of the array elements and separate each one with `lineEnding`.

To demonstrate the method in action, we call the `wrapText()` method with some sample text from Homer's Odyssey:

```
homersOdyssey = "He counted his goodly coppers and cauldrons, his
    gold and all his clothes, but there was nothing missing; still
    he kept grieving about not being in his own country, and
    wandered up and down by the shore of the sounding sea bewailing
    his hard fate. Then Minerva came up to him disguised as a young
    shepherd of delicate and princely mien, with a good cloak folded
    double about her shoulders; she had sandals on her comely feet
    and held a javelin in her hand. Ulysses was glad when he saw
    her, and went straight up to her."

console.log wrapText(homersOdyssey, 40, '<br />\n')
```

Notice that we used CoffeeScript's ability to declare a text variable that spans multiple lines. If we use single double quotes, strings that span multiple lines are joined by a space. If we wish to preserve formatting, including line breaks and indentation, we can use triple double quotes `"""`. Consider the following example:

```
title = """
<title>
    CoffeeScript Strings
</title>
"""
```

This code will produce a string such as `<title>\n     CoffeeScript Strings\n</title>`.

For the preceding example, the output is as follows:

```
He counted his goodly coppers and <br />
cauldrons, his gold and all his clothes, <br />
but there was nothing missing; still he <br />
kept grieving about not being in his own <br />
country, and wandered up and down by the <br />
shore of the sounding sea bewailing his <br />
hard fate. Then Minerva came up to him <br />
disguised as a young shepherd of <br />
delicate and princely mien, with a good <br />
cloak folded double about her shoulders; <br />
she had sandals on her comely feet and <br />
held a javelin in her hand. Ulysses was <br />
glad when he saw her, and went straight <br />
up to her.
```

See also

Our `wrapText()` method made use of a simple regular expression to split text into individual words. See the *Using regular expressions* recipe for more information on using this powerful JavaScript feature.

Truncating text

In this section, we will see how we can truncate text into the desired size without truncating the middle of words.

How to do it...

Truncating text can be handled in much the same way as we handled word wrapping:

1. Define your function:

   ```
   truncateText = (text, maxLineWidth  = 80, ellipsis = '...') ->
   ```

2. Reduce the maximum line width by the length of the ellipsis:

   ```
   maxLineWidth -= ellipsis.length
   ```

3. Create your regular expression:

   ```
   regex = RegExp \
       ".{1,#{maxLineWidth}}(\\s|$)|\\S+?(\\s|$)"
   ```

4. Return the first element of the `match()` result after it has been trimmed with the desired ellipsis:

   ```
   "#{text.match(regex)[0].trim()}#{ellipsis}"
   ```

How it works...

Our `truncateText()` function takes a text parameter representing the text data to be truncated and two optional parameters: `maxLineWidth` representing the maximum width of the text desired, and `ellipsis` representing a string to end our resultant line.

We use the same regular expression as we did in the previous *Wrapping text* recipe. In this case, however, we reduce the maximum line length by the length of the ellipsis. This will ensure that our result will not exceed the maximum line length.

Because we are not using a regular expression modifier, only the first match is returned.

Consider this example:

```
homersOdessy = 'He counted his goodly coppers and cauldrons, his gold
and all his clothes, but there was nothing missing;'

console.log truncateText homersOdessy, 30
```

The output for this code will be:

```
He counted his goodly...
```

Converting character casing

In this recipe, we will demonstrate how to convert text from one casing scheme to another:

- ▸ Sentence case, for example, *This is an example of sentence case*
- ▸ Title case, for example, *This Is an Example of Title Case*
- ▸ Pascal case, for example, *PascalCase*
- ▸ Camel case, for example, *camelCase*
- ▸ Snake case, for example, *snake_case*

How to do it...

We will define our case conversion methods as a utility module that we can use for any application:

1. Create a constant array with the list of those words that are not capitalized within titles:

   ```
   WORD_EXCEPTIONS_FOR_TITLECASE = \
     ['a','an','and','but','for','nor','or','the']
   ```

2. Create some helper methods to split words on whitespace or capitalization and another to capitalize the first letter of the word:

   ```
   capitalizeWord = (word) ->
     word[0].toUpperCase() + word[1..].toLowerCase()

   upperSplit = (item) ->
     words = []
     word = ''
   ```

```
      for char in item.split ''
        if /[A-Z]/.test char
          words.push word if word.length
          word = char
        else
          word += char

    words.push word if word.length

    return words

  splitStringIntoTokens = (text) ->
    results = []

    for token in text.split /[ _]+/
      token = token.trim()
      words = upperSplit token
      for word in words
        results.push word.toLowerCase()

    results
```

3. Create a function to return a string in title case:

```
  toTitleCase = (text, wordsToIgnore = WORD_EXCEPTIONS_FOR_
  TITLECASE) ->
    words = splitStringIntoTokens text
    words[0] = capitalizeWord words[0]
    for word, index in words[1..]
      unless word in wordsToIgnore
        words[index+1] = capitalizeWord word

    words.join ' '
```

4. Create a function to return a string in sentence case:

```
  toSentenceCase = (text) ->
    words = splitStringIntoTokens text
    words[0] = capitalizeWord words[0]
    words.join ' '
```

5. Create a function to return a string in snake case:

```
  toSnakeCase = (text) ->
    splitStringIntoTokens(text).join '_'
```

6. Create a function to return a string in Pascal case:

```
toPascalCase = (text) ->
  (capitalizeWord word for word in splitStringIntoTokens(text)).
join ''
```

7. Create a function to return a string in camel case:

```
toCamelCase = (text) ->
  text = toPascalCase text
  text[0].toLowerCase() + text[1..]
```

8. Assign your functions to the `module.exports` object so they are made available to your applications:

```
module.exports =
  toSentenceCase: toSentenceCase
  toTitleCase: toTitleCase
  toPascalCase: toPascalCase
  toCamelCase: toCamelCase
  toSnakeCase: toSnakeCase
```

How it works...

The module starts with a `capitalizeWord()` method that takes a single word as a parameter and returns the word capitalized. For example, `capitalizeWord 'hello'` returns `Hello`.

The `splitStringIntoTokens()` method is the workhorse of our module and is responsible for breaking up a string of text into various words. For sentences, this is easily accomplished by splitting the string by spaces. We also want to be able to parse text that contains Pascal and camel case words. This will allow us to convert from Pascal case to snake case, camel case, and so on. We accomplish this by passing each token (word) to the inner `upperSplit()` method, which reviews the letters of each word, looking for an uppercase value representing the start of a new word.

The `splitStringIntoTokens 'Hello world'` annotation will return an array containing two words `['hello', 'world']`. `splitStringIntoTokens 'HelloWorld'`. Notice that the words are all lowercase. This helps to normalize the tokens for later processing.

The following methods are responsible for using the individual words that have been split from the text provided and returning the text in the various casing formats. Each takes a single parameter representing the text to be parsed. The `toTitleCase()` function takes an optional array of words to ignore when performing title case conversion. If no array is provided, the default `WORD_EXCEPTIONS_FOR_TITLECASE` array is used.

We finish by exporting `toTitleCase()`, `toSentenceCase()`, `toPascalCase()`, `toCamelCase()`, and `toSnakeCase()` as the public API for our casing utility module.

The following code is a small application to demonstrate our casing module:

```
caseUtils = require './casing_utils'

console.log 'Title:', caseUtils.toTitleCase 'an author and his book'
console.log 'Sentence:', caseUtils.toSentenceCase 'this should be in
sentence case'
console.log 'Pascal:', caseUtils.toPascalCase 'this should be in
pascal case'
console.log 'Camel:', caseUtils.toCamelCase 'this should be in camel
case'
console.log 'Snake:', caseUtils.toSnakeCase 'this should be in snake
case'
```

The output for this code is as follows:

```
Title: An Author and His Book
Sentence: This should be in sentence case
Pascal: ThisShouldBeInPascalCase
Camel: thisShouldBeInCamelCase
Snake: this_should_be_in_snake_case
```

Using regular expressions

Regular expressions can be used when working with text data and provide a powerful tool to process text. This is accomplished by passing or using processing instructions to the various methods that accept regular expressions as parameters or by executing the regular expression directly.

We have already seen regular expressions used to split strings and test a value. These can be used as parameters to the split() and replace() methods. In these cases, the regular expression is used as a matcher.

How to do it...

Let's look at how we can utilize regular expressions using split(), replace(), and test():

```
# SPLIT() USING A REGULAR EXPRESSION
whiteSpaceRegex = /[\s]/

words = "A happy\tday\nis here"
console.log "Value:", words
console.log (words.split whiteSpaceRegex)
```

```
# REPLACE() USING A REGULAR EXPRESSION
phrase = 'The blue balloon is bright'
console.log "Red balloon:", (phrase.replace /blue/, 'red')

# TEST() USING A REGULAR EXPRESSING
validIpAddress = '192.168.10.24'
invalidIpAddress = '192.168-10.24'
testRegex = /\d+\.\d+\.\d+\.\d+/
console.log "#{validIpAddress} valid?", (testRegex.test
validIpAddress)
console.log "#{invalidIpAddress} valid?", (testRegex.test
invalidIpAddress)
```

How it works...

The following example uses a regular expression to split a string on whitespaces \s including spaces, tabs, newlines, and others. Note that the regular expression is enclosed in two forward slashes /.

The output for the preceding example is:

```
Value: A happy   day
is here
[ 'A', 'happy', 'day', 'is', 'here' ]
```

> Note that regular expressions can also be created using the RegExp constructor. In our example, the whiteSpaceRegex expression could have also been written as follows:
>
> ```
> whiteSpaceRegex = new RegExp '\s'
> ```

In the replace() example, we replace all instances of blue with red. This updates our phrase to The red balloon is bright.

By default, regular expressions are case sensitive. You can make the matching pattern case insensitive by adding the \i modifier. For example, "It's a Wonderful Life".replace /life/i, "Book" will return It's a Wonderful Book.

You can use the RegExp test() method to see whether a string matches the regular expression pattern. In our example, we have two IP addresses, one that is valid and one that is not. We have a pattern that represents a sequence of four numbers separated by periods. Our invalid IP address uses a hyphen.

Running the example, we have:

```
192.168.10.24 valid? true
192.168-10.24 valid? False
```

Note that our test for IP address that the IP address consists of four positive integers separated by periods. To validate that each segment is between 0 and 255, we can use the following regular expression:

```
/(25[0-5]|2[0-4][0-9]|[01]?[0-9][0-9]?)\.(25[0-
5]|2[0-4][0-9]|[01]?[0-9][0-9]?)\.(25[0-5]|2[0-4][0-
9]|[01]?[0-9][0-9]?)\.(25[0-5]|2[0-4][0-9]|[01]?[09]
[0-9]?)/
```

There's more...

There are many great online resources to learn more about regular expressions including the following:

▶   A full overview of regular expressions from the Mozilla Developer Network at `https://developer.mozilla.org/en-US/docs/Web/JavaScript/Guide/Regular_Expressions`

▶   An interactive regular expression tester at `http://regex101.com`

▶   A regular expression visualization tool at `http://www.regexper.com`

Working with numbers

This section looks at various aspects of working with numbers in CoffeeScript. All of this functionality comes from JavaScript but is made better by using CoffeeScript.

Converting between bases

JavaScript provides a `parseInt()` function that is most commonly used to convert strings to numeric values but it can also be used to convert numbers between bases in the range of base 2 to base 32. This section demonstrates converting numbers to and from base 10.

How to do it...

Let's define several base conversion methods in a utility module that we can use in our applications:

```
convertBase = (number, fromBase, toBase) ->
  value = parseInt number, fromBase
  value.toString toBase
```

```
convertToBase2 = (number, fromBase = 10) ->
  convertBase number, fromBase, 2

convertToBase10 = (number, fromBase = 2) ->
  convertBase number, fromBase, 10

convertToBase16 = (number, fromBase = 10) ->
  convertBase number, fromBase, 16

module.exports =
  convertBase: convertBase
  convertToBase2: convertToBase2
  convertToBase10: convertToBase10
  convertToBase16: convertToBase16
```

How it works...

The basic process to convert from one numeric base to another involves using `parseInt()` to get a numeric value for the base we are converting from, and then using that number's `toString()` method to return the value at the desired base.

We also created some helper methods to make our API more convenient for our users. The `convertToBase2()`, `convertToBase10()`, and `convertToBase16()` functions use CoffeeScript's default parameter feature to provide sensible defaults for the `fromBase` parameter. Helper methods like these should be all about convenience.

We can use our convenient helper methods to convert to base 2, 10, and 16. If we need to convert to any other bases, we have the general purpose `convertBase()` method.

Consider the following example:

```
bcu = require './base_conversion_utils'

console.log '153 base 10 to base 2:',
  (bcu.convertToBase2 153)
console.log '10011001 base 2 to base 10:',
  (bcu.convertToBase10 10011001)
console.log '153 base 10 to base 16:',
  (bcu.convertToBase16 153)
console.log '10011001 base 2 to base 16 from base 2:',
  (bcu.convertToBase16 10011001, 2)
console.log '153 base 13 to base 17:',
  (bcu.convertBase 153, 13, 17)
```

Its output will be:

```
153 base 10 to base 2: 10011001
10011001 base 2 to base 10: 153
153 base 10 to base 16: 99
10011001 base 2 to base 16 from base 2: 99
153 base 13 to base 17: dg
```

Generating random numbers

We can generate random numbers by using the JavaScript `Math` object. Of course, we can make some great utility functions using CoffeeScript that will make using random numbers more convenient to work with.

How to do it...

Let's define our randomization methods in a utility module that we can use with our applications:

```
getRandomNumberInRange = (minimum, maximum) ->
  length = maximum - minimum + 1
  randomValue = Math.floor (Math.random() * length)
  minimum + randomValue

getRandomNumber = (maximum) ->
  getRandomNumberInRange 1, maximum

getRandomElementFromCollection = (collection) ->
  randomIndex = getRandomNumberInRange 0, collection.length - 1
  collection[randomIndex]

module.exports =
  getRandomNumber: getRandomNumber
  getRandomNumberInRange: getRandomNumberInRange
  getRandomElementFromCollection: getRandomElementFromCollection
```

How it works...

We have three useful methods to provide randomness to our applications. We begin with a method that calculates a random number between a minimum and maximum value.

The `Math.random()` method is at the heart of our method. `Math.random()` returns a decimal number greater than or equal to zero and less than 1. The result of `Math.random()` is a decimal value with 16 digits of precision.

We normally want a whole number as our random number, so we use the `Math.floor()` method to reduce our fractional value to a whole number.

We then created two other methods that make working with our module more convenient.

The `getRandomNumber()` method is a specialized form of our more general `getRandomNumberInRange()` method for when the user wants to get a random value between 1 and some number.

The `getRandomElementFromCollection()` method takes an array and returns a random element from that array.

Consider the following example:

```
random = require './random_utils'

console.log 'Random number between 1 and 1,000:',
  (random.getRandomNumber 1000)
console.log 'Random number between 10 and 50:',
  (random.getRandomNumberInRange 10, 50)
console.log "Random element from ['Cat', 'Dog', 'Hamster']:",
  (random.getRandomElementFromCollection ['Cat', 'Dog', 'Hamster'])
```

Its output will be:

```
Random number between 1 and 1,000: 93
Random number between 10 and 50: 26
Random element from ['Cat', 'Dog', 'Hamster']: Hamster
```

Converting between degrees and radians

We commonly need to convert numeric values from one unit of measure to another. This is a great candidate for a utility module. In this section, we will look at creating utility methods to convert angles between degrees, radians, and gradians.

How to do it...

Let's define our conversion routines in a utility module we can use with our applications:

```
PI = Math.PI
DEGREES_IN_RADIAN = 180 / PI
RADIANS_IN_GRADIAN = 200 / PI

radiansToDegrees = (radians) ->
  radians * DEGREES_IN_RADIAN
```

```
radiansToGradians = (radians) ->
  radians * RADIANS_IN_GRADIAN

degreesToRadians = (degrees) ->
  degrees / DEGREES_IN_RADIAN

degreesToGradian = (degrees) ->
  radians = degreesToRadians degrees
  radiansToGradians radians

gradiansToRadians = (gradians) ->
  gradians / RADIANS_IN_GRADIAN

gradiansToDegrees = (gradians) ->
  radians = gradiansToRadians gradians
  radiansToDegrees radians

module.exports.angles =
  degreesToRadians: degreesToRadians
  degreesToGradian: degreesToGradian
  radiansToDegrees: radiansToDegrees
  radiansToGradians: radiansToGradians
  gradiansToDegrees: gradiansToDegrees
  gradiansToRadians: gradiansToRadians
```

How it works...

Our module begins by defining three constants: `PI`, `DegreesInRadians`, and
`RadiansInGradian`. `PI` is used to calculate the ratios required to convert between degrees,
radians, and gradians. The methods that follow will show you how to perform the conversions.

Notice that at the end of this module, we export our conversion methods to an object named
`angles`. This allows us to namespace our methods to convert angles. We may want to add
additional conversion methods converting temperatures, lengths, weights, speeds, and so on.

The following is a demonstration of our conversion utilities in action:

```
convUtils = require './conversion_utils'

console.log '360 deg:',
  "#{convUtils.angles.degreesToRadians 360} rad"
console.log '360 deg:',
  "#{convUtils.angles.degreesToGradian 360} grad"
console.log '6.28 rad:',
  "#{convUtils.angles.radiansToDegrees 6.28} deg"
```

```
console.log '6.28 rad:',
  "#{convUtils.angles.radiansToGradians 6.28} grad"
console.log '400 grad:',
  "#{convUtils.angles.gradiansToDegrees 400} deg"
console.log '400 grad:',
  "#{convUtils.angles.gradiansToRadians 400} rad"
```

Its output will be:

```
360 deg: 6.283185307179586 rad
360 deg: 400 grad
6.28 rad: 359.817495342157 deg
6.28 rad: 399.79721704684107 grad
400 grad: 360 deg
400 grad: 6.283185307179586 rad
```

Checking a credit card checksum

Validating credit cards might require an expensive call to a payment authorization gateway. Before we make the call for authorization, we should verify that the number is at least a valid credit card number.

We can match formats using regular expressions, but this does not give us the full picture.

Credit card numbers (Visa, MasterCard, American Express, and many others) use a formula to calculate a credit card number's check digit. If the check digit is evenly divisible by 10, the number is at least a possible number. If, on the other hand, the check digit is not evenly divisible by 10, the number is not valid, and we won't have to make our call to the payment authorization service.

How to do it...

Let's implement this process as follows:

```
reduceNumber = (number) ->
  value = 0
  digits = (Number x for x in number.toString().split '')
  value += digit for digit in digits

  if value > 9
    return reduceNumber value
  else
    return value
```

```
calculateCheckDigit = (creditCardNumber) ->
  value = 0
  index = 0
  digits = (Number x for x in creditCardNumber.split '')
  for digit in digits.reverse()
    if index % 2 is 1
      value += reduceNumber digit * 2
    else
      value += digit
    index += 1

  return value

isValidCreditCardNumber = (cardNumber) ->
  calculateCheckDigit(cardNumber) % 10 is 0
module.exports =
  isValidCreditCardNumber: isValidCreditCardNumber
```

How it works...

We calculate the credit card number's check digit by adding every even number digit to every odd digit and then multiplying it by 2. If the odd digit is greater than 10, you add the tens and ones place values together (that is, if the odd number is 8, then *2 x 8 = 16* and *1 + 6 = 7*).

If the check digit is evenly divisible by 10 with no remainder, the credit card number may actually be a valid credit card and we can proceed with the payment authorization.

For example, the number 4,012,888,888,881,881 would be:

```
(4 x 2) + 0 + (1 x 2) + 2 + (8 x 2) + 8 + (8 x 2) + 8 + (8 x 2) + 8 +
(8 x 2) + 8 + (1 x 2) + 8 + (8 x 2) + 1
```

This becomes:

```
8 + 0 + 2 + 2 + 16 + 8 + 16 + 8 + 16 + 8 + 16 + 8 + 2 + 8 + 16 + 1
```

Now, all of the 16s become *1 + 6 = 7* and our calculation becomes the following:

```
8 + 0 + 2 + 2 + 7 + 8 + 7 + 8 + 7 + 8 + 7 + 8 + 2 + 8 + 7 + 1
```

Finally, our check digit is 90, so 4,012,888,888,881,881 could be a valid card number.

We demonstrate this by using the check digit validator as follows:

```
ccv = require './credit_card_validator'

# VALID CARD NUMBERS
visa1Sample = '4012888888881881'
mc1Sample = '5105105105105100'

# INVALID CARD NUMBERS
visa2Sample = '4012788888881881'
mc2Sample = '5555655555554444'

console.log "#{visa1Sample} valid? ",
  (ccv.isValidCreditCardNumber visa1Sample)
console.log "#{mc1Sample} valid? ",
  (ccv.isValidCreditCardNumber mc1Sample)
console.log "#{visa2Sample} valid? ",
  (ccv.isValidCreditCardNumber visa2Sample)
console.log "#{mc2Sample} valid? ",
  (ccv.isValidCreditCardNumber mc2Sample)
```

Its output will be:

```
4012888888881881 valid?  true
5105105105105100 valid?  true
4012788888881881 valid?  false
5555655555554444 valid?  False
```

There's more...

For more information regarding credit card check digits, see the Wikipedia article on the Luhn or modulus 10 algorithm at `http://en.wikipedia.org/wiki/Luhn_algorithm`.

Working with dates and times

Working with dates is a very common task in our software. This section describes how we can perform date calculations in our CoffeeScript applications and provides some useful utility methods that you can use in your own applications.

Performing date calculations

Performing date calculations is not as intuitive as one would like in JavaScript. For example, subtracting two dates returns the number of milliseconds between the two dates. JavaScript does not provide methods to add hours, days, months, and so on for a date. In the next section, we will create methods to address each of these complications.

How to do it...

Let's define methods to calculate the difference between two dates and add a timespan to a date as follows:

```
MILLISECONDS_PER_SECOND = 1000
MILLISECONDS_PER_MINUTE = MILLISECONDS_PER_SECOND * 60
MILLISECONDS_PER_HOUR  = MILLISECONDS_PER_MINUTE * 60
MILLISECONDS_PER_DAY   = MILLISECONDS_PER_HOUR * 24
MILLISECONDS_PER_WEEK  = MILLISECONDS_PER_DAY * 7
MILLISECONDS_PER_YEAR  = MILLISECONDS_PER_WEEK * 52

dateDifference = (startDate, endDate, units = 'days') ->
  elapsed = endDate - startDate
  switch units
    when 'days'
      return elapsed / MILLISECONDS_PER_DAY
    when 'weeks'
      return elapsed / MILLISECONDS_PER_WEEK
    when 'months'
      return elapsed / MILLISECONDS_PER_YEAR * 12
    when 'years'
      return elapsed / MILLISECONDS_PER_YEAR
    when 'hours'
      return elapsed / MILLISECONDS_PER_HOUR
    when 'minutes'
      return elapsed / MILLISECONDS_PER_MINUTE
    when 'seconds'
      return elapsed / MILLISECONDS_PER_SECOND

  return elapsed

dateAdd = (date, amount, units = 'days') ->
  workingDate = new Date(date.valueOf())
  switch units
    when 'days'
      workingDate.setDate date.getDate() + amount
```

```
    when 'weeks'
      workingDate.setDate date.getDate() + amount * 7
    when 'months'
      workingDate.setMonth date.getMonth() + amount
    when 'years'
      workingDate.setFullYear date.getFullYear() + amount
    when 'hours'
      workingDate.setHours date.getHours() + amount
    when 'minutes'
      workingDate.setMinutes date.getMinutes() + amount
    when 'seconds'
      workingDate.setSeconds date.getSeconds() + amount
  return workingDate

module.exports =
  dateAdd: dateAdd
  dateDifference: dateDifference
```

How it works...

First, define some useful constants to help convert milliseconds to days or years.

Next, we define a method to calculate the difference between two dates. The `dateDifference()` method takes a `startDate` and `endDate` parameter as well as an optional `units` parameter (which defaults to `days`) that represents the units to be returned.

The `dateDifference()` method essentially subtracts the two dates and converts the resultant milliseconds to the desired units.

We then define the `dateAdd()` method. This method accepts `date`, `amount`, and an optional `units` parameter representing the units of the amount being added (which defaults to `days`).

To add time to a date, you must use a little trick to set the proper date unit to its value and the amount to be added. For example, to add 5 days to the current date, you would use the following code:

```
currentDate = new Date()
currentDate.setDays currentDate.getDays() + 5
console.log currentDate
```

You can subtract amounts from the given date by using negative values. For example, 7 days ago would be as follows:

```
currentDate = new Date()
console.log dateAdd currentDate, -7
```

An example of using these `date math` functions is shown as follows:

```
dm = require './date_math'

zeroPad = (value, length = 2) ->
  return "00000000000000#{value}".split('')[-length..].join('')

formatDate = (date) ->
  year   = date.getFullYear()
  month  = date.getMonth() + 1
  day    = date.getDate()
  hour   = date.getHours()
  minute = date.getMinutes()

  return "#{year}-#{zeroPad month}-#{zeroPad day} #{zeroPad
hour}:#{zeroPad minute}"

currentDate = new Date()
newCentury = new Date(2000, 0)

console.log 'Current date: ', formatDate currentDate

console.log 'Days since Jan. 1, 2000: ',
  dm.dateDifference newCentury, currentDate
console.log 'Years since Jan. 1, 2000: ',
  dm.dateDifference newCentury, currentDate, 'years'

console.log '3 days from now: ',
  formatDate dm.dateAdd currentDate, 3
console.log '3 days ago: ',
  formatDate dm.dateAdd currentDate, -3
console.log '3 months from now: ',
  formatDate dm.dateAdd currentDate, 3, 'months'
console.log '3 years from now: ',
  formatDate dm.dateAdd currentDate, 3, 'years'
console.log '3 hours from now: ',
  formatDate dm.dateAdd currentDate, 3, 'hours'
```

Its output will be:

```
Current date:  2013-10-21 18:54
Days since Jan. 1, 2000:  5042.746363993056
Years since Jan. 1, 2000:  13.806287101965928
3 days from now:  2013-10-24 18:54
3 days ago:  2013-10-18 18:54
3 months from now:  2014-01-21 18:54
3 years from now:  2016-10-21 18:54
3 hours from now:  2013-10-21 21:54
```

Measuring elapsed time

Using what we covered about working with dates and times, we can easily take it one step further and create a performance measurement tool that can clock the start and end times to execute a function and display execution statistics once complete.

How to do it...

In this section, we define helper methods to format and display results, and a `timer()` method that performs the timing function:

```
dm = require './date_math'

padRight = (value, zeroPadding) ->
  "00000000000000#{value}".split('')[-zeroPadding..].join('')

padLeft =  (value, zeroPadding) ->
  "#{value}00000000000000"[0...zeroPadding]

formatNumber = (value, decimalPlaces = 0, zeroPadding = 0) ->
  valueParts = (value + '').split '.'
  resultParts = []
  resultParts.push padRight valueParts[0], zeroPadding
  if decimalPlaces
    resultParts.push padLeft valueParts[1], decimalPlaces

  return resultParts.join '.'

formatTime = (value) ->
  hours   = 0
  minutes = 0
  seconds = value / 1000
```

```
    if seconds > 60
      minutes = Math.floor seconds / 60
      seconds -= minutes * 60

    if minutes > 60
      hours = Math.floor minutes / 60
      minutes -= hours * 60

    return "#{formatNumber hours, 0, 2}:" + \
      "#{formatNumber minutes, 0, 2}:" + \
      "#{formatNumber seconds, 4, 2}"

displayResults = (results) ->
  totalTime   = 0
  minimumTime = Number.POSITIVE_INFINITY
  maximumTime = 0

  for result in results
    minimumTime = result if result < minimumTime
    maximumTime = result if result > maximumTime
    totalTime += result

  console.log "Statistics"
  console.log "Times run: #{results.length}"
  console.log "Total:     #{formatTime totalTime}"
  console.log "Minimum:   #{formatTime minimumTime}"
  console.log "Maximum:   #{formatTime maximumTime}"
  console.log "Average:   #{formatTime totalTime / results.length}"

timer = (func, numberOfTimesToExecute = 1) ->
  timerResults = []
  console.log 'Running...'

  for lap in [1..numberOfTimesToExecute]
    start = new Date()
    func()
    end = new Date()
    timerResults.push \
      dm.dateDifference(start, end, 'milliseconds')

  displayResults timerResults
```

```
module.exports =
    timer: timer
```

How it works...

This little performance utility module begins by requiring our `date_utils` library as we will be using the `dateDifference()` method to calculate how long a method takes to execute.

Then, we have some formatting helper methods. The `formatNumber()` method will format a number for display and includes optional parameters for the number of decimal places and zero padding. For example, `formatNumber(5.4, 3, 2)` will produce `05.400`.

The `formatTime()` method will take a value in milliseconds and display it as hours, minutes, and seconds. For example, `formatTime(5680)` will be displayed as `00:00:05.680`.

 You may have noticed we need to define our helper methods before they are used. This is a requirement of JavaScript due to its dynamic nature.

After our formatting helper methods, we have a method that displays the performance measurement results, but let's look at the `timer()` method first.

The `timer()` method is really the heart of our module. It is responsible for executing the function being measured and gathering timing statistics with each run. The method takes a function (`func`) as a parameter and a `numberOfTimesToExecute` optional parameter representing the number of times to execute the function, which defaults to 1.

The `timer()` method then declares a `timerResults` array to store our execution times.

We then loop between 1 and `numberOfTimesToExecute`. With each iteration, we perform the following tasks:

- Store the current date and time in a variable called `start`
- Execute the function that is being measured
- Store the current date and time after the execution of a variable called `end`
- Push the results into our `timerResults` array

Once the function execution has been measured, the `timer()` method calls `displayResults()` to pass the `timerResults` array. The `displayResults()` method displays the number of executions, the total time, minimum time, maximum time, and the average time.

It is worth noting that the act of measuring performance negatively impacts the performance, however minimally. When working to improve performance in your code, it is better to compare results between tests with the understanding that each test executes with roughly the same overhead.

Let's try running our timer as follows:

```
tu = require './timer_utils'

test = () ->
  for i in [1..1000000]
    d = new Date()

tu.timer test, 5
```

Our little timer demo declares a `test` method that simply iterates from one to a million, and with each iteration, the current date/time is stored in the `d` variable.

 Why a million? Turns out `d = new Date()` happens very quickly. If we do it a million times, it takes about 0.5 seconds.

We then pass our `test()` method to `timer()` and have it execute five times.

The output for the preceding code is:

```
Running...
Statistics
Times run: 5
Total:     00:00:02.2810
Minimum:   00:00:00.4220
Maximum:   00:00:00.4920
Average:   00:00:00.4562
```

Working with arrays

Our applications will almost always make use of data and in some cases a lot of data. In this section, we will investigate some useful ways to work with collections of data using CoffeeScript and its list comprehension feature and various JavaScript methods made available on the `array` object.

Iterating over arrays

CoffeeScript provides convenient operators to iterate through collections of data by using loops and comprehensions.

Getting ready

For our example, we will be working with the following array of employee objects:

```
employees = [
  { id: 10, firstName: 'Tracy', lastName: 'Ouellette', salesYtd: 22246
}
  { id: 2, firstName: 'Chris', lastName: 'Daniel', salesYtd: 3876 }
  { id: 3, firstName: 'Jason', lastName: 'Alexander', salesYtd: 4095 }
  { id: 4, firstName: 'Jennifer', lastName: 'Hannah', salesYtd: 8070 }
  { id: 5, firstName: 'Maxx', lastName: 'Slayde', salesYtd: 2032 }
]
```

How to do it...

We can iterate through an array using the `for item in array` format as follows:

```
# Listing Employees
for employee in employees
  console.log "Employee No. #{employee.id}: #{employee.firstName}"
```

We can also use the `doSomethingWith item for item in array` format:

```
displayEmployee = (emp) ->
  console.log "Employee No. #{emp.id}: #{emp.firstName}"

displayEmployee employee for employee in employees
```

How it works...

Both of these looping expressions iterate though the array one element at a time, and each of the previous examples produces the same result as can be seen in the following output:

```
Employee No. 1: Tracy
Employee No. 2: Chris
Employee No. 3: Jason
Employee No. 4: Jennifer
Employee No. 5: Maxx
```

These can be used to return augmented arrays through the use of CoffeeScript comprehensions. For example, if we had an array of integers, we could return an array of these integers squared in the following manner:

```
array = [1, 2, 3, 4, 5]
result = (i * i for i in array)
```

The value of `result` is [1, 4, 16, 9, 25].

It is important to wrap your comprehension inside parentheses, otherwise the value being assigned will be the last item processed. For example, we can omit the parentheses in the previous example as follows:

```
result = i * i for i in array
```

Now, the value of `result` will be 5.

There's more...

There are a number of useful variations when working with loops and comprehensions. For example, we can use an optional indexing value as shown in the following code:

```
fruit = ['apples', 'bananas', 'oranges']
console.log "#{index}: #{item}" for item, index in fruit
```

This will produce the following output:

```
0: apples
1: bananas
2: oranges
```

We can also omit some items from being processed by adding a when clause to our loop operation:

```
names = ['Chris', 'Tracy', 'Jason', 'Jennifer', 'Maxx']
console.log name for name in names when name[0] is 'J'
```

This will only operate on names that begin with J, as can be seen in the following output:

```
Jason
Jennifer
```

Lastly, we can also skip items and process every *n*th (second, third, and so on) value by including a by clause as shown in the following code:

```
names = ['Chris', 'Tracy', 'Jason', 'Jennifer', 'Maxx']
console.log name for name in names by 2
```

This loop will display every second name as seen in the following code:

```
Chris
Jason
Maxx
```

Sorting arrays

Sorting a collection is a very common task. Some collections, such as an array of numbers or strings, are simply sorted by value. Complex objects can be sorted by a property or method value. Sorting may not just be alphabetical or by numeric value; the logic may be more complicated than that. We will look at each of these scenarios.

How to do it...

When sorting a simple array of values, we can take advantage of JavaScript's `Array.prototype.sort()` function. By default, arrays are sorted in alphabetical order by string value.

For an array of strings, we can do the following.

```
names = ['Chris', 'Tracy', 'Jason', 'Jennifer', 'Maxx']
console.log "Sorted: #{names.sort()}"
```

Executing this code produces `Sorted: Chris,Jason,Jennifer,Maxx,Tracy`.

For numbers, we need to use a version of `sort` that accepts a function as an argument that returns a negative, 0, or positive value based on two values being compared:

- ▶ **Negative**: A is less than B
- ▶ **0**: A is equal to B
- ▶ **Positive**: A is greater than B

We can see the simple `a - b` comparer in the following code:

```
values = [3,63,56,4,65,3,555,9]
console.log "Sorted: #{values.sort (a,b) -> a - b}"
```

In this example, we compare A and B through simple subtraction, which produces `Sorted: 3,3,4,9,56,63,65,555`.

How it works...

In our example, we use the `sort()` function to sort both strings and numeric values. Because `sort()` operates on strings by default, we had to provide a comparer function for `sort()` to compare numeric values.

We can sort numeric arrays in descending order by subtracting A from B, as shown in the following code:

```
values = [3,63,56,4,65,3,555,9]
console.log "Sorted descending: #{values.sort (a,b) -> b - a}"
```

This will produce `Sorted descending: 555,65,63,56,9,4,3,3`.

We can use a comparer to sort objects as well. For example, if we want to sort an array of employees in descending order by year-to-date sales, we can accomplish this with the following code:

```
displayEmployee = (emp) ->
  console.log "#{emp.firstName}: $#{emp.salesYtd}"

employeeSortBySalesYtd = (a, b) ->
  b.salesYtd - a.salesYtd

console.log '\nEmployees Sorted by YTD Sales'
displayEmployee emp \

  for emp in employees.sort(employeeSortBySalesYtd)
```

This will display the following output:

```
Employees Sorted by YTD Sales
Tracy: $22246
Jennifer: $8070
Jason: $4095
Chris: $3876
Maxx: $2032
```

Note that the easiest way to sort an array of strings in descending order is to combine the `sort()` function with the `Array.prototype.reverse()` function, which will reverse the order of an array. For example, consider the following array:

```
names = ['Chris', 'Tracy', 'Jason', 'Jennifer', 'Maxx']
```

We can sort this in descending order with `names.sort().reverse()`, which will produce `['Tracy','Maxx','Jennifer','Jason','Chris']`.

Shuffling an array

There are times when we may want to randomize a collection of data. For example, if we were developing a game involving a deck of cards, we would want to shuffle the cards before dealing them.

In this section, we will look at ways to accomplish this using CoffeeScript.

Getting ready

We will be shuffling an array representing a deck of cards. We will define our card suits and values as string arrays and assemble an array of card objects representing a deck by iterating through each.

```
suits = ['Diamonds', 'Hearts', 'Clubs', 'Spades']
values = ['Ace', 'Two', 'Three', 'Four', 'Five', 'Six', 'Seven',
  'Eight', 'Nine', 'Ten', 'Jack', 'Queen', 'King']

assembleDeck = (deck) ->
  for suit in suits
    for value in values
      card = { suit: suit, value: value }
      deck.push card
```

We will also create two helper functions; one that is able to display the first five cards of the deck and another that returns a random number, as follows:

```
displayDeck = (deck) ->
  for card in deck[0..4]
    console.log "#{card.value} of #{card.suit}"

getRandomNumber = (maximumValue) ->
  Math.floor (Math.random() * maximumValue)
```

How to do it...

We can shuffle the array of cards using the following code:

```
shuffle = (array) ->
  for i in [1..(array.length * 100)]
    indexOne = getRandomNumber array.length
    indexTwo = getRandomNumber array.length
    tempItem = array[indexOne]
    array[indexOne] = array[indexTwo]
    array[indexTwo] = tempItem
```

How it works...

The shuffle() function takes an array of values of any length and type. It proceeds to loop 100 times for any number of items in the deck. This is an arbitrary number and can be modified as needed. For a small array such as ours, it gives us a good shuffle while taking very little time.

During each iteration, we retrieve two random index values based on the length of the array and swap the values in each index.

We can create a new deck of cards by issuing the following commands:

```
deck = []
assembleDeck deck
```

After the deck is assembled, we can display the first five cards with the following command:

```
displayDeck deck
```

As you can see from the following output, the cards have not been shuffled:

```
Ace of Diamonds
Two of Diamonds
Three of Diamonds
Four of Diamonds
Five of Diamonds
```

We can shuffle the deck using out `shuffle()` function in the following way:

```
shuffle deck
```

Once it has been shuffled, we can again display the first five cards in the deck and see they are indeed shuffled in following output:

```
Eight of Diamonds
Two of Spades
Ace of Clubs
Five of Hearts
Ten of Spades
```

Mapping and reducing arrays

Mapping involves iterating through a collection and transforming each element in some way and returning these transformed values as a collection.

Reducing an array is the act of deriving a single value from the array. This involves processing each element of the collection and performing some calculation on it and returning a value to be used while processing the next element.

In this section, we will look at some mapping and reducing examples.

Getting ready

In our examples, we will be using an array of strings and an array of numeric values as follows:

```
names = ['Chris', 'Tracy', 'Jason', 'Jennifer', 'Maxx']
values = [3, 63, 56, 4, 65, 3, 555, 9]
```

How to do it...

We can map our arrays using CoffeeScript list comprehensions.

We can convert our array of names to an array of integers representing the length of each name in the following manner:

```
nameLengths = (name.length for name in names)
```

After executing this statement, the nameLengths array will contain [5, 5, 5, 8, 4].

To reduce an array, we will use the Array.prototype.reduce() function:

```
sum = values.reduce (runningTotal, value) -> runningTotal + value
```

Once the reduce() statement is executed, sum is assigned the value of 758.

Of course, we can reduce other types of arrays besides numeric arrays. For example, if we want to find the longest word in a string array, we can do the following:

```
words = ['Once', 'upon', 'a', 'time', 'there', 'was', 'a', \
  'beautiful', 'mountain']
reduceWords = (value, word) ->
  if word.length > value.length then word else value

longestWord = words.reduce reduceWords, ''
```

In this example, we seed our reduce() function with an empty string. When this is executed, the value of longestWord is beautiful.

Filtering and testing arrays

Before we leave arrays, we will look at ways to filter elements that match specific criteria and testing collections to determine whether elements meet specific criteria.

Getting ready

In our example, we will reference the following array:

```
testScores = [27, 44, 39, 37, 41, 48, 37, 34, 40, 43, 30, 43, \
  29, 27, 37]
```

How to do it...

In our example, we will use list comprehensions to filter our arrays and test elements using the CoffeeScript `when` construct.

If we wanted to filter only the even test scores, we can do the following:

```
evenScores = (i for i in testScores when i % 2 is 0)
```

We can reverse our `when` expression to filter only odd test scores:

```
oddScores = (i for i in testScores when i % 2 isnt 0)
```

 Note that we use CoffeeScript's `is` and `isnt` filters to check for equality. This makes the code read more like English. CoffeeScript offers a number of English keywords like this.

We can build tests around list comprehensions that will test that any or all elements match specific criteria:

```
any = (array, testFunc) ->
  matches = (m for m in array when testFunc m)
  matches.length isnt 0

all = (array, testFunc) ->
  matches = (m for m in array when testFunc m)
  matches.length is array.length
```

How it works...

Using list comprehensions makes filtering and testing arrays a breeze.

For example, we can call our `any()` function with our array of test scores to see whether any test scores were greater than `40`:

```
anyGreaterThan40 = any testScores, (n) -> n > 40
```

The `any()` function executes the `testFunc()` function with each element in the provided array and collects the elements where this returns a truthy value. Given our `testScores` array, this is will return `true` because one or more matches exist.

The `all()` function also executes `testFunc()` for each element. In this case, however, we will only return `true` if every `element` returns truthy.

Working with classes

Traditional classes do not exist in JavaScript. They can be very useful in decomposing your code into reusable component-like blocks. This is especially true if you are used to working with classes in other languages.

CoffeeScript classes are compiled into constructor functions that allow us to instantiate JavaScript objects. Using CoffeeScript classes makes use of best practices to define objects by keeping private variables private and making proper use of function prototypes.

In this section, we will look at defining classes with properties and methods, using class inheritance, and some of the hurdles we can run into when using CoffeeScript classes.

Defining classes

Creating a class involves using the `class` CoffeeScript keyword to define our class name, prototype properties and methods, as well as class variables and methods.

In this section, we will define a number of CoffeeScript class examples and see how they are used.

How to do it...

We can create a simple CoffeeScript class by giving it a name. For example `class Employee` is all it takes to define an `Employee` class.

This will create the following JavaScript code when compiled:

```
var Employee;
Employee = (function() {
  function Employee() {}

  return Employee;
})();
```

We can create an instance of our `Employee` class in the following way:

```
emp = new Employee()
```

A slightly more complex example of our `Employee` class defines three functions that allow you to set the employee's ID, and first and last names as follows:

```
class Employee
  setId: (value) ->
    @id = value
```

```
setFirstName: (value) ->
  @firstName = value


setLastName: (value) ->
  @lastName = value
```

In the previous example, we used the @ character. This is shorthand for `this`.

CoffeeScript classes provide a special `constructor` function that can be used to initialize member properties. Let's modify our `Employee` class to make use of `constructor`:

```
class Employee
  constructor: () ->
    @id = 0
    @firstName = ''
    @lastName = ''
```

Constructors can also take parameters such as other methods:

```
class Employee
  constructor: (id, firstName, lastName) ->
    @id = id
    @firstName = firstName
    @lastName = lastName
```

This is such a common task that CoffeeScript provides an initialization shorthand that will allow us to construct new objects and assign property values with very little code:

```
class Employee
  constructor: (@id, @firstName, @lastName) ->
```

How it works...

When classes are compiled, they become constructor functions that are wrapped within a closure. This provides the mechanism to keep private members private.

We can easily define instance methods in our class definitions:

```
class Employee
  constructor: (@id, @firstName, @lastName) ->
    @salesByMonth = [0, 0, 0, 0, 0, 0, 0, 0, 0, 0, 0, 0]

  totalSales: ->
    @salesByMonth.reduce (t, n) -> t + n
```

When we define methods in our class definition, they are compiled into functions on the object's prototype. In the previous example, `totalSales()` will exist as `Employee.prototype.totalSales()`. Functions defined on the object's prototype are used by all instances of the `Employee` objects. In other words, regardless of the number of `Employee` instances, there will only ever be one copy of `totalSales()` in memory.

We can create a new `Employee` instance and retrieve the employee's year-to-date sales in the following manner:

```
emp = new Employee(13, 'Tracy', 'Ouellette')
emp.salesByMonth[0] = 504.43
emp.salesByMonth[1] = 389.56
emp.salesByMonth[2] = 493.23
console.log "YTD sales:  ", emp.totalSales()
```

When we execute this, we see the following output:

```
YTD sales:    1387.22
```

Dealing with inheritance

CoffeeScript classes support inheritance by making use of JavaScript's native prototype inheritance. This allows you to create generalized classes and then derive more specific classes when needed.

For example, if we continue with our `Employee` example we created in the previous section, we can extract the first and last names into a `Person` class, and then create an employee class that extends the `Person` class.

How to do it...

Let's look at an example of how to use class inheritance:

```
class Person
  constructor: (@firstName, @lastName) ->

  fullName: ->
    "#{@firstName} #{@lastName}"

# Create a more specific type of person (Employee)
class Employee extends Person
  constructor: (@id, @firstName, @lastName) ->
    @salesByMonth = [0, 0, 0, 0, 0, 0, 0, 0, 0, 0, 0, 0]

  totalSales: ->
    @salesByMonth.reduce ((t, n) -> t + n), 0
```

First, we define a simple `Person` class. A person has a first name and last name. We also define a simple instance method to return the person's full name.

We then create a specific kind of `Person` by defining the `Employee` class as an extension of the `Person` class as `class Employee extends Person`.

How it works...

We can create an instance of an `Employee` class in the same manner as we did previously, but because `Employee` extends `Person`, we get the added features provided by the `Person` class:

```
emp = new Employee(13, 'Tracy', 'Ouellette')
emp.salesByMonth[0] = 504.43
emp.salesByMonth[1] = 389.56
emp.salesByMonth[2] = 493.23


displayEmployee emp
```

Its output will be:

```
Employee
  Id:          13
  Name:        Tracy Ouellette
  YTD sales:   1387.22
```

In this example, `Employee` inherited the `fullName()` method from `Person`.

What if we needed to override a method found in the parent class? This can be easily accomplished by simply creating a method with the same name as the parent class method:

```
# Create general person class with a toString() method
class Person
  constructor: (@firstName, @lastName) ->

  fullName: ->
    "#{@firstName} #{@lastName}"

  toString: ->
    @fullName()

# Create an employee class from person, overriding toString()
class Employee extends Person
  constructor: (@id, @firstName, @lastName) ->
    @salesByMonth = [0, 0, 0, 0, 0, 0, 0, 0, 0, 0, 0, 0]
```

```
      totalSales: ->
        @salesByMonth.reduce ((t, n) -> t + n), 0

      toString: ->
        "#{@fullName()} (#{@id})"

   # Create employee instance and display
   console.log "#{ new Employee(13, 'Tracy', 'Ouellette') }"
```

Its output will be:

```
   Tracy Ouellette (13)
```

Notice that our `Employee.prototype.toString()` function still has access to its base `Person.prototype.toStirng()` function.

CoffeeScript also provides a `super()` method to access instance methods from the parent class from within the overriding child method.

For example, if we wanted `Employee.prototype.toString()` to be an extension of the `Person.prototype.toString()` method, we can define `Employee.prototype.toString()` in this way:

```
   class Employee extends Person
     constructor: (@id, @firstName, @lastName) ->
       @salesByMonth = [0, 0, 0, 0, 0, 0, 0, 0, 0, 0, 0, 0]

     totalSales: ->
       @salesByMonth.reduce ((t, n) -> t + n), 0

     toString: ->
       "#{super()} (#{@id})"
```

In this example, `Employee.toString()` calls `super()`, which in this case is `Person.toString()`, and then uses the output from `Person.toString()` as a part of the output from `Employee.toString()`.

Class properties and methods

In this section, we will look at how to define class-level variables and methods. These are available only on the class object itself and not on instances of a class.

How to do it...

Let's look at how to define class-level variables and methods:

```
class Employee extends Person
  constructor: (@id, @firstName, @lastName) ->
    @salesByMonth = [0, 0, 0, 0, 0, 0, 0, 0, 0, 0, 0, 0]

  totalSales: ->
    @salesByMonth.reduce ((t, n) -> t + n), 0

  toString: ->
    "#{super()} (#{@id})"

  @departments: [
    'Sales'
    'Customer Service'
    'I.T.', 'Finance'
    'Marketing'
    'Human Resources'
    'Research and Development'
  ]
```

How it works...

In our class definition, we define a class-level variable for `Employee` named `departments`.

When we use `Employee`, we can access `Departments` without using an `Employee` instance as `Employee.departments`, as follows:

```
console.log "Employee class has #{Employee.departments.length}
departments."
```

Its output will be:

```
Employee class has 7 departments.
```

If we try to access `Departments` from an `employee` instance, you'll see that it is `undefined`.

```
emp = new Employee(13, 'Tracy', 'Ouellette')
console.log "#{emp} instance departments? #{emp.departments}"
```

Its output will be:

```
Tracy Ouellette (13) instance departments? Undefined
```

If we derive a class from `Employee` (such as a `Manager` class), `Manager` also has access to `Departments` on its parent `Employee` class, as follows:

```
class Manager extends Employee
  constructor: (@id, @firstName, @lastName) ->

console.log "Manager class has #{Manager.departments.length}
departments."
```

Its output will be:

```
Manager class has 7 departments.
```

We can create class-level methods as well. Here is a `Numbers` class, which defines an `avg()` method that returns the average from a numeric collection:

```
class Numbers
  @avg: (collection) ->
    sum = collection.reduce ((t, n) -> t + n), 0
    sum / collection.length
```

We can then call this method using `Numbers.avg()`:

```
data = require '../working_with_collections/sample_data'
roundWithDecimals = (value, decimalPlaces = 0) ->
  multiplier = Math.pow(10, decimalPlaces)
  Math.round(value * multiplier) / multiplier

avgTestScore = Numbers.avg testScores
```

Its output will be:

```
Average test score:  37.07
```

Dealing with the this keyword

In JavaScript, `this` can sometimes trip us up. This is because the value of `this` depends on the context in which it is being used.

Getting ready

When defining classes in CoffeeScript, instance methods will execute on the current `this` context. For normally instantiated objects, `this` refers to the object itself.

If the instance method is instead passed as a function callback, `this` represents the object that is executing the callback.

For example, consider the following code:

```
class Person
  constructor: (@firstName, @lastName) ->

  displayFullName: ->
    console.log "#{@firstName} #{@lastName}"

person = new Person('Tracy', 'Ouellette')
person.displayFullName()
```

If you run this code, `person.displayFullName()` will give the following output:

```
Tracy Ouellette
```

However, consider what would happen if you used `person.deplayFullName()` as a callback:

```
func = (callback) ->
  callback()

func(person.displayFullName)
```

Its output would be:

```
undefined undefined
```

What's going on here? The problem is that `displayFullName()` was executed under the context of `func()` (that is, `this` is `func`) and `func()` does not have `firstName` or `lastName` associated with it; they are bound to `person`.

To address this, we must use CoffeeScript's **fat-arrow** operator `=>`.

How to do it...

Let's look at how to use CoffeeScript's `@` helper as shown in the following code:

```
class Person
  constructor: (@firstName, @lastName) ->

  displayFullName: =>
    console.log "#{@firstName} #{@lastName}"
```

How it works...

There is a very subtle change to our `Person` class. We defined the `displayFullName()` method using the fat-arrow operator.

This will bind `displayFullName()` to the instance of `Person` instead of the default context of `this`.

Let's see if using the fat-arrow addresses our binding problem, as follows:

```
person = new Person('Tracy', 'Ouellette')
func(person.displayFullName)
```

Its output will be:

```
Tracy Ouellette
```

Using the fat-arrow to bind the method to its instance did indeed address our binding problem.

You may be asking yourself, "why not just use the fat-arrow operator to define all instance methods on classes?"

If you look at the JavaScript code that gets generated, you will see that using the fat-arrow generates more JavaScript code. This is code that is needed to bind the instance method to the object's instance itself.

It is recommended to only use the fat-arrow operator when the method may be used as an event callback and needs access to instance variables and methods.

Consider the following example where `Person` is compiled to JavaScript using a thin-arrow operator:

```
var Person;
Person = (function() {
  function Person(firstName, lastName) {
    this.firstName = firstName;
    this.lastName = lastName;
  }

  Person.prototype.displayFullName = function() {
    return console.log("" + this.firstName + " " + this.lastName);
  };

  return Person;

})();
```

Consider the following example where `Person` is compiled to JavaScript using the fat-arrow operator:

```
var Person,
  __bind = function(fn, me){ return function(){ return fn.apply(me,
arguments); }; };

Person = (function() {
  function Person(firstName, lastName) {
    this.firstName = firstName;
    this.lastName = lastName;
    this.displayFullName = __bind(this.displayFullName, this);
  }

  Person.prototype.displayFullName = function() {
    return console.log("" + this.firstName + " " + this.lastName);
  };

  return Person;

})();
```

3
Creating Client Applications

In this chapter, we will cover the following recipes:

- ▶ Working with jQuery
- ▶ Working with Backbone
- ▶ Working with AngularJS
- ▶ Communicating in real time with Socket.io

Introduction

One of the most important aspects of developing an application is the user interface. In this chapter, we will look at many popular frameworks and libraries that can be used with CoffeeScript when developing the user interfaces and client-side application code for our applications.

We will look at several options for creating views, handling UI events, and routing using Backbone and AngularJS specifically.

We will also see how we can implement real-time communications between our client application and server using the Socket.io library.

Working with jQuery

jQuery is undoubtedly one of the most widely used JavaScript libraries in use today. It alone is used by nearly 57 percent of all websites in the world and has a whopping 92 percent market share in the JavaScript library space.

 For more information on jQuery, you can visit the project home page at `http://jquery.com/`.

In this section, we will look at writing jQuery code to use with jQuery and some of jQuery's most popular plugins.

Executing on load

When a web page first loads, jQuery will trigger a `document.ready` event allowing you to execute code before the page begins rendering. This is the opportune time to execute any initialization code.

Getting ready

Our jQuery examples will be based on a basic HTML file with the following structure:

```
<!doctype html>

<html lang="en">

<head>
  <meta charset="utf-8">
  <title>jQuery Examples</title>
</head>

<body>

  <!-- Your CoffeeScript code goes here -->
  <script type="text/coffeescript">

  </script>

  <!-- Reference jQuery and CoffeeScript -->
  <script src="http://cdnjs.cloudflare.com/ajax/libs/jquery/1.11.2/
jquery.min.js"></script>
  <script src="http://coffeescript.org/extras/coffee-script.js"></
script>
</body>

</html>
```

Using this template you can add your CoffeeScript code inside the `<SCRIPT TYPE="text/coffeescript">` tag.

How to do it...

There are two basic methods to handle the document ready event:

1. You can assign a ready event handler to a jQuery-wrapped document object:

    ```
    $(document).ready ->
        console.log 'Document ready...'
    ```

2. You can use the shortcut provided by jQuery:

    ```
    $ ->
        console.log 'Document ready (shortcut)...'
    ```

How it works...

In the previous code, we saw two ways to listen to the `document.ready` event.

The first method listens for the ready event triggered by the document object. In this example, our code displays **Document ready...** in the browser's console.

The second method accomplishes the exact same task using jQuery's shortcut to handle the `document.ready` event as can be seen in the following screenshot:

Handling DOM events

Much in the same way that we listened for the `document.ready` event, we can also add various event listeners to DOM elements. This section describes a number of common ways that jQuery allows us to do this.

How to do it...

DOM event handlers can be added to a specific element, a set of existing elements, or to elements that have yet to be created.

Let's look at an example of how to add a jQuery `click()` listener to a DOM element:

- ▸ Adding a click handler to a specific element:

```
$('#first-button').click (e) ->
  e.preventDefault()
  alert 'You have clicked first-button'
```

- ▸ Adding a click handler to a set of similar elements:

```
$('ul#color-list a').click (e) ->
  e.preventDefault()
  color = $(e.target).data('color')
  alert "Thank you for selecting #{color}."
```

- ▸ Adding a click handler to an element that does not yet exist

```
$(document).on 'click', 'button.new-button', (e) ->
  e.preventDefault()
  buttonValue = $(e.target).data 'counter'
  alert "You clicked button ##{buttonValue}"
```

How it works...

Our example demonstrates three common ways to use jQuery to add event listeners to DOM elements.

In the first example, we simply attach a handler to a specific instance of a DOM element identified by using a `#id` selector. In this example, we assign an event handler to the first-button element's `click` event.

Our event handlers receive an event object (e, in our example) that provides additional information our handler may need. It also provides a method to prevent the default behavior. For example, we can capture the click of a form submission button to perform validation of the data provided and, if there is a validation error, prevent the default action of the form being submitted by executing `e.preventDefault()`. This is very handy when assigning a click handler to anchor elements and buttons.

Our second example applies an event handler to all DOM elements that match the query selector; `ul#color-list a`, in this case. Any anchor element found inside the unordered list with the ID of `color-list` will listen for a click event and execute our event handler. This handler uses the `e.target` property and jQuery's `data()` method to retrieve the `data-color` value and displays an alert to the user informing them of the color that was clicked.

When working with CoffeeScript, it can be difficult to know when to use parenthesis. If you are calling a method with no parameters, then parenthesis are required. We have also seen cases in some of our examples where parentheses were used to clarify our intensions to the CoffeeScript compiler. There are other cases where they may make code intent clear to you, the developer. If using parenthesis makes the code intent clear, by all means, use them. One aspect you might have noticed was the way that I make use of the jQuery function. For example, `$('button#add-button').doSomething()` is the same as `$('button#add-button').doSomething()`, but I personally find the former pattern a little more readable; however, you may find the latter more suitable.

Our third example uses a feature of jQuery that allows you to register an event handler to DOM elements that do not yet exist. This is very handy in **Single Page Applications (SPA)**, where we load DOM elements into our application at runtime. jQuery's `on()` method takes advantage of the browsers behavior of bubbling events. You use `on()` to attach an event listener to a container element (`document`, in our example). We then tell the listener what type of event we are interested in and the scope we are interested in (`click` and `button.new-button`, respectively).

Clicking on the `add-button` button will add a new button with the CSS class of `.new-button` to the DOM. Using `on()`, we set an event handler that will listen for click events on any button contained in the document with the `.new-button` class. When detected, we grab the target's `data-counter` value and display a message to the user.

Using this approach allows us to create listeners for elements that our application will create dynamically. This provides an enormous amount of flexibility when using jQuery for our applications.

We can see our demo page loaded in the following screenshot:

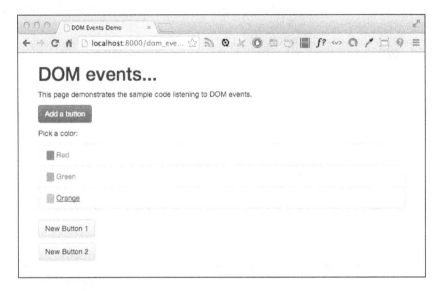

Modifying the DOM

jQuery is an excellent library to add, change, and remove DOM elements. Using jQuery methods such as `append()`, `prepend()`, `after()`, and `before()` allows us to add new elements to the DOM.

We can use jQuery's `remove()`, `empty()`, and `detach()` methods to remove elements from the DOM.

jQuery also provides many methods to change element attributes and has `addClass()`, `removeClass()` and `toggleClass()` to deal with CSS classes, `data()`, `css()`, and `attr()` to use the `data-dash` values, CSS properties, and general element attributes.

You can view all of jQuery's documentation on their jQuery API site at `http://api.jquery.com`.

How to do it...

Let's look at how we can use jQuery to modify our document object model by adding, modifying, and removing DOM elements:

> ▸ Adding a DOM element:

```
itemHtml = "<li class='list-group-item'>
  <label>
  <input type='checkbox' class='complete-checkbox'>
    #{description}
  </label>
  <button class='delete-button btn btn-danger btn-xs'>Delete</
button>
</li>"
$('#todo-list').append itemHtml
```

> ▸ Deleting a DOM element:

```
$('#todo-list').on 'click', '.delete-button', (e) ->
  if (confirm 'Delete this item?')
    $(e.target).parent('li').remove()
```

> ▸ Modifying a DOM element:

```
$('#todo-list').on 'click', '.complete-checkbox', (e) ->
  $(e.target).parent('label').toggleClass 'completed'
```

How it works...

In the preceding example, we work with a sample to-do list. The functionality is pretty simple. You can add a new item by entering a description and clicking on the add button. You can mark items as complete by clicking on the checkbox next to the item in the list. You can also delete an item by clicking on its delete button.

We wire up three event handlers. One to handle the add action, one to handle the delete action, and the third to handle the toggle of clicking on the checkbox.

When adding a to-do item, the following thing happens:

1. The event handler grabs the task description using jQuery's `val()` method.

2. We then call the `addTodoItem()` method to pass our description.

3. The `addTodoItem()` method prepares the HTML to be added to the DOM as a simple string.

4. We finish by using jQuery's `append()` method, which adds a new DOM element to `todo-list`.

Our delete handler confirms the user's action, which is always recommended when the user performs a destructive action. If confirmed, we remove the `LI` element that contains the delete button that was clicked. We accomplish this using jQuery's `remove()` method. The delete button that was clicked is `e.target`. We really want to remove `LI` that contains the delete button so we use jQuery's `parent()` method to find that element and remove it.

We can see the page loaded in our browser in the following screenshot:

There's more...

You may have noticed that we used inline HTML strings. Having inline HTML in this simple example is not much of a problem, but imagine how messy a larger application could become. A better solution is to use a **template engine**. There are a number of very good libraries that can help with this. Some of the most popular libraries include Handlebars (`http://handlebarsjs.com/`), Underscore (`http://documentcloud.github.io/underscore/#template`), and the jQuery `tmpl` plugin (`https://github.com/BorisMoore/jquery-tmpl`).

If you are using a JavaScript framework, it may have a built-in template engine or its community may have a preferred engine.

 Note that Underscore is an amazing utility library created by CoffeeScript creator Jeremy Ashkenas. At 5 KB, this library packs some fantastic methods to manipulate collections, arrays, functions, objects, and has a built-in template engine as well.

In our previous example, we created DOM elements by creating HTML. In the following example, we use the Underscore template engine:

1. Initialize a new template variable:

```
itemTemplate = null
```

2. Get the HTML to be used by our template:

```
$ ->
  # Grab item template
  itemTemplate = _.template $('#item-template').html()
```

3. Register an event handler to add an item:

```
# Add new todo
$('#add-button').click (e) ->
  description = $('#todo-description').val()
  addTodoItem description
```

4. Register an event handler to remove an item:

```
# Delete an item
$('#todo-list').on 'click', '.delete-button', (e) ->
  if (confirm 'Delete this item?')
    $(e.target).parent('li').remove()
```

5. Register an event handler to mark an item as complete:

```
# Mark an item complete
$('#todo-list').on 'click', '.complete-checkbox', (e) ->
  $(e.target).parent('label').toggleClass 'completed'
```

6. Create some sample items:

```
# Pre-populate our list with some tasks
todos = [
  'Pick up milk',
  'Take the car in for an oil change',
  'Pick up tickets for Jenn\'s show'
]
```

7. Add our sample items using the item template:

```
(addTodoItem description) for description in todos

addTodoItem = (description) ->
  $('#todo-list').append itemTemplate(description: description)
```

8. Add a reference to the Underscore library:

```
<script src="http://cdnjs.cloudflare.com/ajax/libs/underscore.
js/1.8.2/underscore-min.js"></script>
```

In this version, we begin by grabbing a copy of the template from our HTML file by the `#item-template` ID. Underscore's `template()` method takes HTML and returns a function that can be called, which will generate an HTML representation of the template with the appropriate values substituted.

For example, you can see in the following HTML template, we use a code nugget, `<%= description %>`, representing an expression that will be evaluated and injected into the template's output. These expressions are evaluated using an object passed as an argument to the template's function. In this case, we execute our template function passing an object with a description property:

```
<script type="text/x-template" id="item-template">
<li class="list-group-item">
  <label>
    <input type="checkbox" class="complete-checkbox">
    <%= description %>
  </label>
  <button class="delete-button btn btn-danger btn-xs">
    Delete
  </button>
</li>
</script>
```

 Note that our HTML template was contained in a script tag. By providing a type that is not recognized by the browser, we can include the HTML template with an ID and the browser will simply ignore its contents.

Communicating with the server using AJAX

jQuery offers several AJAX methods that can be used to send requests to a backend service and handle the server's response asynchronously. jQuery provides several methods to perform AJAX requests, including the very flexible `ajax()` method and various specialized methods such as `get()`, `post()`, and `getJSON()`.

How to do it...

In this example, we will demonstrate several methods to retrieve data from the server via AJAX calls:

1. Get the template HTML and compile it to be reusable:

```
departmentsTemplate = null

$ ->
  templateHtml = $('#departments-template').html()
  departmentsTemplate = _.template templateHtml
```

2. Make a call using `ajax()`:

```
# Using ajax() the old way
$('#first-button').click (e) ->
  method = 'ajax() the old way'
  $.ajax 'data/departments.json',
    dataType: 'json',
    complete: (res) ->
      displayDepartments method, res.responseJSON
    error: (res) ->
      displayError method, res.statusCode, res.statusText
```

3. Make a call using `ajax()` with promises:

```
# Using ajax() with promises
$('#second-button').click (e) ->
  method = 'ajax() with deferred'
  xhr = ($.ajax 'data/departments.json', {dataType: 'json'})
  xhr.done (data) ->
      displayDepartments method, data
  xhr.fail (res) ->
     displayError method, res.statusCode, res.statusText
```

4. Make a call using `get()`:

```
# Using get()
$('#third-button').click (e) ->
  method = 'get()'
  xhr = ($.get 'data/departments.json', dataType: 'json')
  xhr.done (data) ->
    displayDepartments method, data
  xhr.fail (res) ->
     displayError method, res.statusCode, res.statusText
```

5. Make a call using `getJSON()`:

```
# Using getJSON()
$('#fourth-button').click (e) ->
  method = 'getJSON()'
  xhr = ($.getJSON 'data/departments.json')
  xhr.done (data) ->
      displayDepartments method, data
  xhr.fail (res) ->
    displayError method, res.statusCode, res.statusText
```

6. Create helper functions to display results and/or errors:

```
displayDepartments = (method, departments) ->
  $('#output').html departmentsTemplate
    method: method
    departments: departments

displayError = (method, code, text) ->
  alert "#{method} failed: #{code} - #{text}"
```

How it works...

In our example, we have four examples to load data from our server via AJAX.

The first example uses the classic approach to use the flexible `ajax(url, settings)` method. Our settings contain a few common properties, including `dataType` (we want to load `json` as opposed to the `text` data), a `complete()` event handler, and an `error()` event handler.

The event handlers are the same for each of our examples. Upon success, the departments are displayed using an Underscore template and upon failure, we display an alert to provide some useful feedback to the user.

Our second example also uses the `ajax()` method. In this example, however, we use the new XHR object that is returned by `ajax()`. The XHR object provides three deferred methods:

▶ `done()`: This is fired when the action completes successfully.

▶ `failed()`: This is fired if the action fails (that is, it returns a non-success status code).

▶ `always()`: This is fired regardless of success or failure. This is a great place to clean up any necessary objects, and so on.

Our third example uses the specialized `get()` method that is used when making `GET` requests to our server. This is similar to using `ajax()` with the settings type property set to `GET`, which happens to be the default type value.

There is also a similar `post()` method to submit data to the server.

Our last example uses `getJSON()`, an even more specialized form of `get()`, that is used to retrieve JSON-formatted data from the server:

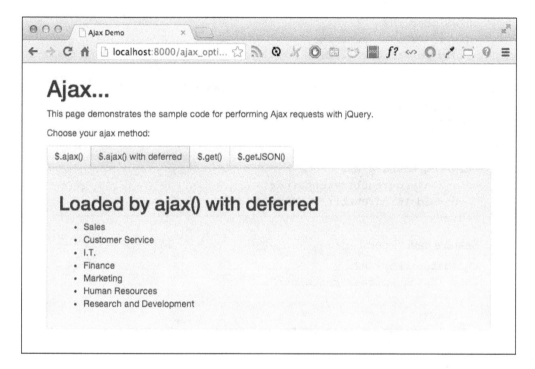

Using jQuery UI widgets

jQuery UI is a popular user interface framework built on top of jQuery. The jQuery UI library provides a number of widget-style controls and UI paradigms that can be used when building your user interfaces.

 For more information on jQueryUI, you can visit the project home page at `http://jqueryui.com/`.

In this section, we will examine how we can use jQuery UI to spice up our applications.

How to do it...

Let's look at how we can use jQuery UI to display useful widgets within our HTML page:

1. Add a reference to the jQuery UI and theme CSS files:

    ```
    <link rel="stylesheet" href="css/theme/jquery-ui.min.css">
    <link rel="stylesheet" href="css/theme/jquery.ui.theme.css">
    ```

2. Define a slider:

    ```
    <h2>Slider</h2>
    <div id="slider-container">
      <div id="slider"></div>
      <p>
        Change the slider and the progressbar below will
        update.</p>
    </div>
    ```

3. Define a progress bar:

    ```
    <h2>Progressbar</h2>
    <div id="progressbar-container">
      <div id="progressbar"></div>
    </div>
    ```

4. Define a date picker:

    ```
    <h2>Datepicker</h2>
    <div id="datepicker-container">
      <p>
        Date:
        <input type="text" id="datepicker">
      </p>
    </div>
    ```

5. Define an autocomplete textbox:

    ```
    <h2>Autocomplete</h2>
    <div id="autocomplete-container">
      <label>
        Department:
        <input type="text" id="autocomplete">
      </label>
    </div>
    ```

6. Lastly, include a reference to the jQuery UI JavaScript:

    ```
    <script src="js/vendor/jquery-ui.min.js"></script>
    ```

In the preceding HTML, we reference the jQuery UI stylesheets. We then define the DOM elements that will become our widget instances. We end by referencing the jQuery UI JavaScipt file. Once defined, we can execute jQuery UI methods to transform our DOM elements into actual widgets as can be seen in the following CoffeeScript code:

1. Create a handler for the DOM ready event:

   ```
   $ ->
   ```

2. Initialize the progress bar widget:

   ```
   # Create a progress bar
   $('#progressbar').progressbar { value: 50 }
   ```

3. Initialize the slider widget with a value and a change event handler:

   ```
   # Create a slider
   $('#slider').slider
     value: 50
     change: (e, ui) ->
       $('#progressbar').progressbar 'option', \
         'value', ui.value
   ```

4. Initialize the date picker widget:

   ```
   # Create a date picker
   $('#datepicker').datepicker()
   ```

5. Initialize the autocomplete textbox widget with departments loaded from the server:

   ```
   # Load departments from server and create auto-complete
   ($.getJSON 'data/departments.json')
     .done (data) ->
       ($ '#autocomplete').autocomplete { source: data }
     .fail (res) ->
       alert 'Cannot load departments. ' + res.statusText
   ```

How it works...

In order to use the jQuery UI widgets, you must link the desired jQuery UI theme CSS and the `jquery-ui.js` JavaScript library.

Once the necessary jQuery UI files are included, you can use the related methods to create the desired widgets.

jQuery UI widgets are created by selecting the DOM element that acts as the widget placeholder using a jQuery selector, and then call the function that converts the placeholder into the widget itself.

In the example, we first create a progress bar by selecting `#progressbar` and executing jQuery UI's `progressbar()` method. The `progressbar()` method accepts an optional object that defines properties and methods used to customize the behavior and settings of the progress bar. In our case, we set its initial value to 50. By default, the minimum value is 0 and the maximum value is 100.

We then create a slider control. Again, we set its initial value to 50. This time, however, we also provide a handler for the slider's change event. The event handler takes two parameters. The first parameter is a generic jQuery event object. The second parameter is an instance of the widget itself, which is very helpful to retrieve selected values, and so on. In our example, we set the progress bar's value to the user-selected value of the slider.

In the next example, we create a simple date picker. This is a very representative example of the power of jQuery UI. With a single `$('#datepicker').datepicker()` statement, we have a fully functioning date picker. It really is that easy.

Last, we create an autocomplete `INPUT` box. This is an excellent widget to offer suggestions to a user as they are typing. In this example, we ask the user for the name of a department.

We first load our sample department data using `getJSON()` and then pass the array as the source option for the autocomplete widget.

We can see these jQuery UI widgets loaded in our browser in the following screenshot:

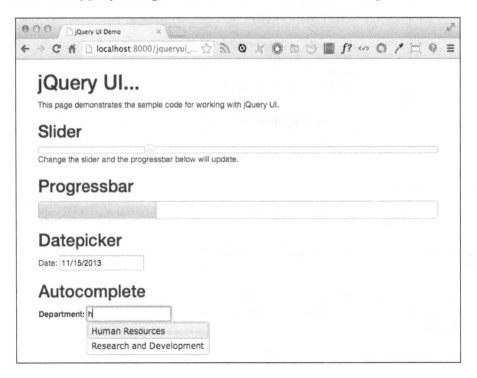

There's more...

jQuery UI allows you to create custom themes using their ThemeRoller tool at `http://jqueryui.com/themeroller`.

You might have noticed that the `jquery-ui.min.js` file is still very large at almost 290 KB. This might be acceptable for our example but a large file such as this is likely too large for a real application. The jQuery UI team has created a tool that allows you to select only the components you are interested in using and downloading only the code required for the components you are using. You can find this tool at `http://jqueryui.com/download`.

Displaying an image gallery using Lightbox

Lightbox is a popular jQuery plugin to display images in a user-friendly yet still visually pleasing way.

> For more information on the Lightbox plugin, you can visit the project home page at `http://lokeshdhakar.com/projects/lightbox2/`.

How to do it...

Let's look at how we can use Lightbox to display a gallery of photos in our HTML page.

1. Add a reference to the Lightbox CSS file:

    ```
    <link rel="stylesheet" href="css/lightbox.css">
    ```

2. Define a `DIV` element to hold the image gallery:

    ```
    <div id="gallery" class="well">
    </div>
    ```

3. Define a template to be used for the album:

    ```
    <script type="text/x-template" id="album-template">
      <h2><%= album.title %></h2>
      <div>
      <% _.each(album.images, function(img){ %>
        <a href="<%=
          album.imageRootPath + img.filename %>"
          data-lightbox="<%= album.title %>"
          title="<%= img.description %>">
          <img src="<%=
            album.imageRootPath + 'tn_' + img.filename %>"
            alt="<%= img.description %>"
            class="img-thumbnail">
        </a>
    ```

```
<% }); %>
</div>
</script>
```

4. Add references to the necessary JavaScript libraries:

```
<script src="js/vendor/jquery.min.js"></script>
<script src="js/vendor/lightbox-2.6.min.js"></script>
<script src="js/vendor/underscore-min.js"></script>
<script src="js/lightbox_demo.js"></script>
```

In the preceding HTML, we reference the Lightbox style sheet and then define DIV to contain our gallery. We then define a template that will iterate through a collection of images. We then reference the necessary JavaScript libraries, including jQuery, Lightbox, and UnderscoreJS to process our template.

In the following CoffeeScript code, we initialize the template, load our images via jQuery's getJSON() method, and finally append our gallery to the gallery DIV:

```
$ ->
  # Grab gallery template
  galleryTemplate = _.template $('#album-template').html()

  # Load images
  ($.getJSON 'data/images.json').done (data) ->
    # Render gallery template and append the HTML
    galleryHtml = galleryTemplate {album: data}
    $('#gallery').append galleryHtml
```

How it works...

To use the Lightbox library, you simply add a link to the `lightbox.css` and `lightbox-2.6.min.js` files.

Once these files are included, you simple add the appropriate attributes to our HTML file. In our case, we use an Underscore template that defines a gallery with HTML that will display an album title and then iterate over a collection of images and create the basic Lightbox image structure:

```
<a href="path-to-fullsize-image"
   data-lightbox="gallery-name"
   title="image-description">
   <img src="path-to-thumbnail-image"
     alt="image-description" class="img-thumbnail" />
</a>
```

We then load the album data from data/images.json using $.getJSON(). We then execute the template and append the resultant HTML to the #gallery DOM element.

Note our use of the img-thumbnail class on our image tag. This is a Bootstrap class that will add a border and some padding around the image, which is perfect for our needs here.

We can see our gallery displayed in the following screenshot:

When we click on a thumbnail, Lightbox will expand it. This can be seen in the following screenshot:

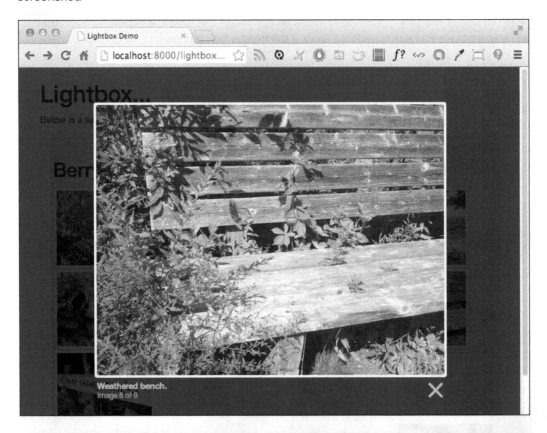

Working with Backbone

Backbone was created by CoffeeScript creator Jeremy Ashkenas in 2010. The project itself was extracted from Jeremy's work for DocumentCloud as a client-side application framework. It was originally a lightweight client-side **Model-View-Control** (**MVC**) framework. It has evolved from it's original 0.1.0 release to remain lightweight, but is no longer an MVC framework strictly speaking. It is instead an MV-Star framework having replaced the notion of a controller with a router instead.

For more information on Backbone, you can visit the project home page at http://backbonejs.org/.

In this section, we will demonstrate how CoffeeScript can be used to create the various building blocks of an Angular application including the following:

- Creating models
- Creating collections
- Creating views
- Handling UI events
- Creating routers

Creating models

In Backbone, the models represent the heart of our application. Models contain our application's interactive data as well as much of the logic surrounding it, such as static properties and methods to provide computed properties, validation, and security access.

Getting ready

Our models are created completely in CoffeeScript code. To begin, create an empty CoffeeScript file or open an existing CoffeeScript file.

How to do it...

We can create Backbone models in two ways:

- Extending the Backbone model:

```
Employee = Backbone.Model.extend
  # define your class structure
```

- Extending using the CoffeeScript syntax sugar:

```
class Employee extends Backbone.Model
  # define your class structure
```

We will follow the second approach to defining Backbone models as this is a more idiomatic way to write our CoffeeScript objects.

In both approaches, we define our structure as an object literal.

For example, we can define our `Employee` model as follows:

```
class Employee extends Backbone.Model
  defaults:
    id: 0
    firstName: ''
    lastName: ''
    salesYtd: 0.0000

  fullName: ->
    "#{@get 'firstName'} #{@get 'lastName'}"

  validate: ->
    return 'First name required' if (@get 'firstName').length is 0
    return 'Last name required' if (@get 'lastName').length is 0

window.app =
  models:
    Employee: Employee
```

How it works...

Here we create a Backbone model to represent our sample `Employee` object. By extending the `Backbone.Model` object, we gain a number of methods that we can use to manage our object and state.

We then define a class with some default attributes. Defaults are applied to new objects when they are created. For example, `emp = new Employee()` will create a new employee instance that has `id`, `firstName`, `lastName`, and `salesYtd` with their default values.

We can override these defaults or add any number of properties to our object's initialization by providing an object literal to our object's construction. For example, `emp = new Employee { id: 99, salary: 50000 }` will create an employee instance with an ID of 99, empty `firstName` and `lastName` values, `salesYTd` of 0, and a salary of 50,000.

Next, we created a method that returns the employee's full name. In this method, we use Backbone's `get()` method to get the model's `firstName` and `lastName` property values. Conversely, if we wanted to set a model's values, we would use `set()`. For example, setting the employee's `salesYtd` can be accomplished as `emp.set 'salesYtd', 40000`.

Lastly, we add a validate method. Backbone will use this method to determine whether a model contains valid data or not. If the model's values are invalid, we simply return a non-undefined value. In our example, the `firstName` and `lastName` values are required. If either are empty, the model state is invalid.

Creating collections

A Backbone collection represents a collection of model instances. This section looks at defining Backbone collections and some of the benefits of using one.

Getting ready

Our collections are created completely in CoffeeScript code. To begin, create an empty CoffeeScript file or open an existing CoffeeScript file.

How to do it...

Collections represent collections of model instances. Like models, these can be defined using the `class` approach:

```
class EmployeeList extends Backbone.Collection
  model: Employee
```

When defining a collection, the only requirement is to specify the type of models the collection will contain.

Once a collection has been defined, it can be easily instantiated using the new operator. For example, to instantiate a collection of `Employee` objects, we can do the following:

```
empList = new EmployeeList [
  { "id": 1, "firstName": "Tracy" }
  { "id": 2, "firstName": "Chris", }
  { "id": 3, "firstName": "Jason", salesYtd: 2000 }
  { "id": 4, "firstName": "Jennifer" }
]
```

How it works...

Like Backbone models, when we extend `Backbone.collection`, we gain a number of methods and properties that allow us to manage and extract information from our collection of objects.

Some of the common methods and properties include:

▶ `add()`, `push()`: Adds an item or items to the collection

▶ `set()`: Adds or updates the collection with the item or items passed to the method

▶ `remove()`, `pop()`: Removes an item from the collection

▶ `pluck()`: Returns an array of values from the property being plucked

▶ `length`: Provides the count of items in the collection

▶ `toJSON()`: Returns the collection as a JSON array

Using `EmployeeList` we defined previously, we can get the number of items in the collection using the `length` property:

```
empList.length        # 4
```

We can add and remove items from our collection using the `add()` and `remove()` methods, respectively:

```
empList.add { id: 5, firstName: "Maxx" }
empList.length        # 5

empList.remove { id: 4, firstName: "Jennifer" }
empList.length        # 4
```

We can use the `at()` method to retrieve a model at a specified location:

```
firstEmp = empList.at 0
firstEmp.get 'firstName'  # "Tracy"
```

We can use the `where()` method to find items by matching attributes:

```
findResults = empList.where { salesYtd: 0 }
findResults.length        # 3
```

We can use the handy `pluck()` method to extract values from our collection. For example, we can use `pluck()` to retrieve the `firstName` values from each of the items in our collection as follows:

```
firstNames = empList.pluck 'firstName'
(firstNames.join ', ')  # "Tracy, Chris, Jason, Maxx"
```

There's more...

There are dozens more methods and properties available. You can view them all on the Backbone website at `http://backbonejs.org/#Collection`.

Once a collection is instantiated, we can perform actions against it.

Creating views

In Backbone, views represent logical pieces of code that can render HTML that is based on a model. It is common to use a template engine to render the HTML for our views. We will use the engine that is built into Underscore.

Getting ready

A view is typically defined in code and associated with an HTML template. For our example, we will have a collection of employees and display them in an HTML table.

Create an HTML file with the following HTML that defines our table container and table row template:

```html
<table id="employee-table"
  class="table table-compact table-bordered table-striped">
  <thead>
    <tr>
      <th>Id</th>
      <th>First name</th>
      <th>Last name</th>
      <th>Sales YTD</th>
    </tr>
  </thead>
  <tbody></tbody>
</table>

<script id="employee-template" type="text/x-template">
  <td><%= id %></td>
  <td><%= firstName %></td>
  <td><%= lastName %></td>
  <td><%= salesYtd %></td>
</script>
```

Next, create a CoffeeScript script file to contain our Backbone view.

How to do it...

As the other Backbone components, views are defined by extending a base Backbone object. For a view, this is the `Backbone.View` object:

1. In our web page, define a table to serve as the container for our rendered views:

    ```html
    <table id="employee-table"
      class="table table-compact table-bordered table-striped" >
      <thead>
        <tr>
          <th>Id</th>
          <th>First name</th>
          <th>Last name</th>
          <th>Sales YTD</th>
        </tr>
      </thead>
      <tbody></tbody>
    </table>
    ```

2. Define a template to be used by our view:

```
<script id="employee-template" type="text/x-template">
  <td><%= id %></td>
  <td><%= firstName %></td>
  <td><%= lastName %></td>
  <td><%= salesYtd %></td>
</script>
```

3. Open a `SCRIPT` tag for our CoffeeScript code:

```
<script type="text/coffeescript">
```

4. Create a view class that extends `Backbone.View`:

```
class EmployeeView extends Backbone.View
```

5. Use a `tr` tag as the HTML container for our view:

```
tagName: 'tr'
```

6. Define the template our view will use:

```
template: _.template $('#employee-template').html()
```

7. Define a `render()` function responsible for rendering our view:

```
render: ->
  @$el.html ($ (@template @model))
  return this
```

8. Add an array of employee objects as sample data:

```
employees = [
  { id: 1, firstName: "Tracy", lastName: "Ouellette", \
    salesYtd: 22246 }
  { id: 2, firstName: "Chris", lastName: "Daniel", \
    salesYtd: 3876 }
  { id: 3, firstName: "Jason", lastName: "Alexander", \
    salesYtd: 4095 }
  { id: 4, firstName: "Jennifer", lastName: "Hannah", \
    salesYtd: 8070 }
  { id: 5, firstName: "Maxx", lastName: "Slayde", \
    salesYtd: 2032 }
]
```

9. Iterate through the employee items and append each rendered view to the employee table:

```
for emp in employees
  employeeView = new EmployeeView model: emp
    $('#employee-table tbody').append \
      employeeView.render().el
```

10. Close our CoffeeScript SCRIPT tag and add references for our library JavaScript files:

```
</script>
<script src="js/vendor/jquery.min.js"></script>
<script src="js/vendor/underscore-min.js"></script>
<script src="js/vendor/backbone-min.js"></script>
<script src="js/vendor/coffee-script.min.js"></script>
```

How it works...

In Backbone, a view is responsible for generating HTML by combining a model or collection with a template and appending this to the DOM. In this example, we will iterate through a collection of employees and add each item as a table row to the employees table.

When a Backbone view is rendered, it will be wrapped by a DIV tag by default. For our example, we want each table row to be wrapped by a TR tag. We specify this in our view by using the tagName property:

```
tagName: 'tr'
```

We then define a template property to be used when rendering an employee:

```
template: _.template $('#employee-template').html()
```

We finally define a render() method that will be responsible for adding HTML to the root element (the tr tag in this case):

```
render: ->
  @$el.html ($ (@template @model))
  return this
```

All Backbone views have a root element named el. No changes are made to the DOM on our page. Instead, all changes are applied to this root element. Backbone provides a jQuery-wrapped version of this root element named $el. This is simply a shorthand of performing $(el). This allows us to call jQuery's html(), append(), and other DOM manipulation methods when preparing our HTML.

Once render() is called, we can then use the view's el property to append, insert, or otherwise modify our page's DOM.

Note that it is best practice to return this at the end of the render() method as this allows the render processes to be chained.

With our HTML table and template defined inside the web page, we iterate through each employee object and create an instance of `EmployeeView` passing the employee as the view's model. This is the model that will be used by our view's `render()` method.

We finish by calling the view instance's `render()` method and appending the view's `el` DOM to our table's `TBODY` element.

When loaded in our browser, the employee views are appended to our table as shown in the following screenshot:

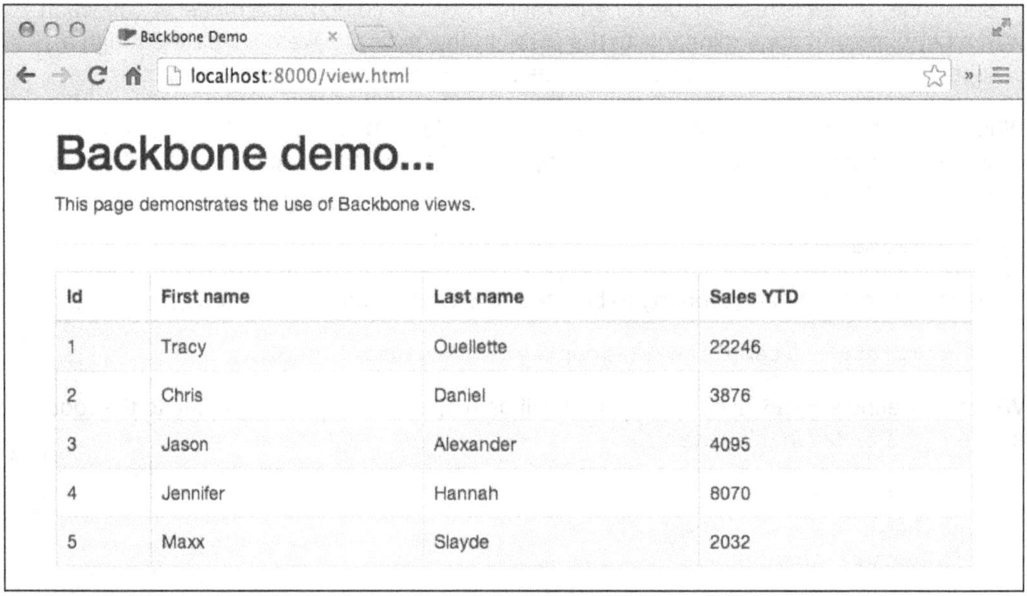

Handling UI events

Even the most basic of applications built upon Backbone will have some form of user interaction. In this section, we will demonstrate how to listen for client-side UI events and take action on them.

Getting ready

Create an empty CoffeeScript file and add the following view code:

```coffeescript
class EditView extends Backbone.View
  template: _.template $('#employee-edit-template').html()

  render: ->
    @$el.html(@template @model)
    return this
```

This view is nearly identical to `EmployeeView` we defined in our previous section on views.

How to do it...

Backbone allows us to define an events property in our view. The value of this property is a collection of an event signature and handling method named pairs.

Let's add an event that will listen for a click event on an update button:

1. Begin by defining a view as we saw previously:

```
class EditView extends Backbone.View
    template: _.template $('#employee-edit-template').html()
```

2. Add an `events` property to listen for a `click` event on the update button:

```
events:
    'click #update-button': 'updateEmployee'
```

3. Add the `updateEmployee()` function:

```
updateEmployee: ->
    alert 'Update button has been clicked'
```

How it works...

Backbone allows us to define our event handlers in our Backbone views using the view's events property. Each event is defined using an `event selector: call back` format.

Event selectors are based on jQuery delegates. A selector includes an event type and a DOM selector that indicates which element(s) should trigger the event.

Other event selector examples include:

```
events:
    'click #emp-edit button'    : 'updateEmployee'
    'mouseover #emp-edit label' : 'highlight'
    'mouseout  #emp-edit label' : 'unhighlight'
```

Event callbacks receive a jQuery event object. If your callback requires additional information about the item that triggered the event, you can use jQuery's `data()` method to retrieve values from `event.target`:

```
events:
    'click #employee-edit button': 'updateEmployee'

updateEmployee: (e) ->
    id = $(e.target).data 'id'
    alert "Update button has been clicked for ID: #{id}"
```

Creating routers

Backbone provides a routing mechanism that allows us to watch for routing changes and then take the necessary actions. For even moderately complex applications, it is common to use routing to switch between various application states.

For example, if the user is looking at a list of employees, they can click on an **Add** button, which will navigate the user to the `#/add-employee` state, at which time we can render a form to allow the user to add the information for a new employee.

In this section, we will see how Backbone allows us to register routes and handle the navigation event they raise.

How to do it...

We create a router by extending the `Backbone.Router` object. We then define a `routes` property that contains a route table:

1. Define a class that extends the Backbone `Router` object:

   ```
   class AppRouter extends Backbone.Router
   ```

2. Add a `routes` property to define our routes:

   ```
   routes:
     ''                                : 'displayList'
     'employees/:id'                   : 'displayEmployee'
     'employees/:id/departments/:id': 'displayEmployeeDepartment'
     'payroll/giveRaise/*ids'        : 'giveEmployeesRaise'
   ```

3. Add our route handlers as functions:

   ```
   displayList: ->
     $('#output-list').append '<li>Displaying employee list.</li>'

   displayEmployee: (id) ->
     $('#output-list').append \
       "<li>Displaying employee with id of #{id}</li>"

   displayEmployeeDepartment: (empId, deptId) ->
     $('#output-list').append \
       "<li>Displaying employee #{empId}, department #{deptId}</
   li>"

   giveEmployeesRaise: (ids) ->
     $('#output-list').append \
       "<li>Employees #{ids} thank you</li>"
   ```

4. Finish by adding an instance of the router to the application object and start Backbone's `history` service:

```
router = new AppRouter()
Backbone.history.start()
```

How it works...

Our router defines a route property representing the routes our application will recognize. Routes are added as `path:value` pairs where the path represents the URL to be matched and the value represents the method to be called.

Paths can include URL parameters using the `/:param` format. Backbone will automatically parse these parameters and pass them to the method to be called. For paths that contain more than one parameter such as `employees/:id/departments/:id`, the parameters will be passed in the order they are provided in the path.

Paths can also include splats. A splat represents an unknown number of parameters and is essentially everything that occurs after the splat in the path. For example, the path `payroll/giveRaise/*ids` will call the method passing everything after `giveRaise/` as a single argument. This allows us to define very flexible routes, but the parsing of splats is our responsibility.

Once the routes are defined, we create the methods to be called when the browser navigation matches the various defined routes.

In the example, our routes simply append a `LI` element to our `#output-list` `UL` element for the sake of demonstration. In a real application, our routes would instantiate the various views used in our system and append them to the DOM.

To kick start our application routing, we create an instance of our `AppRouter`, saving it as `app.router` if we need access to it later in our application and then we start Backbone's history service. The history is responsible for listening for URL changes and dispatching them accordingly.

There's more...

Once instantiated, a Backbone router provides a `navigate()` method that allows us to navigate to a URL from within our application code. For example, `app.router.navigate '#/employees/45'` will update our application URL and trigger the route handling.

You can also register event listeners for route changes using the router's `on()` method. We simply pass a string that represents the name of the routing event and an event handler function.

The name of the routing event follows a simple pattern of `route:methodName`. For example, we can create an event listener for our `'employees/:id' : 'displayEmployee'` route in the following manner:

```
router.on 'route:displayEmployee', (id) ->
  alert 'Displaying employee ' + id
```

Working with AngularJS

AngularJS is a fully featured client-side MVC framework from Google. Its popularity has exploded in recent months.

 For more information on AngularJS, you can visit the project home page at `http://angularjs.org/`.

In this section, we will demonstrate how CoffeeScript can be used to create the various building blocks of an Angular application including the following:

- ▶ Creating an Angular application module
- ▶ Creating Angular controllers
- ▶ Creating Angular providers
- ▶ Creating Angular directives
- ▶ Creating Angular routers
- ▶ Handling inter-controller events

Creating an Angular application module

In Angular, the application module contains all of our applications controllers, services, directives, and routing. This allows us to limit the scope of our application to a specific application instance and consequently allows us to have multiple applications within the same page.

Getting ready

Angular is an extensive framework and contains almost everything you would ever need to create your applications. On top of that, there are a number of official plugins developed by the Angular team that can be brought in as needed.

For our example, we will use a basic HTML5 template with the following code:

```html
<!doctype html>
<html>
<head>
  <title>AngularJS Demo</title>
  <link rel="stylesheet" href="css/bootstrap.min.css">
  <link rel="stylesheet" href="css/lightbox.css">
</head>
<body>
  <div class="container">
    <h1>AngularJS demo...</h1>
    <p>
      This page demonstrates using AngularJS.
    </p>
  </div>
</body>
<script src="js/vendor/angular.min.js"></script>
<script type="text/coffeescript" src="coffee/app.coffee"></script>
<script src="js/vendor/coffee-script.min.js"></script>
</html>
```

How to do it...

To create an Angular application, we execute the `angular.module()` method providing a name and list of the external dependencies needed by Angular:

1. Create a file named `coffee/app.coffee` with the following code:

    ```coffee
    window.app = angular.module('demoApp', [])
    ```

2. Add a SCRIPT block to bootstrap Angular:

    ```html
    <script type="text/coffeescript">
      angular.bootstrap document, ['demoApp']
    </script>
    ```

How it works...

As you can see, the process of creating an Angular application is quite easy.

After loading, Angular will scan the DOM for an element with an `ng-app` attribute. It will then begin the application Bootstrap process.

Note that it is possible to have more than one Angular application on the same page. For example, an application such as Gmail could have an Angular application to handle the inbox, and another Angular application to handle Google Hangouts in the sidebar. In this case, we could have two DIV tags, each with their own `ng-app` attribute.

We use the `Angular.module()` function to define a new Angular application called demoApp. The empty array tells Angular that we have no dependencies (yet).

Angular provides an impressive dependency injection mechanism that is also used quite extensively. We will see this in the next section when we discuss controllers. Remember that if you do not have dependencies, you still need to pass along an empty array, or else Angular's dependency injection mechanism will fail in odd ways.

We then add our application module to the global window namespace so it will be available to our other modules as demoApp.

We call the `angular.bootstrap()` method, the element to which the application should be scoped (the entire document in this case), and the array of our dependencies (demoApp).

There's more...

The application module can be used for much more than our simple example. For example, it is common to use the application module to perform any initialization or application configuration. We will see an example of these in our upcoming section on creating Angular routes.

Even though the application module's source file can contain controllers, services, and all manner of Angular components, it is recommended to keep our applications modular and define the controllers, services, and so on in their own files.

Creating Angular controllers

Angular controllers represent a logical application component responsible for exposing models and functions to your views and for monitoring your models for changes so that they can take appropriate actions.

Getting ready

In this recipe, we have an `app.coffee` file that defines the application object with the following code:

```
window.app = angular.module('demoApp', [])
```

How to do it...

To create a controller, we create a CoffeeScript class that provides a constructor that includes the controller's dependencies. Angular will resolves those dependencies for you and inject them into your controller's constructor. One such dependency you will use with most controllers is the `$scope` provider:

1. Create a file named `controller.coffee` and add a class to represent our controller:

```
class window.MyController
```

2. Add a constructor function that receives a scope object:

```
constructor: ($scope) ->
```

3. Set a title property and event handler for the scope:

```
$scope.title = 'Controllers are Fun'
$scope.onClick = (e) ->
  alert 'Thanks!'
```

4. Add the controller to the application object:

```
app.controller 'myController', MyController
```

5. Add the following HTML to a basic web page:

```
<div ng-controller="myController">
  <h2>{{title}}</h2>
  <a class="btn btn-primary" ng-click="onClick()">
    Click me!
  </a>
</div>
```

6. Add references to Angular, CoffeeScript, and the `app.coffee` and `controller.coffee` files:

```
<script src="js/vendor/angular.min.js"></script>
<script src="js/vendor/coffee-script.min.js"></script>
<script type="text/coffeescript" src="coffee/app.coffee"></script>
<script type="text/coffeescript"
  src="coffee/controller.coffee"></script>
```

7. Finish by bootstrapping Angular:

```
<script type="text/coffeescript">
  angular.bootstrap document, ['demoApp']
</script>
```

How it works...

In this example, we create a controller called `MyController`. Our controller's constructor receives a copy of `$scope` to which we add a title value and an event handler named `onClick`.

`$scope` is a powerful object as it is the glue between the controller and any views that reference it.

Angular provides several methods of hooking into our HTML. We can do this by element, attribute, class, or comment. In our example, we use the attribute method to wire our Angular application to our HTML.

For example, we use the `ng-controller` directive to assign our controller named `myController` to the DIV. Inside of this DIV, we use Angular's built-in data-binding template syntax (double curly braces) to display the title value of `$scope`:

```
<h2>{{title}}</h2>
```

We use another directive named `ng-click` to automatically bind our anchor's click event to the `onClick()` event handler inside `$scope`.

We can see an example of our rendered template in the following screenshot:

There's more...

Angular provides a number of directives to make our lives easier. For example, the `ng-repeat` directive will iterate over a collection of items and render each using the provided template.

Let's create an example that uses `ng-repeat` to display our familiar employee data. For this slightly more advanced example, we will create an `Employee` model:

```
window.demo = window.demo || {}

class Employee
  constructor: (emp) ->
    @id = emp.id
    @firstName = emp.firstName
    @lastName = emp.lastName
    @salesYtd = emp.salesYtd

  fullName: ->
    "#{@firstName} #{@lastName}"

window.demo.models =
  Employee: Employee
```

This is a simple object that has the `id`, `firstName`, `lastName`, and `salesYtd` properties and defines a method that returns an employee's full name.

Our controller can then add a collection of `Employee` instances to our controller's `$scope` object:

```
window.demo = window.demo || {}

Employee = demo.models.Employee

class EmployeeCtrl
  constructor: ($scope) ->
    $scope.title = 'Employee List'
    $scope.employees = [
      new Employee { 'id': 1, 'firstName': 'Tracy', \
        'lastName': 'Ouellette', 'salesYtd': 22246 }
      new Employee { 'id': 2, 'firstName': 'Chris', \
        'lastName': 'Daniel', 'salesYtd': 3876 }
      new Employee { 'id': 3, 'firstName': 'Jason', \
        'lastName': 'Alexander', 'salesYtd': 4095 }
      new Employee { 'id': 4, 'firstName': 'Jennifer', \
        'lastName': 'Hannah', 'salesYtd': 8070 }
      new Employee { 'id': 5, 'firstName': 'Maxx', \
        'lastName': 'Slayde', 'salesYtd': 2032 }
    ]

window.demo.app.controller 'employeeCtrl', EmployeeCtrl
```

Our controller adds a title value and employees collection to our $scope object:

We can then iterate over our employee collection using ng-repeat:

```
<body>
  <div class="container">
    <h1>AngularJS demo...</h1>
    <p>
      This page demonstrates using AngularJS.
    </p>
    <hr>
    <div ng-controller="employeeCtrl" ng-cloak>
      <h2>{{title}}</h2>
      <div class="row">
        <div class="col-md-6">
          <table class="table table-condensed
            table-bordered table-hover">
            <thead>
              <tr>
                <th>Employee</th>
                <th class="numeric">Sales YTD</th>
              </tr>
            </thead>
            <tbody>
              <tr ng-repeat="emp in employees">
                <td>{{emp.fullName()}}</td>
                <td class="numeric">
                  {{emp.salesYtd | currency}}</td>
              </tr>
            </tbody>
          </table>
        </div>
      </div>
    </div>
  </div>
</body>
<script src="js/vendor/angular.min.js"></script>
<script src="js/vendor/coffee-script.min.js"></script>
<script type="text/coffeescript" src="coffee/app.coffee"></script>
<script type="text/coffeescript" src="coffee/models.coffee"></script>
<script type="text/coffeescript" src="coffee/controllers.coffee"></
script>
<script type="text/coffeescript">
angular.bootstrap document, ['demoApp']
</script>
```

Our HTML sets up a Bootstrap table and in TBODY, we add the ng-repeat attribute with the expression of emp in employees.

Then, inside our TR elements, we define the template to be rendered for each employee. In this case, we display the employee's full name and their YTD sales:

```
<td>{{emp.fullName()}}</td>
<td class="numeric">{{emp.salesYtd | currency}}</td>
```

You might have noticed that we're doing something strange with the way we display the employee's sales figures. More specifically, you might have noticed the | (pipe) and currency.

This is called a filter in Angular. Filters are used to convert one value to another. For example, the currency filter will turn a numeric value of 125 into the string $125.00, which is more suitable for display.

Angular comes with a number of scalar value filters including:

Filter	Purpose	Example
Number	Formats a number as text	10000 | number:2 => "10,000.00"
Date	Formats a date as text	1288323623006 | date:'MM/dd/ yyyy' => 10/29/2010
Lowercase	Converts a string to lowercase	'ABCD' | lowercase => 'abcd'
Uppercase	Converts a string to uppercase	'abcd' | uppercase => 'ABCD'

We can see Angular's currency filter in the following screenshot:

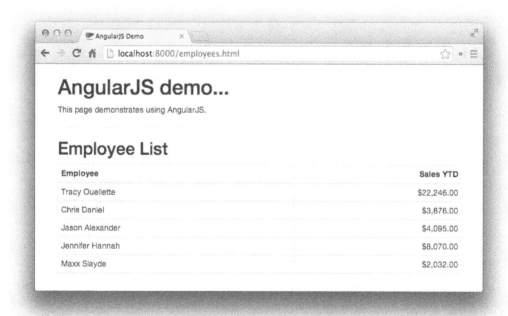

Lastly, you may have noticed a new attribute on our `ng-controller="employeeCtrl"` div called `ng-cloak`.

Occasionally, while Angular loads, we may see flashes of the HTML template before it has been populated by Angular. The `ng-cloak` directive will hide the HTML until the template has been fully populated and it is ready to be displayed.

Creating Angular providers

We can add additional functionality to our Angular application through the use of providers.

Angular providers allow us to create injectable components that return objects and values to our application. Angular has four provider methods: `constant()`, `value()`, `service()`, and `factory()`.

Angular's `constant()` and `value()` methods are used to register values or objects that can be used by Angular's services. Note that values declared with `constant()` are also available to other providers.

Angular's `service()` and `factory()` methods are used to register constructor functions or factory functions, respectively.

How to do it...

We can register a constant provider using the `constant()` function by following these steps:

1. Create a module:

    ```
    app = angular.module 'demoApp', []
    ```

2. Create a constant to store an array of departments:

    ```
    app.constant 'DEPARTMENTS', [
        'Sales', 'Customer Service', 'I.T.'
        'Finance', 'Marketing', 'Human Resources'
        'Research and Development'
    ]
    ```

3. Create a controller and inject our constant as a dependency:

    ```
    class DepartmentCtrl
      constructor: ($scope, DEPARTMENTS) ->
        $scope.title = 'Constant() Demo'
        $scope.departments = DEPARTMENTS.sort()
    ```

4. Add the controller to the application object:

    ```
    app.controller 'departmentCtrl', DepartmentCtrl
    ```

We can register a value provider in the same manner using the `value()` function by following these steps:

1. Create a module:

   ```
   app = angular.module 'demoApp', []
   ```

2. Create a value to contain an array:

   ```
   app.value 'famousCats', [
     'Garfield', 'Felix', 'Butch'
     'Duchess', 'Meowth', 'Scratchy'
   ]
   ```

3. Create a controller and inject our constant as a dependency:

   ```
   class DepartmentCtrl
     constructor: ($scope, DEPARTMENTS, superHeroes) ->
       $scope.title = 'Value() Demo'
       $scope.superHeroes = superHeroes.sort()
   ```

4. Add the controller to the application object:

   ```
   app.controller 'departmentCtrl', DepartmentCtrl
   ```

We can create a service provider by using the `service()` function by following these steps:

1. Create a module:

   ```
   app = angular.module 'demoApp', []
   ```

2. Create an object to be returned by our service:

   ```
   class MathUtils
     areaOfRectangle: (height, width) ->
       height * width
     areaOfSquare: (width) ->
       @areaOfRectangle width, width
     areaOfTriangle: (base, height) ->
       (@areaOfRectangle base, height) / 2.0
     areaOfCircle: (radius) ->
       Math.PI * radius * radius
   ```

3. Register our object as a service provider:

   ```
   app.service 'mathUtils', MathUtils
   ```

We can create a factory provider by using the `factory()` function; perform the following steps:

1. Create a module:

   ```
   app = angular.module 'demoApp', []
   ```

2. Create an object to be returned by the factory provider:

   ```
   class StringUtils
     toUpper: (value) ->
       value.toUpperCase()
     toLower: (value) ->
       value.toLowerCase()
     length: (value) ->
       value.length
   ```

3. Register our object as a service provider:

   ```
   app.factory 'stringUtils', -> new StringUtils
   ```

How it works...

In the first example, we declared a constant named DEPARTMENTS. We then injected our DEPARTMENTS constant into our DepartmentCtrl controller. Constants are great to deal with configuration settings.

"What happens if you try to replace a constant?" you might ask. Well, no error is raised, but any attempts to reassign a constant value will be ignored. So, in the following scenario, LETTERS will continue to be A through E:

```
app.constant 'LETTERS', [ "A",  "B",  "C",  "D", "E" ]
app.constant 'LETTERS', [1, 2, 3, 4, 5]
```

LETTERS will continue to be A thru E.

We then defined a system value using the `value()` provider. Values are similar to constants in that they can be easily injected into our controllers. Unlike constants, however, values can be reassigned during the application's life cycle. Lastly, we defined a service and a factory provider.

There is a lot of confusion with regards to Angular services and factories. This confusion stems from the fact that both `service()` and `factory()` can be used to accomplish the same goals.

Services and factories are a means to encapsulate a related set of functionality in the same module that can then be used by our controllers or other services and factories.

Both `service()` and `factory()` return a singleton object. That's an object that gets instantiated only and exactly once. All requests to the service or factory will receive the same object.

We can use our factory and service in our controllers and use Angular's dependency injection. For example, we can use our `mathUtils` service and `stringUtils` factory in the following way:

```
class ServiceFactoryCtrl
  constructor: ($scope, mathUtils, stringUtils) ->
    $scope.title = 'Service and Factory Demo'

    $scope.areaOfRectangle = (mathUtils.areaOfRectangle 4, 5)
    $scope.areaOfTriangle = (mathUtils.areaOfTriangle 4, 5)
    $scope.areaOfCircle = (mathUtils.areaOfCircle 5)

    $scope.toUpper = (stringUtils.toUpper 'abcde')
    $scope.toLower = (stringUtils.toLower 'ABCDE')
    $scope.length = (stringUtils.length 'ABCDE')

app.controller 'serviceFactoryCtrl', ServiceFactoryCtrl
```

> A good rule of thumb is to use a service if the object does not require any configuration once the object is initialized, and use a factory if you need to perform some post initialization work.

In the preceding code, our `ServiceFactoryCtrl` controller uses both `mathUtils` and `stringUtils`.

There's more...

Angular provides a number of powerful built-in providers for our use. These include the following:

Service	Description
`$http`	A service that wraps the browser's AJAX mechanisms to facilitate communication with the HTTP server
`$location`	A service that provides access to `window.location`, including methods to get or set parts of the URL
`$log`	A simple logging service
`$resource`	A factory that provides access to RESTful data services
`$timeout`	A wrapper for the `window.setTimeout` function that provides a promise that allows you to cancel the timeout

Creating Angular directives

Angular directives are primarily responsible for manipulating our DOM elements. In other applications, we may have used jQuery to perform these actions, but Angular directives can wire event handlers, hide/show elements, include/exclude content, and so on, all based on the state of our application's scope.

We saw several built-in directives, including ngController to associate a DOM element with a controller and ngRepeat to iterate over collections. There are dozens of other built-in directives including the following:

Directive	Description
ngHide	Hides a DOM element if the expression evaluates to true.
ngShow	Displays a DOM element if the expression evaluates to true.
ngClass	Evaluated expression sets a DOM element's class attribute.
ngInclude	Includes DOM elements when the evaluated expression is true.
ngStyle	Evaluated expression sets a DOM element's style attribute.
ngSwitch	Include DOM elements when the evaluated expression matches an ng-switch-when value. If no matching values are found, ng-switch-default will be used.
ngBlur	Attaches an onBlur event listener to a DOM element and will call the expression when an element loses focus.
ngClick	Attaches an onClick event listener to a DOM element and will call the expression when clicked.
ngFocus	Attaches an onFocus event listener to a DOM element and will call the expression when an element receives focus.

There are many others as well. Please refer to the Angular documentation for more information.

In this section, we look at creating our own Angular directives.

How to do it...

To define a directive, we call Angular's directive() method with a name and function that returns a configuration object.

1. Create an application:

   ```
   app = angular.module 'demoApp', []
   ```

2. Use the directive() function to register our new directive:

   ```
   app.directive 'greeting', ->
     restrict: 'EA'
     template: '<div>Welcome from <strong>{{from}}</strong></div>'
     scope:
       from: '@grFrom'
     replace: true
   ```

How it works...

In this simple example, we declare a new directive called greeting. Our configuration object has three properties, including restrict, template, and replace.

Directives can exist in four forms: element (E), attribute (A), class (C), and comment (M).

Form	Usage example
Element (E)	`<greeting gr-from="Hello"></greeting>`
Attribute (A)	`<div greeting gr-from="Hello"></greeting>`
Class (C)	`<div class="greeting"></div>`
Comment (M)	`<!-- directive: greeting -->`

In the example, we restrict our greeting directive to only elements and attributes. This is actually recommended by the Angular team as it offers the most flexibility.

 Note that there is one complication to using directives in the element (E) form. Older versions of Internet Explorer do not support custom elements by default. In practice, I recommend that you use the attribute (A) form to define directives.

Our example also defines a template. Angular will use this template to create the necessary DOM elements. In our example, this is a simple string. Templates can be placed into external HTML files on their own and then references in the directive configuration using the `templateUrl` property instead:

```
templateUrl: 'templates/employee.html'
```

Next, we define a scope. Directives, by default, have access to the scope of their parent DOM element. We can, however, create an isolated scope as we have in our example:

```
scope:
  from: '@grFrom'
```

In our example, our scope contains a `from` property that is assigned its value from the `grfrom` attribute value using the following mapping:

```
from: '@grFrom'
```

The @ symbol causes Angular to pass the item by value, which makes it available for data binding.

When we want to use our directive, we can simply include the following in our HTML:

- ▸ In element form it is as follows:

  ```
  <greeting gr-from="element"></greeting>
  ```

- ▸ In attribute form it is as follows:

  ```
  <div greeting gr-from="attribute"></div>
  ```

Creating Angular routers

Angular provides a built-in routing mechanism that allows us to wire URLs to application views and controllers. This is an excellent way to trigger state changes in our applications.

In this section, we will learn how to configure Angular routing.

How to do it...

Let's look at how we can create a router and use route parameters:

1. Create an application:

   ```
   app = angular.module 'demoApp', ['ngRoute']
   ```

2. Create a controller for page A:

   ```
   app.controller 'pageAController', \
     ($scope, $routeParams) ->
       $scope.id = $routeParams.id
   ```

3. Create a controller for page B:

   ```
   app.controller 'pageBController', \
     ($scope, $routeParams) ->
       $scope.id = $routeParams.id
   ```

4. Configure the application's routes using the `$routeProvider` service:

   ```
   app.config ($routeProvider) ->
     $routeProvider
       .when '/page-a/:id',
         templateUrl: 'partials/page-a.html'
         controller: 'pageAController'
       .when '/page-b/:id',
         templateUrl: 'partials/page-b.html'
         controller: 'pageBController'
   ```

How it works...

Angular provides a `config()` method that allows us to perform any necessary application configuration as the application starts. This is the perfect time to configure our routing.

Angular has a `$routeProvider` service that allows us to register our application routes.

First, we must indicate our application's dependency on `ngRoute`. This module contains `$routeProvider`. Note that the `ngRoute` module is not in the standard Angular JavaScript file. You must also add a reference to the `angular-route.js` file in order to load `$routeProvider`.

We then call `config()` on our application object. We pass a function into `config()` that takes `$routeProvider` as a dependency. Within our function, we use the `$routeProvider`'s `when()` method to assign a route configuration object to a specific path in the form of the following:

```
$routeProvider.when('/path/to/resource/:params', configuration)
```

For each route, we defined an object with both `templateUrl` and `controller` properties. The `templateUrl` property points to the template to be loaded as the application's view. The `controller` property specifies the name of the controller the view should use.

Notice that we defined both of our routes with a route parameter named `:id`. Angular's `$routeProvider` service will automatically extract route parameters and make them available through the `$routeParams` provider. We register `$routeParams` as a dependency in our two sample controllers and assign the value of `:id` to our `$scope` object.

We will create two partial templates.

In the first template, named `partials/page-a.html`, we have the following HTML:

```
<h2>Welcome to Page A</h2>
<p>Product Id is {{id}}</p>
```

In the second template, named `partials/page-b.html`, we have the following HTML:

```
<h2>Welcome to Page B</h2>
<p>Product Id is {{id}}</p>
```

In our main HTML page, we have the following HTML:

```
<h1>AngularJS demo...</h1>
<p>
  This page demonstrates using AngularJS routing.
</p>
<a href="#/page-a/23">Load page A</a> <br>
<a href="#/page-b/72">Load page B</a>
<hr>
<div ng-view></div>
...
<script src="js/vendor/angular-route.min.js"></script>
```

Our HTML has a new directive, `ng-view`. This directive acts as a placeholder where our views will be displayed.

When loaded, we can click on the **Load page A** link, which will navigate to the `/page-a` route passing the value of 23 for the ID. The `page-a.html` file will be displayed in the `ng-view` element. Clicking on the **Load page B** link, on the other hand, will display `page-b.html` instead.

We can see an example in the following screenshot:

Handling inter-controller events

Angular allows us to build very sophisticated applications. It is not uncommon to have more than one controller on a page at any given time. There are times when some action in one controller will need to affect another controller.

In this section, we will look at how to accomplish inter-controller communication.

How to do it...

The recommended way to pass events through our Angular applications is to use the `$emit()` and `$on()` methods of the `$rootScope` provider.

The root scope represents the initial scope of the application and acts as a wrapper scope for the entire application. The root scope is made available through the $rootScope provider.

The $rootScope provider has two event methods that can act as an event bus. The $emit() method allows you to trigger an event from any controller, or provider:

```
# something interesting happened
$rootProvider.$emit 'watch-me', { interesting: true }

# something uninteresting happened
$rootProvider.$emit 'watch-me', { interesting: false }
```

How it works...

The $emit() method takes a name and an optional argument representing the event details.

In the preceding example, we emit two notifications. Both will trigger the watch-me event. One passes event arguments with interesting = true, while the other with interesting = false.

Then, we can subscribe to these events in our application using the $rootScope $on() method:

```
# subscribe to watch-me event
$rootProvider.$on 'watch-me', (event, args) ->
  console.log "Was it interesting? #{args.interesting}"
```

There's more...

Using the $emit() and $on() methods of $rootScope is convenient and they also excel in performance.

Let's now look at how to use $emit() and $on() inside a controller:

```
class FirstCtrl
  constructor: ($scope, $rootScope) ->
    $scope.message = 'This is the message of FirstCtrl'
    $scope.onClick = ->
      $rootScope.$emit 'firstCtrlClick',
        message: '[nudged by FirstCtrl]'

    unbind = $rootScope.$on 'secondCtrlClick', (event, args) ->
      $scope.message += '<br />' + args.message
    $scope.$on '$destroy', unbind
```

```
class SecondCtrl
  constructor: ($scope, $rootScope) ->
    $scope.message = 'This is the message of SecondCtrl'
    $scope.onClick = ->
      $rootScope.$emit 'secondCtrlClick',
        message: '[nudged by SecondCtrl]'

    unbind = $rootScope.$on 'firstCtrlClick', (event, args) ->
      $scope.message += '<br />' + args.message
    $scope.$on '$destroy', unbind
```

Here, we have two controllers, FirstCtrl and SecondCtrl. Each one has $scope and the application's $rootScope passed through Angular's dependency injection.

Inside each controller, we define a message property and an onClick event handler on the controller's $scope object. In the onClick event handler, we use the $emit() method of $rootScope to emit a message with a name and an event argument:

```
# FirstCtrl
$rootScope.$emit 'firstCtrlClick',
  message: '[nudged by FirstCtrl]'
# SecondCtrl
$rootScope.$emit 'secondCtrlClick',
  message: '[nudged by SecondCtrl]'
```

We then register a listener on $rootScope for a message posted by the other controller using the $on() method of $rootScope. We will need to dispose of this event listener when the controller is destroyed. So we keep a handle to our registered $on() listener that can be used when the controller is disposed. We capture this event using $scope.$on to listen for the controller's destroy event.

Note that we do not need to dispose of our $on() event listeners inside providers such as services or factories. This is because providers create only one instance of the object unlike controllers.

It is also worth noting that $emit() and $on() are not particular to $rootScope. They are available on all scope objects including our controller's $scope object.

Communicating in real time with Socket.io

Socket.io is a node library that facilitates real-time two-way communication between the HTTP server and the web client. It has support for platforms, browsers, and devices.

In this section, we will see how to configure Socket.io with the express server and process messages between the client and server.

You can get more information on Socket.io from the project's home page at `http://socket.io/`.

Getting ready

We will be using an express server as our HTTP server configured to use the Jade view engine.

We begin by defining our application's node dependencies in a file named `package.json`:

```
{
  "name": "socket-demo",
  "description": "Socket.io Demo",
  "dependencies": {
    "express": "~3.4",
    "jade": "~0",
    "socket.io": "~0.9"
  }
}
```

Besides our express and Jade dependencies, we also take a dependency on the Socket.io node library.

Install the necessary packages by running the following command:

npm install

Now, let's create our `app.coffee` file to create our HTTP server:

```
express = require 'express'
app = express()
port = 8080

# configure Jade view engine
app.set 'views', __dirname + '/tpl'
app.set 'view engine', 'jade'
app.engine 'jade', (require 'jade').__express
```

```
# expose static assets from /public folder
app.use (express.static __dirname + '/public')

# routes
app.get '/', (req, res) ->
  res.render 'index'

# listen for requests
console.log "Listening on port #{port}"
app.listen port
```

This is a fairly straightforward express server. We require express and create an instance for our application. Next, we configure the Jade view engine. It is worth noting that we assign our view template folder to be /tpl. This is where we will store our Jade templates. Then, we configure express to serve static assets from inside the /public folder. We will use this for our client scripts, CSS, images, and so on. Lastly, we start our application listening on the specified port.

We define one route. It renders index.jade:

```
!!!
html
  head
    title= "Socket.io Example"
    link(rel="stylesheet", href="css/bootstrap.min.css")
  body
    .container
      h1= "Socket.io Example"
      p
        | This page demonstrates the use of Socket.io
      hr
```

Launch the HTTP server by running the following command:

app.coffee

Navigate to http://localhost:8080/ and you should see the index page shown in the following screenshot:

How to do it...

We will update our express server's `app.coffee` file in the following ways:

1. Load the Socket.io library:

   ```
   socket  = require 'socket.io'
   ```

2. Add a new route to load a page to be used as our client:

   ```
   app.get '/count', (req, res) ->
     res.render 'counter'
   ```

3. Replace the `app.listen port` line with the following:

   ```
   server = app.listen port
   io = socket.listen server
   ```

4. At the end of `app.coffee`, add the following:

   ```
   io.sockets.on 'connection', (socket) ->
     value = 0
     setInterval ->
       value += 1
       socket.emit 'update', value: value
     , 1000

     socket.on 'add', (data) ->
       value += data.amount
       socket.emit 'update', value: value
   ```

5. Create a new Jade template called `counter.jade` with the following contents:

   ```
   !!!
   html
     head
       title= "Socket.io Example"
       link(rel="stylesheet", href="css/bootstrap.min.css")
     body
       .container
         h1= "Socket.io Example"
         p
           | This page demonstrates the use of Socket.io
         hr
         .well
           #output= "Waiting..."
   ```

```
          .btn-toolbar
            button#add-1000.btn.btn-primary= "Add 1000"
            button#add-500.btn.btn-primary= "Add 500"
            button#disconnect.btn.btn-warning= "Disconnect"

        script(src="js/vendor/jquery.min.js")
        script(src="js/vendor/coffee-script.min.js")
        script(src="/socket.io/socket.io.js")
        script(src="/coffee/count-client.coffee", type="text/
coffeescript")
```

6. Create a CoffeeScript file named `public/coffee/count-client.coffee` with the following contents:

```
$ ->
  socket = io.connect 'http://localhost:8080'
  socket.on 'update', (data) ->
    $('#output').html "From the server: #{data.value}"
```

7. Add a click event handler for the `add-1000` button:

```
$('button#add-1000').click ->
  socket.emit 'add', amount: 1000
```

8. Add a click event handler for the `add-500` button:

```
$('button#add-500').click ->
  socket.emit 'add', amount: 500
```

9. Add a click event handler for the disconnect button:

```
$('button#disconnect').click ->
  socket.disconnect()
```

How it works...

We updated `app.coffee` to reference the Socket.io library and created a new route to handle requests for `/count`. Lastly, we instructed Socket.io to listen to the HTTP server and save this to a variable named `io`. We will use this to hook into the sending and receiving process.

We then defined a simple view template that references the jQuery and CoffeeScript JavaScript libraries. We then added a reference to the Socket.io client library and to our `count-client.coffee` file.

You might be wondering where the Socket.io.js file comes from. Socket.io actually handles this request for us at `/socket.io/socket.io.js`. This is very convenient as it ensures that the version of the client library always matches the version of Socket.io running on the server.

Inside our `count-client.coffee` file, we call the `io.connect()` function to establish a connection to Socket.io running on the sever.

In the `app.coffee` file, we registered an event handler to watch for connection events using `io.sockets.on 'connection'`. When this is triggered, it calls our event handler passing an instance of `socket` as an argument.

Inside our connection event handler, we use `setInterval()` to register a method to run every 1,000 milliseconds.

When `setInterval()` triggers, we increment a `value` variable by 1 and then execute Socket's `emit()` function to send a message to all the connected clients. The `emit()` function takes a message name and an object representing the message payload.

In our example, we emit an `update` message. The message's payload is an object with a `value` property assigned to our counter's value.

Inside `count-client.coffee`, we register a listener for update messages using `socket.on 'update'`. This event handler listens specifically for update messages. When an update message is received, our handler is called with the message payload from the server.

In this example, we simply display the counter value that was received from the server as shown in the following screenshot:

In `count-client.coffee`, we also registered DOM event listeners to handle click events for our **Add 1000**, **Add 500** and **Disconnect** buttons.

When we click on **Add 1000** or **Add 500**, we use Socket.io's client `emit()` function to send a message back to the server in exactly the same way we sent our `update` message to the client. In this case, we emit an `add` message with an object representing `amount` to increase `value` on the server. Once value has been updated, we then emit an `update` message with the updated value, immediately displaying the new value on the client.

In `app.coffee`, we registered a Socket.io listener for `add` messages. When received, we simply increment the value by the amount specified in the message object.

Our last client event handler for click events on our **Disconnect** button executes the `disconnect()` function of the Socket.io client. This closes the socket and we no longer receive `update` messages on the client.

4
Using Kendo UI for Desktop and Mobile Applications

In this chapter, we will cover the following recipes:

- ▸ Using the Kendo UI Core widgets
- ▸ Using the Kendo UI Core mobile widgets

Introduction

Kendo UI Core is an exciting open source framework from Telerik to implement user interfaces in pure HTML5, JavaScript, and CSS3.

Kendo UI Core provides many out-of-the-box features including:

- ▸ More than 20 jQuery-based widgets
- ▸ A powerful data source object
- ▸ An MVVM framework
- ▸ A template engine
- ▸ Drag-and-drop
- ▸ Globalization
- ▸ A complete mobile framework

In this chapter, we will demonstrate how to use the Kendo UI framework to create compelling UIs for both the desktop and mobile applications.

Using the Kendo UI Core widgets

In this recipe, we will look at some of the common widgets that come with Kendo UI Core, a free library provided by Telerik to the open web.

Getting ready

Begin by downloading a copy of the Kendo UI Core library from the Telerik website at `http://www.telerik.com/download/kendo-ui-core`.

Once downloaded, extract the contents of the ZIP file into a directory called `kendo`.

Our demo will use the Bootstrap and Lightbox libraries but these will be linked from a CDN.

Create a file named `index.html` with the following contents:

```html
<!DOCTYPE html>
<html>
<head>
  <title>KendoUI Widget Demo</title>
  <link rel="stylesheet" href="https://cdnjs.cloudflare.com/ajax/libs/
twitter-bootstrap/3.0.1/css/bootstrap.min.css">
  <link rel="stylesheet" href="https://cdnjs.cloudflare.com/ajax/libs/
lightbox2/2.7.1/css/lightbox.css">
  <!-- Add Kendu CSS here -->
  <style>
    .value {
      color: red;
    }
  </style>
</head>
<body>
  <div class="container">
    <h1>KendoUI widgets...</h1>
    <p>
      This page demonstrates various KendoUI widgets.
    </p>
    <!-- Add controls here -->
  </div>
</body>
<script src="https://cdnjs.cloudflare.com/ajax/libs/lightbox2/2.7.1/
js/lightbox.min.js"></script>
<!-- Add Kendo JavaScript libs here -->
<script type="text/coffeescript" src="coffee/app.coffee"></script>
<script src="http://coffeescript.org/extras/coffee-script.js"></
script>
</html>
```

Create a file named `data/gallery.json` with the following contents:

```json
{
    "title": "Berry Picking 2012",
    "imageRootPath": "img/albums/berries-2012/",
    "images": [
        {
            "filename": "WP_001740.jpg",
            "description": "Path to tranquility."
        },
        {
            "filename": "WP_001745.jpg",
            "description": "Vines on rocks."
        },
        {
            "filename": "WP_001749.jpg",
            "description": "Weathered tree stump."
        }
    ]
}
```

How to do it...

We will add the Kendo assets to `index.html`:

1. Add a link to the Kendo common CSS file:

   ```html
   <link rel="stylesheet" href="kendo/styles/kendo.common.min.css">
   ```

2. Add a link to a Kendo theme CSS file:

   ```html
   <link rel="stylesheet" href="kendo/styles/kendo.default.min.css">
   ```

3. Add the jQuery library:

   ```html
   <script src="kendo/js/jquery.min.js"></script>
   ```

4. Add the Kendo Core library:

   ```html
   <script src="kendo/js/kendo.ui.core.min.js"></script>
   ```

5. Create a new CoffeeScript file named `coffee/app.coffee` with the following contents:

```
DEPARTMENTS = [
  'Sales', 'Customer Service', 'I.T.'
  'Finance', 'Marketing', 'Human Resources'
  'Research and Development'
]

$ ->
  # our initialization code goes here
```

6. We will define our Kendo components in our HTML page and then initialize them in `app.coffee`:

7. Create a HTML placeholder for a Kendo progress bar control in `index.html`:

```
<h2>Progress bar</h2>
<div class="well">
  <div id="progressbar" style="width: 100%"></div>
</div>
```

8. Add the initialization code to `app.coffee` for the progress bar by calling the `kendoProgressBar()` function on the jQuery `#progressbar` element:

```
progressBar = $('#progressbar')
  .kendoProgressBar value: 50
  .data 'kendoProgressBar'
```

9. Create a Kendo slider control and SPAN to display the selected value in `index.html`:

```
<h2>Slider</h2>
<div class="well">
  <input id="slider" style="width: 100%" />
  <div style="margin-top: 2em;">
    Selected value:
    <span id="slider-value" class="value">None</span>
  </div>
</div>
```

10. Add the initialization code to `app.coffee` for the progress bar by calling the `kendoSlider()` function on the jQuery `#slider` element. Set `max` and initial `value` properties and add a `change` event handler:

```
$('#slider').kendoSlider
  max: 100, value: 50
  change: ->
    $('#slider-value').text @value()
    progressBar.value @value()
```

11. Create a Kendo date picker control and SPAN to display the selected value in `index.html`:

```
<h2>Date picker</h2>
<div class="well">
  <label>
    Date:
    <input type="text" id="datepicker">
  </label>
  <br>Selected value:
  <span id="datepicker-value" class="value">None</span>
</div>
```

12. Add the initialization code to `app.coffee` for the progress bar by calling the `kendoDatePicker()` function on the jQuery `#datepicker` element. Add a `change` event handler:

```
$('#datepicker').kendoDatePicker
  change: ->
    $('#datepicker-value').text  @value()
```

13. Create a Kendo drop-down list control and SPAN to display the selected value in `index.html`:

```
<h2>Drop down list</h2>
<div class="well">
  <label>Department:
    <input id="dropdownlist" style="width: 300px;" />
  </label>
  <br>Selected value:
  <span id="dropdownlist-value" class="value">None</span>
</div>
```

14. Add the initialization code to `app.coffee` for the progress bar by calling the `kendoDropDownList()` function on the jQuery `#dropdownlist` element. Set the `dataSource` and `optionLabel` properties and add a `change` event handler:

```
$('#dropdownlist').kendoDropDownList
  dataSource:
    data: DEPARTMENTS
    sort:
      dir: 'asc'
  optionLabel: 'Select...'
  change: ->
    $('#dropdownlist-value').text @value()
```

15. Create a Kendo autocomplete textbox control and SPAN to display the selected value in `index.html`:

```
<h2>Auto-complete</h2>
<div class="well">
  <label>
    Department:
    <input type="text" id="autocomplete" style="width: 300px;">
  </label>
  <br>Selected value:
  <span id="autocomplete-value" class="value">None</span>
</div>
```

16. Add the initialization code to `app.coffee` for the progress bar by calling the `kendoAutoComplete()` function on the jQuery `#autocomplete` element. Set the `dataSource` and `filter` properties and add a change event handler:

```
$('#autocomplete').kendoAutoComplete
  dataSource:
    data: DEPARTMENTS
    sort:
      dir: 'asc'
  filter: 'contains'
  change: ->
    $('#autocomplete-value').text @value()
```

17. Create a Kendo list view control and SPAN to display the selected value in `index.html`:

```
<h2>ListView</h2>
<div class="well">
  <h3>Berry Picking 2012</h3>
  <div id="listview"></div>
  <div style="margin-top: 1em;">
    Selected item:
    <span id="listview-value" class="value">None</span>
  </div>
</div>
```

18. Add a template to define the markup for each item of the list view in `index.html`:

```
<script type="text/x-template" id="album-template">
  <a href="img/albums/berries-2012/#= filename #"
    data-lightbox="Berry Picking 2012"
    title="#= description #">
    <img src="img/albums/berries-2012/tn_#= filename #"
    alt="#= description #" class="img-thumbnail">
  </a>
</script>
```

19. Define a Kendo data source object to load data from the server by defining a `read` transport pointing to a JSON file of gallery data:

```
imageDataSource = new kendo.data.DataSource
  transport:
    read:
      url: 'data/gallery.json'
      dataType: 'json'
  schema:
    data: (data) ->
      return data.images
```

20. Add the initialization code to `app.coffee` for the progress bar by calling the `kendoListView()` function on the jQuery `#listview` element. Set the `dataSource`, `template`, and `selectable` properties, and add a `change` event handler:

```
$('#listview').kendoListView
  dataSource: imageDataSource
  template: kendo.template $('#album-template').html()
  selectable: true
  change: ->
    selectedIndex = @select().index()
    image = @dataSource.view()[selectedIndex]
    $('#listview-value').text image.description
```

How it works...

Kendo, like jQueryUI, can be defined within our HTML. We then use Kendo methods, defined as jQuery plugins.

We start by adding references to the Kendo CSS files; a common CSS file and a theme CSS file.

> The Kendo UI Core ships with 13 themes. In the previous code, we used Kendo's default theme by adding the `kendo.common.min.css` style sheet. You can use a different theme by referencing a different theme file (`kendo.flat.min.css` for example).

We then added references to the Kendo JavaScript library and jQuery.

When creating our widgets, we first defined a DOM element with an ID in our `index.html` file to act as a placeholder and then created the code in `app.coffee` to instantiate and initialize the Kendo widget, which then replaces the DOM element with the desired widget.

We followed this pattern to define a progress bar, slider, date picker, drop-down list, autocomplete text box, and even a list view.

For the progress bar, we defined a `DIV` element with the ID of `#progressbar`. Then, in our code, we use jQuery to select the DOM element by ID and called Kendo's `kendoProgressBar()` function as seen in the following code:

```
progressBar = $('#progressbar')
  .kendoProgressBar value: 50
  .data 'kendoProgressBar'
```

This follows a very basic pattern for the Kendo UI that allows us to construct a widget and also save this new widget object by calling jQuery's `data()` function passing a string representing the type of widget as the argument.

> We can also get the widget object after it has been instantiated using jQuery, as seen in the following code:
>
> ```
> progressBar = $('#progressbar').data 'kendoProgressBar'
> ```

When creating a Kendo widget in code, we can pass a configuration object to the `kendoWidget()` function that can set default values, property settings, and event handlers.

When creating the progress bar, we set the initial value to `50`. By default, the progress bar has a min value of `0` and a max value of `100`.

Once executed, the `kendoProgressBar()` function replaces the `#progressbar` DIV element with the necessary DOM elements to display the progress bar as seen in the following figure:

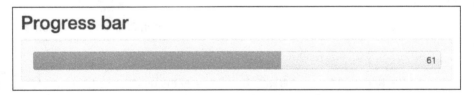

We then created a slider in much the same way with the exception that we provided a max setting and a change event handler that will be called when the slider's value changes.

Inside this change event handler, we update the `SPAN` element to display the new value (`@value()`) and we pass the new value to the progress bar's `value()` function, which will get or set the progress bar's value. This ties the slider and the progress bar together. As the slider value changes, the progress bar's progress value will also change accordingly.

Once rendered, the slider is displayed as seen in the following figure:

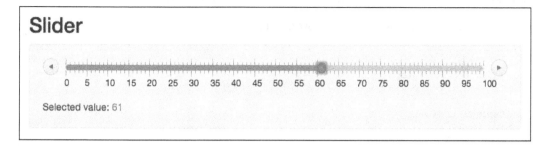

We created a date picker with a `change` event handler. When the user selects a different date from the date picker, the event handler will display the selected date in the `#datepicker-value` SPAN we provided.

Once created, the date picker will display an `INPUT` textbox and a little calendar icon, which, when clicked, displays a calendar view as can be seen in the following figure:

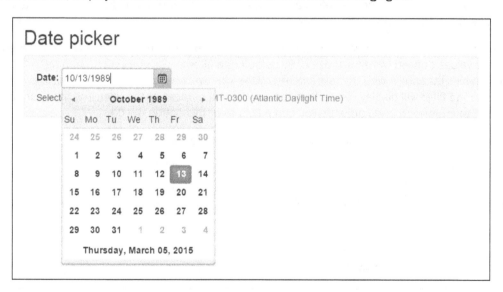

The next control we created was a drop-down list. This control takes a `dataSource` property that defines the data for the drop-down list items as well as an optional `optionLabel` property that defines the default string to be displayed to the user, prompting them to choose.

We set `dataSource` to an object with a data property and a `sort` property. The data property is simply our static `DEPARTMENTS` array, an array of strings representing the various departments found in a company. The `sort` property ensures that the items are sorted alphabetically in the ascending order.

We also provide a `change` event handler so if the user selects a department from the dropdown, the `#dropdownlist-value` span is updated with the selected item.

Once created, the drop-down list is displayed as follows:

The autocomplete textbox allows a user to start typing into a text box and the system will try to narrow down a possible list of choices based on what they typed in.

The autocomplete textbox is similar to the drop-down list in that we use our DEPARTMENTS array as `dataSource`, and we define a `change` event handler that will display our selected values in the `#autocomplete-value` span.

We also pass a `filter` option that determines how the text entered by the user is compared to the values defined by `dataSource`. By default, the filter is `startswith`, meaning only values that begin with the text entered by the user will be displayed to the user. The `contains` filter will display values that contain the text entered by the user. The filter can also be set to `endswith` and I am sure you can guess what this option will do.

When rendered, the autocomplete textbox looks like the following:

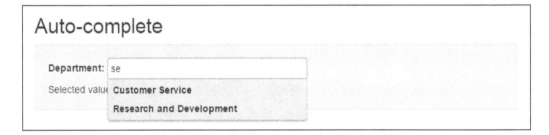

The last widget we create is a list view. The list view widget is a great choice to display a list of complex items. In our example, we display a list of thumbnails images as a Lightbox gallery.

There are two new concepts we used with this widget. First, we used an actual Kendo DataSource object. We define `imageDataSource` as a new instance of `kendo.data.DataSource`. We pass a configuration object that defines the `transport` and `schema` options.

The `transport` configuration object defines the parameters of our read operation. In this case, we define the read object by giving it the URL of our backend endpoint and the type of data to be expected; `dataType: 'json'` in this case.

The `schema` configuration option is used to override the data to be returned. In this case, when our list view requests its data, the data source will return the array of images loaded from the `data/gallery.json` file.

> The Kendo DataSource is a comprehensive data provider that supports a variety of data formats, including JSON (default), JSONP, XML, script and HTML, and a variety of HTTP actions, including POST, GET (default), PUT, and DELETE. See the Kendo UI official documentation at `http://docs.kendoui.com/api/` for more information.

Second, we used a template to define the HTML related to displaying a single item in the list view (a thumbnail image in this demo). We then used Kendo's template engine to compile this template and assign the result to the list view's initialization function as the template property.

The template itself is fairly simple, as follows:

```
<script type="text/x-template" id="album-template">
  <a href="img/albums/berries-2012/#= filename #"
    data-lightbox="Berry Picking 2012"
    title="#= description #">
    <img src="img/albums/berries-2012/tn_#= filename #"
    alt="#= description #" class="img-thumbnail">
  </a>
</script>
```

Kendo templates use a `#=    #` notation to indicate the placeholders that will be replaced with actual values as the template is rendered. In our template, we will be injecting the image's filename and description.

We use the built-in `kendo.template()` method to compile our template.

By default, list view items are for display only and are not selectable. You can easily override this by setting the `selectable` property to `true` as we did.

Lastly, we created a `change` event handler that will be triggered whenever a user selects (clicks) an item in the list view. In the `change` handler, we use the `@select()` method to get the selected item, and call `index()` to get the selected item's index. Lastly, we get the selected image from the `@dataSource.view()` object by index. The `@dataSource.view()` object returns an array containing our source data for the given view.

We can see our rendered list view in the following figure:

There's more...

It's worth noting that the `kendo.all.min.js` file, though minified, is still a pretty heavy file. For our purposes, it is perfect. Kendo does, however, provide individual files for each of the components allowing you to only reference the specific files you need for your application. For an application that specifically needs to be tuned for performance (running on a mobile device for example), using only the control libraries you need can greatly reduce the download size.

There are two ways of instantiating Kendo widgets: declaratively and explicitly.

In our example, we created our widgets explicitly by writing code to create our widgets and passing configuration objects to our Kendo initialization functions to set options for max, value, filter, dataSource, and so on.

Kendo also allows us to define our widgets declaratively by decorating our HTML tags with data attributes that define the type of widget and its configuration options.

For example, we could define our slider declaratively in the following manner:

```
<input id="slider" data-role="slider"
    data-max="100" data-value="50"
    style="width: 100%" />
```

When defining your widgets declaratively, you add a `data-role` attribute to your HTML element with a value representing the type of widget you wish to create. This defines `#slider` as a Kendo slider widget with a `max` value of `100` and an initial `value` of `50`.

To render our Kendo widgets, we only need to call the `kendo.init()` function as shown in the following:

```
$ ->
  kendo.init(document.body)
```

You can also pass a root element to the `kendo.init()` method to limit the DOM tree scanning to a particular subset of the DOM:

```
$ ->
  kendo.init $('payment-window')
```

You can also specify event handlers as a data-dash attribute as well. For example, to define a change handler, you can add a `data-change="methodToCall"` attribute to our DOM element:

```
<input id="slider" data-role="slider"
  data-max="100" data-value="50"
  data-change="app.slider.change"
  style="width: 100%" />
```

Note that because CoffeeScript wraps each file in a closure, we need to expose the event handler on a globally accessible object. In this case, we defined an app object/namespace on the global window object as seen here:

```
change = ->
  $('#slider-value').text @value()

window.app =
  slider:
    change: change
```

We have only touched the surface of what we can do with Kendo UI Core. You can find out more from Telerik's website at `http://www.telerik.com/kendo-ui/open-source-core`.

You may also want to download a trial copy of Telerik's Kendo UI Professional, which includes all of the components found in the core package as well as a fantastic grid component, a powerful WYSIWYG HTML editor, impressive data visualizations, including charts and gauges, a fully functional scheduling component, and much more.

Using the Kendo UI Core mobile widgets

Along with the widgets we saw in the previous recipe, the Kendo UI Core library includes an entire framework targeting mobile platforms known as Kendo UI Mobile. This library provides the basic building blocks to build cross-platform applications that can mimic the native platform's look and feel. For example, when running the application on an iOS device, the application looks like a native iOS application. However, if this same application runs on Android, Blackberry, or Windows Phone, the application looks like a native application for the supported platform.

In this recipe, we will look at various aspects of using Kendo to create mobile applications in HTML, CSS, and CoffeeScript.

Getting ready

Kendo mobile applications are created using HTML, CSS, and JavaScript or CoffeeScript.

For simplicity, we will develop our code with CoffeeScript to be run locally, but you should compile your CoffeeScript code to JavaScript before deploying your Kendo application to production. See *Chapter 10, Hosting Our Web Applications*, for more information.

As we saw in the previous recipe on Kendo widgets, components can be created declaratively or explicitly in code. For Kendo mobile, it is advised to create your mobile widgets declaratively.

Creating our application declaratively is accomplished by using various `data-dash` attributes.

For example, we can create a simple button by defining anchor data with the `data-role` attribute with the value of the button:

```
<a href="#some-action" data-role="button">Click Me!</a>
```

This will render the anchor as a button that is styled to the native platform upon which it is being displayed.

In this recipe, we will use a standard HTML file with the following content:

```html
<!DOCTYPE html>
<html>
<head>
  <title></title>
  <meta charset="UTF-8" />
  <link
    rel="stylesheet"
    href="kendo/styles/kendo.mobile.all.min.css">
</head>
<body>
  <!-- interesting things go here -->

  <script src="kendo/js/jquery.min.js"></script>
  <script src="kendo/js/kendo.ui.core.min.js"></script>
  <script
    type="text/coffeescript"
    src="coffee/app.coffee"></script>
  <script type="text/coffeescript">
    app.init document.body
  </script>
  <script src="http://coffeescript.org/extras/coffee-script.js"></script>
</body>
</html>
```

In this basic HTML5 template, we add a CSS reference to `kendo.mobile.all.min.css` and script references to jQuery and `kendo.ui.core.min.js`. We also include a script reference to `coffee/app.coffee`, the file we will use for our application code.

The `coffee/app.coffee` file has the following code:

```coffeescript
application = null
init = (element) ->
  application = new kendo.mobile.Application(element)

window.app =
  application: application
  init: init
```

In our HTML file, we call the `app.init()` function passing the document body as an argument. This will initialize all declarative widgets defined in the DOM of the document body.

In our samples, we will place HTML contents immediately following the `<!-- interesting things go here -->` comment and occasionally the code in the `coffee/app.coffee` file.

How to do it...

The main building blocks of a Kendo mobile application include the View, Layout, NavBar, and TabStrip. Also included are more than a dozen other components.

Kendo views represent a page or screen of information displayed to the user. They are the fundamental container for text, images, forms, and widgets.

Views have three basic regions: a header, content area, and a footer.

To create a view, follow these steps, inserting the HTML into `index.html`:

1. Add a `DIV` with a `data-role` attribute of `view`:

   ```
   <div id="foo" data-role="view" data-title="My First View">
   ```

2. Define a header with a `data-role` value of `header`:

   ```
   <!-- view header -->
   <header data-role="header">
     <div data-role="navbar">
       <span data-role="view-title"></span></div>
   </header>
   ```

3. Add some content:

   ```
   <h1>This is my view content</h1>
   ```

4. Define a footer with a `data-role` value of `footer`:

   ```
   <!-- view footer -->
   <footer>
     <div data-role="navbar">
       <span>Footer</span>
     </div>
   </footer>
   </div>
   ```

When this is rendered on the mobile device, it will look similar to the following figure:

In the previous figure, our view on the left is rendered on a Samsung Galaxy S4 and on an Apple iPhone 5 on the right. Kendo mobile will detect the type of device being used and will apply styles (color, layout, icons, and so on) that are suitable for the native platform. You can optionally choose from other mobile styles to maintain a consistent brand across all devices.

 Note that for testing purposes, you can use Google Chrome's built-in developer tools. Chrome provides an emulation mode to simulate rendering on a number of devices.

Kendo provides a layout component that allows us to create general views that can be used essentially as a default template for a view:

1. Create a DIV tag with a data-role attribute of layout:

    ```
    <div data-id="standard-layout" data-role="layout">
    ```

2. Add a default header:

    ```
    <header data-role="header">
      <div data-role="navbar">
        <span data-role="view-title"></span>
      </div>
    </header>
    ```

3.   Add a footer and include a tab strip widget:

```
<div data-role="footer">
  <div data-role="tabstrip">
    <a href="#first" data-icon="home">First</a>
    <a href="#second" data-icon="contacts">Second</a>
    <a href="#third" data-icon="info">Third</a>
  </div>
</div>
</div>
```

4.   Add three views that use the standard layout:

```
<div id="first" data-role="view" data-title="First View"
  data-layout="standard-layout">
  <h1>First view content</h1>
</div>

<div id="second" data-role="view" data-title="Second View"
  data-layout="standard-layout">
  <h1>Second view content</h1>
</div>

<div id="third" data-role="view" data-title="Third View"
  data-layout="standard-layout">
  <h1>Third view content</h1>
</div>
```

If we load this on our device, we will see something similar to the following figure:

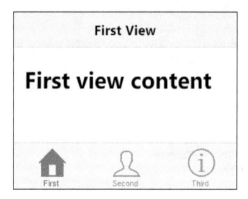

How it works...

Our view contains a header and footer element as well as the view content.

When the application is initialized, the initial view is rendered for the mobile platform.

Views provide a number of properties and events that you can hook into in order to tailor them to your needs.

For example, a view can provide a title using the `data-title` attribute:

```
<div id="foo" data-role="view" data-title="My First View">
```

We can display the view's title in a `navbar` component by adding `SPAN` with a `data-role` value of `view-title`:

```
<header data-role="header">
  <div data-role="navbar">
    <span data-role="view-title"></span></div>
</header>
```

Layouts use a `data-id` attribute to provide a name to the layout. An application can have many layouts.

When using layouts, we can create a view that references the view by setting its `data-layout` attribute to the name given to the view.

In our layout example, we also used a tab strip control. This is a great way to provide navigation between views in your mobile application. Tapping a button in the tab strip will navigate to the desired view. By using a layout, all of our views can secure the tab strip. This can save considerable time coding our mobile applications.

Kendo mobile is very good at rendering its components to match the native platform. This is especially true for the tab strip widget. On iOS, Blackberry, and Windows Phone, our tab strip displays at the bottom of our view. If we load this on the Android platform however, it will display across the top of the view. This may seem odd given we defined our tab strip in our layout footer but this is the extent that Kendo goes to make our application blend in with the native platform.

As you can see in the following figure, Android has rendered our tab strip at the top of the screen:

Notice the data-icon attribute. Kendo provides more than 300 icons for use in our applications for Button or ListView components. You can see these icons on the Kendo site at `http://docs.kendoui.com/getting-started/mobile/icons`.

Navigation is provided through simple anchor tags. We can navigate to a view on the current page using the `#view-id` notation as we saw in our tab strip. We can also navigate to pages that are remote using a URL such as `http://mysite.com/views/contact-us.html`. Taking this approach, Kendo will load the contents of `contact-us.html` via AJAX and inject its view DOM into the current page. Kendo manages all these DOM manipulations for us.

There's more...

Views provide two events that we can hook into in our code to handle view initialization and display. These are the `data-init` and `data-show` events, respectively:

```html
<div id="foo" data-role="view" data-title="View Event Demo"
  data-init="app.view.viewInit"
  data-show="app.view.viewShow">
  <!-- view header -->
  <header data-role="header">
    <div data-role="navbar">
      <span data-role="view-title"></span></div>
  </header>

  <h1>This is my view content</h1>
  <div id="output"></div>

  <!-- view footer -->
  <footer>
    <div data-role="navbar">
      <span>Footer</span>
    </div>
  </footer>
</div>
```

When a view is initialized, the method defined in the view's `data-init` attribute is called. This allows us to prepare everything needed for the view.

When a view is about to be displayed, the method defined in the view's `data-show` attribute is called.

The following code snippet defines our view's `init()` and `show()` methods:

```
window.app = window.app || {}

viewInit = (e) ->
  view = e.view
  (view.element.find '#output').append(
    '<pre>viewInit() called</pre>'
  )

viewShow = (e) ->
  view = e.view
  (view.element.find '#output').append(
    '<pre>viewShow() called</pre>'
  )

window.app.view =
  viewInit: viewInit
  viewShow: viewShow
```

Notice that our events are provided a parameter that represents the event object. This object provides a view property that represents the view that is calling the event. We used the view's element property, which is a jQuery object wrapping the view's root element.

When using layouts, we can use a layout for a view and still override the header or footer if needed. For example, the following code defines a view based on our standard layout that we created, but overrides the header to include a back button:

```
<div id="second" data-role="view" data-title="Second View"
  data-layout="standard-layout">
  <header data-role="header">
    <div data-role="navbar">
      <a data-role="backbutton"
        data-align="left">Back</a>
      <span data-role="view-title"></span>
    </div>
  </header>
  <h1>Second view content</h1>
</div>
```

In this case, our second view defines its own header element. This header will override the default header defined in the layout. In this customized header, we added a back button using the `data-role` of `backbutton`.

In the following figure, we can see the back button rendered as a part of the second view's header:

The tab strip control provides several properties and methods allowing us to configure the behavior of our tab strip.

One especially useful function is the badge() function. This function allows us to display useful information to the user. For example, we might have a button to view our calls. We can use badge() to display the number of missed calls:

```
<div data-role="footer">
  <div data-role="tabstrip">
    <a href="#home" data-icon="home">Home</a>
    <a href="#inbox" data-icon="phone">Calls</a>
    <a href="#settings" data-icon="settings">Settings</a>
  </div>
</div>
```

Our tab strip definition has different HREFs and icons, but it's identical to the previous tab strip example.

Our #home view defines a data-init value of a function to add the badge to our tab strip:

```
<div id="home" data-role="view" data-title="First View"
  data-layout="standard-layout"
  data-init="app.view.all.viewInit">
  <h1>Home view content</h1>
</div>
```

Our event handler can then call `badge()`:

```
window.app = window.app || {}

viewInit = (e) ->
  footer = e.view.footer
  tabstrip = (footer.find '.km-tabstrip') \
    .data('kendoMobileTabStrip')
  tabstrip.badge 1, 5

window.app.view =
  all:
    viewInit: viewInit
```

In this example, we call the `badge()` method passing two parameters. The first parameter is the numerical index of the anchor to be decorated. The second parameter represents the number to be displayed on the badge (five unread emails in our case).

You can call badge with a single argument representing the index of the anchor. This will return the current badge value for that anchor:

```
console.log (tabstrip.badge 1)
```

We can see our badge count displayed in the following figure:

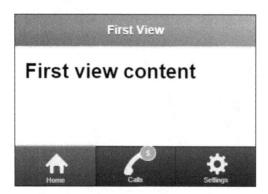

Kendo mobile contains many other very useful widgets and mobile application services that make Kendo a strong competitor when choosing a framework to deliver a mobile application via the mobile web.

You can find more information on Telerik's *Getting Started* page for Kendo Mobile at `http://docs.telerik.com/kendo-ui/mobile`. You can also see dozens of polished demos on Telerik's demo page for Kendo UI at `http://demos.telerik.com/kendo-ui`. You can find out more about Apache Cordova from the official project website at `http://cordova.apache.org`.

5
Going Native with Cordova

In this chapter, we will cover the following recipe:

- ▶ Creating a basic Cordova application
- ▶ Using the camera
- ▶ Using geolocation
- ▶ Using contacts
- ▶ Getting device information

Introduction

Cordova is a framework from the Apache foundation that allows you to wrap your web applications inside a native wrapper that can be packaged and made available via the various app marketplaces.

Cordova currently supports iOS, Android, Blackberry, Windows Phone, and FireFoxOS.

Cordova is not only a native wrapper, but it also provides a JavaScript interface, allowing it to provide access to native hardware and services such as:

- ▶ Access to a camera to take photos and/or videos
- ▶ Access to geolocation information
- ▶ Access to contacts
- ▶ Access to device information

You can find out more about Apache Cordova from the official project website at
`http://cordova.apache.org`.

Creating a basic Cordova application

In this recipe, we will run through the steps to create a basic Cordova application.

Getting ready

Before getting started with Cordova, we must install the Cordova library. Cordova can be installed as a Node package.

Open a terminal window and install the Node package with the following code:

```
npm install -g cordova
```

This will install the Cordova package into Node's global space and allows us to use the Cordova command-line utilities to create and manage our mobile application.

How to do it...

Once Cordova has been installed, we can use the `cordova` command-line tool to create a mobile application.

At a terminal window, perform the following steps:

1. Execute the `cordova create` command:

    ```
    cordova create HelloWorld com.csbook.helloworld
    ```

2. Switch to the `HelloWorld` directory:

    ```
    cd HelloWorld
    ```

3. Add a target platform using the `cordova platform add` command:

    ```
    cordova platform add android
    ```

How it works...

Issuing the `cordova create` command will create a simple folder structure and Cordova libraries, most notably a folder called www. This is where we build our web-based mobile applications.

Adding a platform will create a folder for each platform added. For example, adding the Android platform created a `/platforms/android` directory that has all of the necessary files needed to provide support for the Android platform.

You will see a www folder inside the `/platforms/android` folder. This is automatically built based on the contents of the `/www` folder. Do not make changes to the platform's www files as your changes will be overwritten when the application is rebuilt.

Using the camera

Cordova provides access to the hardware camera via the `org.apache.cordova.camera` plugin.

Getting ready

Plugins are added to our application via the `cordova plugin add` command.

To add the camera plugin, enter the following command in a terminal window at the root directory of our application:

`cordova plugin add org.apache.cordova.camera`

Once installed, the camera methods are made available via the `navigator.camera` object.

Our example will use the Kendo UI mobile framework. To get set up, follow these steps:

1. Copy the Kendo UI `kendo` directory into the www directory of our Cordova application.

2. Replace the contents of `index.html` with the following code:

```html
<!DOCTYPE html>
<html>

<head>
  <meta charset="utf-8" />
  <meta name="format-detection" content="telephone=no" />
  <meta name="msapplication-tap-highlight" content="no" />
  <link rel="stylesheet"
    href="kendo/styles/kendo.mobile.all.min.css">
  <title>CoffeeScript - Cordova</title>
</head>

<body>
  <!-- add your html here -->

  <script src="cordova.js"></script>
  <script src="kendo/js/jquery.min.js"></script>
  <script src="kendo/js/kendo.ui.core.min.js"></script>
  <script src="coffee/app.coffee"
    type="text/coffeescript"></script>

  <!-- add your CoffeeScript files here -->
```

```
<script type="text/coffeescript">
  app.init()
</script>

<script src="js/vendor/coffee-script.js"></script>
</body>

</html>
```

3. Create a directory named `coffee` for our CoffeeScript files.

4. Create a file named `coffee/app.coffee` with the following code:

```
init = (element) ->
  application = new kendo.mobile.Application(element)

window.app =
  init: init
  demos: {}
```

How to do it...

The camera plugin provides a `getPicture()` method that takes success and failure callbacks as well as optional configuration objects:

1. Add the following HTML to `index.html`:

```
<div data-role="view" id="app-camera" data-title="Camera"
  data-layout="layout">
  <h3>Camera</h3>
  <p>
    <a data-role="button"
      data-click="app.demos.camera.onTakePhoto">
    Take Photo</a>
  </p>
  <ul data-role="listview" data-style="inset"></ul>
  <div id="photo-view" data-role="scroller">
    <div data-role="page">
      <img id="photo" src="" />
    </div>
  </div>
</div>
```

2. Create a file named `coffee/camera.coffee` with the following code:

```
displayPhoto = (img) ->
  photo = (document.getElementById 'photo')
  photo.src = 'data:image/jpeg;base64,' + img

onTakePhoto = ->
  success = (img) ->
    displayPhoto img

  fail = (msg) ->
    alert 'Camera failed: ' + msg

  options =
    quality: 50
    destinationType: Camera.DestinationType.DATA_URL

  navigator.camera.getPicture success, fail, options
```

3. Add a reference to our `coffee/camera.coffee` file:

```
<script type="text/coffeescript"
  src="coffee/camera.coffee"></script>
```

How it works...

Our `index.html` file sets up a Kendo mobile view with a button with a `data-click` attribute set to call `app.demos.camera.onTakePhoto`.

Our `onTakePhoto()` method defines a `success()` and a `fail()` callback function. It then prepares a configuration option object that sets the image `quality` to be 50 percent and `desintationType` to be a data URL.

When `navigator.camera.getPicture()` is called, the camera is displayed and the user can use the device's native camera options to adjust the camera settings and take a photo. If successful, the `success()` callback is called with the image's data URL as a parameter.

If the device does not have a camera or if the user cancels the camera function, the `fail()` callback will be called:

There's more...

You can load a photo from the device's photo library. To accomplish this, you can set the `sourceType` option value to `Camera.PictureSourceType.PHOTOLIBRARY` or `Camera.PictureSourceType.SAVEDPHOTOALBUM`:

```
onSelectPhoto = ->
  success = (img) ->
    displayPhoto img

  fail = (msg) ->
    alert 'Load failed: ' + msg

  options =
```

```
    destinationType: Camera.DestinationType.DATA_URL
    sourceType: Camera.PictureSourceType.PHOTOLIBRARY

    navigator.camera.getPicture success, fail, options
```

When `getPicture()` is called with `sourceType` set to `PHOTOLIBRARY` or `SAVEDPHOTOALBUM`, the device's photo library is displayed, allowing the user to select a photo from the library.

Using geolocation

We can use Cordova's `org.apache.cordova.geolocation` plugin to access the hardware's geolocation services.

Getting ready

Begin by installing the geolocation plugin using the following command:

cordova plugin add org.apache.cordova.geolocation

Once installed, we can use Cordova's `navigator.geolocation` object to access the hardware's geolocation services.

How to do it...

To access the device's geolocation information, we use the `getCurrentPosition()` method:

1. Add the following HTML to `index.html`:

```html
<div data-role="view" id="app-location"
  data-title="Location"
  data-layout="layout">
  <h3>Location</h3>
  <p>
    <a data-role="button"
      data-click="app.demos.location.onFetchLocation">
      Fetch Location</a>
  </p>
  <p id="location-status" style="display: none;">
    <i>Fetching position...</i>
  </p>
  <p id="location-error" style="display: none;"></p>
  <ul id="location-info" data-role="listview"
    data-style="inset" style="display: none;">
  </ul>
</div>
```

2. Create a file named `coffee/location.coffee` with the following code:

```
$locationStatus = $ '#location-status'
$locationError  = $ '#location-error'
$locationInfo   = $ '#location-info'

onFetchLocation = ->
  onSuccess = (pos) ->
    $locationInfo.empty()
    $locationStatus.hide()

    $locationInfo.append \
      "<li>Latitude: #{pos.coords.latitude}</li>"
    $locationInfo.append \
      "<li>Longitude: #{pos.coords.longitude}</li>"
    $locationInfo.append \
      "<li>Altitude: #{pos.coords.altitude}</li>"
    $locationInfo.append \
      "<li>Accuracy: #{pos.coords.accuracy}</li>"
    $locationInfo.append \
      "<li>Heading: #{pos.coords.heading}</li>"
    $locationInfo.append \
      "<li>Speed: #{pos.coords.speed}</li>"
    $locationInfo.append \
      "<li>Timestamp: #{pos.timestamp}</li>"

    $locationInfo.show()

  onError = (err) ->
    $locationStatus.hide()

    errorMessage =
      "<h4>Error: #{err.code}</h4><p>#{err.message}</p>"
    $locationError.html errorMessage
    $locationError.show()

  $locationStatus.show()

  navigator.geolocation.getCurrentPosition \
    onSuccess, \
    onError, \
    { timeout: 30000, enableHighAccuracy: true }

app.demos.location =
  onFetchLocation: onFetchLocation
```

3. Add a reference to `coffee/location.coffee` to our `index.html` file.

How it works...

In our HTML page, we create a Kendo mobile view with a button to fetch the user's current position via the button's `data-click` attribute. Clicking on the button will call the `app.demos.locaiton.onFetchLocation()` method.

In our code file, we create an event handler for the location fetch event.

The heart of this module is the call to `navigator.geolocation.getCurrentPosition()`. To this method, we pass a success and fail callback function.

If successful, the success callback is passed a position object. The position has a `coords` object and a `timestamp` property. In our example, we display the `latitude`, `longitude`, `altitude`, `accuracy`, `heading`, and `speed` properties of `coords`. We also display the position's `timestamp`. This can be seen in the following figure:

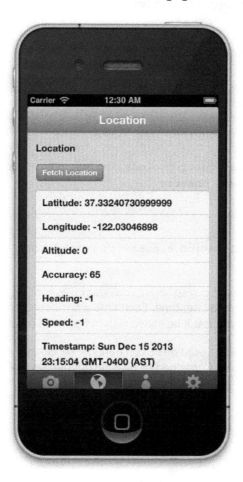

There's more...

The geolocation object provides `geolocation.watchPosition()` and `geolocation.clearWatch()` to set up an event listener that will be called if the position changes and clears/cancels the listener:

```
onWatch = ->
  positionChanged = (pos) ->
    $locationInfo.empty()
    $locationInfo.append \
      "<li>Latitude: #{pos.coords.latitude}</li>"
    $locationInfo.append \
      "<li>Longitude: #{pos.coords.longitude}</li>"
    $locationInfo.append \
      "<li>Timestamp: #{pos.timestamp}</li>"

  onError = (err) ->
    $locationStatus.hide()

    errorMessage =
      "<h4>Error: #{err.code}</h4><p>#{err.message}</p>"
    $locationError.html errorMessage
    $locationError.show()

  watchHandle = navigator.geolocation.watchPosition \
    positionChanged, onError

onWatchCancelled = ->
  if watchHandle
    navigator.geolocation.clearWatch watchHandle
    watchHandle = null
```

In our code, we call `navigator.geolocation.watchPosition()` and save the handle so we can cancel it at a later time. Each time a position change is detected, our `positionChanged()` function will be called with the position object.

When we want to cancel our `watchPosition` handler, we can call the `navigator.geolocation.clearWatch()` method by passing our handle to it.

Using contacts

Cordova provides access to the contacts on the user's device through the `org.apache.cordova.contacts` plugin.

Getting ready

Install the contacts plugin using the following command:

`cordova plugin add org.apache.cordova.contacts`

Once installed, a contacts object will be added to the navigator, which provides the `contacts.create()` and `contacts.find()` methods.

How to do it...

To create a contact, we use the `navigator.contacts.create()` method. It returns a contact object that can be used by your application. You can pass an object literal to this `create()` method, which will initialize the various contact properties:

1. Add the following HTML to `index.html`:

```html
<div data-role="view" id="app-contact"
  data-title="Contacts"
  data-layout="layout">
  <h3>Contacts</h3>
  <p>
    <a data-role="button"
      data-click="app.demos.contacts.onAddContact">
      Add Contact</a>
    <a data-role="button"
      data-click="app.demos.contacts.onFetchContacts">
      Fetch Contacts</a>
  </p>
  <p id="contact-status" style="display: none;">
    <i>Fetching contacts...</i>
  </p>
  <p id="contact-error" style="display: none;"></p>
  <ul id="contact-info" data-role="listview"
    data-style="inset"
    style="display: none;">
  </ul>
</div>
```

2. Create a file named `coffee/contact.coffee` with the following code:

```coffeescript
$contactStatus = ($ '#contact-status')
$contactError =  ($ '#contact-error')
$contactInfo =   ($ '#contact-info')

onFetchContacts = ->
  addContact = (contact) ->
    if contact.displayName
      $contactInfo.append "<li>#{contact.displayName}</li>"

  onSuccess = (contacts) ->
    $contactStatus.hide()
    $contactInfo.empty()
    (addContact item) for item in contacts
    $contactInfo.show()

  onError = (err) ->
    $contactStatus.hide()

    errorMessage = "<h4>Error: #{err.code}</h4>
      <p>#{err.message}</p>"
    $contactError.html errorMessage
    $contactError.show()

  $contactStatus.show()
  fields = ['displayName']
  findOptions =
    filter: ''
    multiple: true

  navigator.contacts.find fields, \
    onSuccess, \
    onError, \
    findOptions
```

3. Add a reference to `coffee/contact.coffee` to our `index.html` file:

```html
<script type="text/coffeescript"
  src="coffee/contact.coffee"></script>
```

How it works...

Our Kendo mobile view has two buttons. The first button defines a `data-click` attribute that will call our `app.demos.contacts.onAddContact()` method. The second button defines a data-click attribute that will call our `app.demos.contacts.onFetchContacts()` method.

In our contacts code, we define our `onAddContact()` method. This method calls the `navigator.contacts.create()` method, passing an object literal that provides `displayName`, `nickname`, and `name`, which is itself an object literal with the `givenName` and `familyName` properties.

When we create a contact, it does not save the contact to the contact list on the device. This allows you to add or modify additional properties before persisting the contact. To persist the contact, we call the object's `save()` method.

There's more...

Along with creating contacts, we can also find an existing contact or all contacts in the user's contact list; we can use Cordova's `navigator.contacts.find()` method for this:

```
onFetchContacts = ->
  addContact = (contact) ->
    if contact.displayName
      $contactInfo.append "<li>#{contact.displayName}</li>"

  onSuccess = (contacts) ->
    $contactStatus.hide()
    $contactInfo.empty()
    (addContact item) for item in contacts
    $contactInfo.show()

  onError = (err) ->
    $contactStatus.hide()

    errorMessage = "<h4>Error: #{err.code}</h4><p>#{err.message}</p>"
    $contactError.html errorMessage
    $contactError.show()

  $contactStatus.show()
  fields = ['displayName']
  findOptions =
    filter: ''
    multiple: true

  navigator.contacts.find \
    fields, onSuccess, onError, findOptions
```

Our `onFetchContacts()` method first defines an array of contact fields we are interested in. This must have at least one element. In our example, we are only interested in accessing the contact's `displayName` value.

We then define a `searchOptions` object literal that has two properties: `filter` and `multiple`.

The `filter` property defines an object literal representing our search criteria. For example, `findOptions.filter = 'Mike'` will find all contacts where the contact's `displayName` contains Mike. The `filter` property is `' '` (an empty string) by default. This will match all records.

By default, our search option's `multiple` property is `false`. We set it to `true` so we get more than one result.

Lastly, we call Cordova's `navigator.contacts.find()` method, passing our search fields (required), our success and fail callbacks (both required), and our find options (optional).

If successful, our success callback is passed an array of matching contact objects. Our `onSuccess()` method iterates through the results and adds them to the `contact-info` list-view control seen in the following figure:

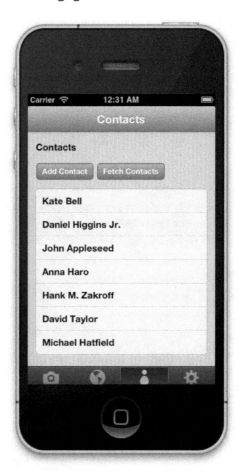

Getting device information

It is sometimes helpful to have specific information about the user's device. Cordova provides a device object that provides such information.

Getting ready

To retrieve device information, we must install the device plugin with the following command:

```
cordova plugin add org.apache.cordova.device
```

How to do it...

To get device information, follow these steps:

1. Add the following HTML to index.html:

   ```html
   <div data-role="view" id="app-device"
     data-title="Contacts"
     data-layout="layout">
     <h3>Device Information</h3>
     <p>
       <a data-role="button"
         data-click="app.demos.device.onFetchInfo">
         Fetch Device Info</a>
     </p>
     <ul id="device-info" data-role="listview"
       data-style="inset" style="display: none;">
     </ul>
   </div>
   ```

2. Create a file named coffee/device.coffee with the following code:

   ```coffee
   $deviceInfo =   $('#device-info')

   onFetchInfo = ->
     $deviceInfo.empty()
     $deviceInfo.append "<li>Name: #{device.name}</li>"
     $deviceInfo.append "<li>Cordova: #{device.cordova}</li>"
     $deviceInfo.append "<li>Model: #{device.model}</li>"
     $deviceInfo.append "<li>Platform:
       #{device.platform}</li>"
     $deviceInfo.append "<li>UUID: #{device.uuid}</li>"
     $deviceInfo.append "<li>Version: #{device.version}</li>"
     $deviceInfo.show()

   app.demos.device =
     onFetchInfo: onFetchInfo
   ```

3. Add a reference to `coffee/device.coffee` to our `index.html` file:

    ```
    <script type="text/coffeescript"
      src="coffee/device.coffee"></script>
    ```

How it works...

We begin by including the HTML defining a Kendo mobile view containing a button with a `data-click` attribute that will call our `app.demos.device.onFetchInfo()` method.

Our CoffeeScript code displays the device's name, Cordova version, model, platform, UUID (universally unique device ID), and OS version.

We can use these values if we need to adjust our application for specific device conditions. Our sample can be seen in the following figure:

6
Working with Databases

In this chapter, we will cover the following recipes:

- ▶ Working with SQLite
- ▶ Working with Redis
- ▶ Working with MongoDB
- ▶ Working with CouchDB

Introduction

In this chapter, we will cover how to use CoffeeScript to perform common **create, read, update, and delete** (**CRUD**) operations against a variety of data storage options.

We will use Node modules to facilitate our database connections and CRUD operations. As with most open source software, there are often times a number of modules that we can use for any given database platform. We will use a single module for each platform, selecting the particular module based on its popularity and ease of use. You may want to investigate other available options for the database platform you are using to see if there is a module that works better for you.

Working with SQLite

SQLite is a lightweight, schema-based relational database engine that executes within the memory context of our application. This proves to be very convenient when developing your application, as SQLite does not require a database server.

Getting started

We will be using the sqlite3 Node module. You can install this module using NPM as follows:

```
$ npm install sqlite3
```

Once installed, you can require it in your application using the following:

```
sqlite = require 'sqlite3'
```

Once required, you can create a connection to an existing database by filename:

```
db = new sqlite3.Database('sample.db')
```

If the database does not exist, an empty database will be created for you.

We will be using a sample database for our examples, which contains a simple `Employees` and `Departments` table. We can see these tables in the following diagram:

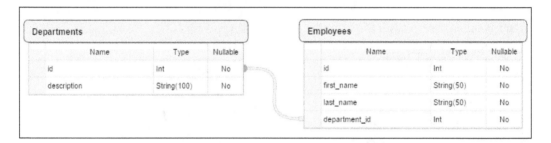

Inserting and updating records, and executing commands

Now that we have an empty database, we will create our tables and insert some records.

We will use the Node sqlite3 provider's `exec()` and `run()` functions to insert, update, and delete records as well as to execute database commands such as the `CREATE TABLE` statements.

How to do it...

The `exec()` method takes a SQL statement as a parameter and an optional callback. When the query is completed or if an error occurs, the callback will be called with a single error parameter.

We will use the `exec()` function to create our sample `Departments` and `Employees` tables and again to populate both with data:

1. Require the sqlite3 package:

    ```
    sqlite = require 'sqlite3'
    ```

2. Instantiate a database instance for our sample database:

    ```
    db = new sqlite.Database 'sample.db'
    ```

3. Define a function to create our tables:

    ```
    createTables = (callback) ->
      sql = "CREATE TABLE [Departments] (
        id INTEGER PRIMARY KEY AUTOINCREMENT,
        description VARCHAR (100)
      );

      CREATE TABLE [Employees] (
        id INTEGER PRIMARY KEY AUTOINCREMENT,
        first_name VARCHAR (50),
        last_name VARCHAR (50),
        department_id INTEGER REFERENCES Departments (id)
      );"

      db.exec sql, (err) ->
        console.log "Error creating tables: #{err}" if err?
        callback err
    ```

4. Define a function to populate our tables with sample data:

    ```
    populateTables = (callback) ->
      departments = [
        { id: 1, desc: 'Sales' }
        { id: 2, desc: 'Customer Service' }
        { id: 3, desc: 'I.T.' }
        { id: 4, desc: 'Finance' }
        { id: 5, desc: 'Marketing' }
        { id: 6, desc: 'Human Resources' }
        { id: 7, desc: 'Research and Development' }
      ]

      employees = [
        { id: 1, first: 'Tracy', last: 'Ouellette', dept: 1 }
        { id: 2, first: 'Chris', last: 'Daniel', dept: 1 }
    ```

```
        { id: 3, first: 'Jason', last: 'Alexander', dept: 3 }
        { id: 4, first: 'Jennifer', last: 'Hannah', dept: 7 }
        { id: 5, first: 'Maxx', last: 'Slayde', dept: 4 }
      ]

    for item in departments
      sql = "INSERT INTO [Departments] VALUES(?, ?)"
      db.run sql, item.id, item.desc, (err) ->
        callback err if err?

    for item in employees
      sql = "INSERT INTO [Employees] VALUES(?, ?, ?, ?)"
      db.run sql, item.id, item.first, item.last, item.dept, (err)
->
        callback err if err?

    callback()
```

5. Execute our `createTables` and `populateTables` functions:

```
createTables (err) ->
  unless err?
    populateTables (err) ->
      unless err?
        console.log 'Database prepped...'
      else
        console.log err
```

How it works...

In our sample, we use the `exec()` function to execute our SQL statement to create the `Customers` table.

Note that our callback is completely optional. If we do not define a callback and an error occurs, an error is called through the database object.

When we populate the `Departments` and `Employees` tables, we use the `run()` function, which is similar to `exec()` but also allows us to pass parameters to our SQL statements.

We use question marks (?) to represent our parameter placeholders inside the SQL string and then pass our parameter values to the `run()` function.

Parameter values can also be passed as an array:

```
sql = "INSERT INTO [Employees] VALUES(?, ?, ?, ?)"
db.run sql, [6, 'Hannah', 'Belle', 7], (err) ->
```

There's more...

When using the `run()` function to pass parameters using the question mark approach, the order of the parameters is important as the values are used in the order they are provided.

This can be problematic as mistakes can be easily made and difficult to find. The `run()` function also accepts named parameters that can help avoid these issues.

We can rewrite our SQL insert statement to use named parameters as seen in the following:

```
sql = "INSERT INTO [Employees] VALUES($id, $first, $last, $deptId)"
```

Then, we can use `run()` in the following way:

```
sql = "INSERT INTO [Employees] VALUES($id, $first, $last, $deptId)"
record = $id: 13, $first: 'Hannah', $last: 'Belle', $deptId: 7
db.run sql, record, (err) ->
```

Reading records

The sqlite3 provider has three functions to read data from an existing database: `get()`, `all()`, and `each()`.

The `get()` function executes the given query and returns the first row of results.

The `all()` function executes the query and returns a collection containing all rows.

The `each()` function executes the query and returns a collection that can be iterated.

Each of these functions takes a SQL statement and a callback method to handle the returned query results. We will look at each of these in turn.

How to do it...

Since `get()` retrieves a single row, it is the method to use for queries where we only care about the first record. This could include statements that return a row by ID, aggregate functions, or the first record when sorted in ascending or descending order.

In the following example, we count the rows in the `Employees` table:

1. Require the sqlite3 package:

   ```
   sqlite = require 'sqlite3'
   ```

2. Create a database instance opening our database:

   ```
   db = new sqlite.Database 'sample.db'
   ```

3. Use `get()` to execute a `select` statement:

    ```
    sql = "select count(*) as 'count' from Employees"
    db.get sql, (err, row) ->
    ```

4. Use the return object to fetch our query results:

    ```
    unless err?
      console.log "There are #{row.count} employees."
    else
      console.log err
    ```

Executing this query via the `get()` function produces the following output:

There are 5 employees.

The `all()` function will return all records from a query result. This is a great option if you are dealing with a limited or reasonable number of rows or if you need to know how many rows have been returned before you begin processing the result set.

The following sample uses `all()` to retrieve all departments from our database:

1. Require the sqlite3 package:

    ```
    sqlite = require 'sqlite3'
    ```

2. Create a database instance opening our database:

    ```
    db = new sqlite.Database 'sample.db'
    ```

3. Use `all()` to execute a select statement with multiple records:

    ```
    sql = 'select * from Departments order by description'
    db.all sql, (err, rows) ->
    ```

4. We can use the array of rows to process each row of our result:

    ```
    unless err?
      console.log "There are #{rows.length} departments."
      for row in rows
        console.log "#{row.id}: #{row.description}"
    else
      console.log err
    ```

Executing the query via the `all()` function produces the following output:

There are 7 departments.

2: Customer Service

4: Finance

6: Human Resources

3: I.T.

5: Marketing

7: Research and Development

1: Sales

The each() function is a great choice when you want to process a number of records but do not want to keep all rows in memory at once.

For example, we can retrieve all records, and process them as they are read.

1. Require the sqlite3 package:

   ```
   sqlite = require 'sqlite3'
   ```

2. Create a database instance to open our database:

   ```
   db = new sqlite.Database 'sample.db'
   ```

3. Use each() to execute a select statement with multiple records:

   ```
   sql = 'select * from Departments order by description'
   db.each sql, (err, row) ->
   ```

4. Use the return object to fetch our query results:

   ```
   unless err?
     console.log "#{row.id}: #{row.description}"
   else
     console.log err
   ```

Executing the query via the each() function produces the following output:

There are 7 departments.

2: Customer Service

4: Finance

6: Human Resources

3: I.T.

5: Marketing

7: Research and Development

1: Sales

How it works...

In the previous examples, we demonstrated the get(), all(), and each() methods in use.

The main difference between all() and each() is that with all(), our callback is called only once we receive the entire result set as an array of rows, while each() will execute our callback for each row that is returned from our query.

The callbacks for each of these functions follow the typical Node style and take an error object as the first parameter, while the second parameter represents our query result.

It is always a good idea to check to see whether an error was returned. If we tried to count the records from a non-existent `Employees2` table, we would get the following error:

```
Error: SQLITE_ERROR: no such table: Employees2
```

There's more...

The `each()` function also allows us to pass an optional second callback that will be executed once the query is completed. This optional callback receives an error object and a count of rows returned:

```coffeescript
sql = 'select * from Departments order by description'

displayRow = (err, row) ->
  unless err?
    console.log "#{row.id}: #{row.description}"
  else
    console.log err}

displayRowCount = (err, rowCount) ->
  unless err?
    console.log "Processed #{rowCount} rows."
  else
    console.log err}

db.each sql, displayRow, displayRowCount
```

Running this `each()` example produces the following output:

```
2: Customer Service
4: Finance
6: Human Resources
3: I.T.
5: Marketing
7: Research and Development
1: Sales
Processed 7 rows.
```

Executing queries in parallel versus serial

By default, queries execute asynchronously (in a parallel manner). This allows the queries to execute without blocking other actions, but this also means there's no guarantee that one query will execute or complete before another runs. This can cause problems. For example, say you had one query to create table X and another to insert into X. We obviously need to make sure the CREATE TABLE command completes before we perform our INSERT command.

We could also execute statements serially by using nested callbacks. Take the following example:

1. Create a function to create a table:

```
createTable = (callback) ->
  sql = "CREATE TABLE Cities (
      id INTEGER PRIMARY KEY AUTOINCREMENT,
      name VARCHAR(100) NOT NULL
    )"

  db.exec sql, (err) ->
    callback err
```

2. Create a function to insert a record into the table:

```
insertIntoTable = (callback) ->
  sql = "INSERT INTO Cities (name) VALUES ('Halifax')"
  db.exec sql, (err) ->
    callback err
```

3. Create a function to read data from the table:

```
selectFromTable = (callback) ->
  db.get 'SELECT * FROM Cities', (err, row) ->
    console.log "City: #{row.name}" unless err?
    callback err
```

4. Create a function to drop the table:

```
dropTable = (callback) ->
  db.exec 'DROP TABLE Cities', (err) ->
    callback err
```

5. Call each function in order through nested callbacks:

```
createTable (err) ->
  unless err?
    insertIntoTable (err) ->
      unless err?
```

```
selectFromTable (err) ->
  unless err?
    dropTable (err) ->
      unless err?
        console.log 'SUCCESS!'
      else
        console.log 'FAILED'
```

As you can see, this is hardly ideal. The SQLite3 module provides a sequential mode for those times when the order of query execution is indeed important.

To control the query execution flow, you can use the `serialize()` and `parallelize()` methods.

How to do it...

Each of these methods takes a function object. Any queries inside this function will be executed in series or parallel as indicated.

```
sqlite = require 'sqlite3'

db = new sqlite.Database('sample.db')

db.serialize ->
  db.run "CREATE TABLE Cities (
      id INTEGER PRIMARY KEY AUTOINCREMENT,
      name VARCHAR(100) NOT NULL
    )"

  db.run "INSERT INTO Cities (name) VALUES ('Halifax')"

  db.get 'SELECT * FROM Cities', (err, row) ->
    unless err?
      console.log "City: #{row.name}"
    else
      console.log "#{err}"

  db.run 'DROP TABLE Cities'
```

How it works...

In our example, we use `serialize()` to make sure we can create a table, insert a record, read that record, and drop our table, all in the correct order.

If we did not use `serialize()`, it is possible our insert may have attempted to use a table that did not yet exist.

Working with Redis

Redis is an open source key-value database that provides a high-performance cross-platform server to store your application's data.

Unlike Sqlite, Redis does not have a fixed schema and is therefore a **schemaless** data store. It allows us to store objects that can be referenced by a key value.

In this section, we will see how to use CoffeeScript to store, retrieve, and delete data with Redis.

 You can find more information, including documentation and installation instructions at the official Redis website at `http://redis.io/`.

Once you have installed Redis, install the Redis NPM package. It will allow us to connect, store, and retrieve values. It can be installed using the following command:

```
npm install redis --save
```

Connecting to the Redis server

Redis runs as a service and the Redis NPM client connects to a running server.

How to do it...

To connect to a Redis service running on the local machine, perform the following steps:

1. Require the Redit package:

   ```
   redis = require 'redis'
   ```

2. Create an instance of the Redit client:

   ```
   client = redis.createClient()
   ```

3. Add an event listener for error events:

   ```
   client.on 'error', (err) ->
     console.log "Error: #{err}"
   ```

4. Add an event listener for a connect event:

   ```
   client.on 'connect', ->
     console.log 'Connected to Redis successfully.'
     client.quit()
   ```

How it works...

In this example, we require the Redis module and then create a client connection using the createClient() method. If called with no parameters, the connection will be established using the default port of 6379 running on the localhost. We can also specify host and port numbers using the createClient(portAsInteger, hostAsString) syntax.

We then create two event listeners: one for error events and the other for the connect event.

If an error occurs and an error event is raised, we simple display it on the console.

If a connection event is raised, we simply print a notification to the console and then call the quit() method, which closes the Redis connection.

Redis is capable of storing several different types of data structures, including strings, hashes, lists, sets, and sorted sets.

The Redis Node client provides methods to store these structures. In the following examples, we will demonstrate how to do this.

If we execute the sample, we see the following output:

Connected to Redis successfully.

If the service is not running or the connection fails for some other reason, the following error is displayed:

Error: Error: Redis connection to 127.0.0.1:6379 failed - connect ECONNREFUSED

Storing and retrieving single values

We can use the set() function to store scalar values, such as strings, numbers, Boolean values, or any value that can be represented as a string.

We can conversely use the get() function to retrieve these scalar values.

How to do it...

Use the set() function by passing the object's key and value.

1. Require the Redis package:

   ```
   redis = require 'redis'
   ```

2. Create an instance of the Redis client:

   ```
   client = redis.createClient()
   ```

3. Add an event listener for error events:

```
client.on 'error', (err) ->
  console.log "Error: #{err}"
```

4. Store a simple key-value pair:

```
client.set 'sales-001', 4503.40
```

5. Store a simple key-value pair with a callback:

```
client.set 'sales-002', 3406.98, (err, res) ->
  console.log res
```

6. Store an object:

```
employee =
  id: '001'
  firstName: 'Tracy'
  lastName: 'Ouellette'
  salesYtd: 4503.40

client.set employee.id, (JSON.stringify employee)
```

7. Retrieve the `sales-001` value:

```
client.get 'sales-001', (err, value) ->
  unless err?
    console.log "Value: #{value}"
```

8. Retrieve an employee object and close the connection:

```
client.get employee.id, (err, objString) ->
  unless err?
    emp = (JSON.parse objString)
    console.dir emp

client.quit()
```

How it works...

In our preceding examples, we use the set() method in several different ways.

First, we save the value 4503.40 with the key sales-001.

Our second call to set() includes a callback method. If provided, the callback is called once the operation is completed. If the set was successful, the value of res will be **OK**.

Our third call to set() includes a convenient helper callback provided by the Redis module called redis.print. This simply displays the result of Reply: <result> if the call was successful and Error: <error> if unsuccessful.

You might have noticed that our numeric value is saved as a string. All values saved using the `set()` method are saved as string values including objects. We can save a complex object by using `JSON.stringify()` to convert our object to a string value.

To retrieve our object, we used the `get()` function with a callback to retrieve the JSON string we stored previously. The callback, when successful, receives the JSON string, which is then parsed using the native `JSON.parse()` function provided by Node.js.

There's more...

Redis also provides other useful functions that can help when working with single values, including:

- `exists key, callback`: This function checks to see whether the given key exists. If it does, it returns `1`, otherwise it returns `0`.
- `setnx key, value`: This function will only set a key's value if the key does not already exist.
- `getset key, value, callback`: This function sets a value for a key and returns the key's previous value before it was set.

Using counters

All set operations are atomic, meaning only one connection can set a value at a time. This avoids concurrency issues and allows the server to maintain consistent lists or sets while allowing multiple clients.

Redis allows us to easily increment and decrement integer values by using the `incr()` and `decr()` methods, respectively.

Getting ready

Create an integer key called `visits`:

```
# initialize vistis to 0
client.set 'visits', 0
```

How to do it...

We can increment and decrement a `visits` counter in the following way:

1. Create a key called `visits` and set it to the value `0`:

   ```
   client.set 'visits', 0
   ```

2. Increment the value of `visits` twice using `incr()`:

   ```
   client.incr 'visits'
   client.incr 'visits'
   ```

3. Display the current value of `visits`:

   ```
   client.get 'visits', redis.print
   ```

4. Decrement the value of visits using `decr()`:

   ```
   client.decr 'visits'
   ```

5. Display the current value of `visits`:

   ```
   client.get 'visits', redis.print
   ```

How it works...

Our example first sets a key called `visits` to an initial value of `0`. It then executes `incr()` twice to increment the `visits` key.

When we check the value of `visits`, we see that the value is `2`.

We then call `decr()` to decrease the value of `visits`. When we check the value again, it's now `1`.

There's more...

There are also `incrby()` and `decrby()` methods to increase and decrease the values by a specified value. For example, in the following code, we increase `visits` by 5:

```
# initialize visits to 13
client.set 'visits', 13

# increment visits by 5
client.incrby 'visits', 5

# display visit count
client.get 'visits', redis.print
```

By running this, we confirm that value of `visits` is now `18`:

Reply: 18

Storing and retrieving hashes

Redis can store sets of data, including hashes, lists, sets, and sorted sets. In this section, we will see some examples of this.

How to do it...

The Redis client provides the `hset()` method to save a single hash key-value pair for an object, or the `hmset()` method to save multiple hash key-value pairs for an object:

1. Use `hset()` with our collection key, hash keys, and values:

   ```
   client.hset 'settings', 'debug-level', 'info'
   client.hset 'settings', 'smtp-use-ssl', 1
   ```

2. Use `hget()` to retrieve a single value from the hash:

   ```
   client.hget 'settings', 'debug-level', redis.print
   ```

3. Use `hmset()` to set multiple hash values:

   ```
   client.hmset 'settings',
     'email-host', '10.1.1.250',
     'email-use-ssl', 'true',
     'email-from', 'no-reply@domain.com', redis.print
   ```

4. Use `hgetall()` to retrieve all values from a hash set:

   ```
   client.hgetall 'settings', (err, res) ->
     console.dir res
   ```

How it works...

In our example, we use `hset()` to create a new hash container called `settings`. Inside settings, we add a property called `debug-level` with the value of `info`.

We then used `hget()` to retrieve the `email-use-ssl` value from the `settings` hash.

Next, we used `hmset()` to save `email-host`, `email-use-ssl`, and `email-from` to the settings hash we created previously.

Using the `hgetall()` method, we retrieve all keys for the settings hash. We provide a callback that displays the result as seen in the following output:

```
{ 'debug-level': 'info',
  'email-host': '10.1.1.250',
  'email-use-ssl': 'true',
  'email-from': 'no-reply@domain.com' }
```

There's more...

There is another form of `hmset()` that the Redis NPM module provides that allows us to use an object to define the key-value pairs. For example, if we wanted to save an employee object, we could do the following.

```
employee =
    id: '001'
    firstName: 'Tracy'
    lastName: 'Ouellette'
    salesYtd: 4503.40

client.hmset "emp-#{employee.id}", employee, redis.print
```

In this example, we define an object literal named `employee`, which we then add to a hash whose key is based on the employee ID.

Storing and retrieving lists

Besides hashes, Redis also natively supports lists of data by providing a number of list-related functions including the following:

- `lpush`: This function pushes a new item to the top of the list
- `rpush`: This function pushes a new item to the bottom of the list
- `lpop`: This function pops the item off the top of the list (removes it from the list and returns its value)
- `rpop`: This function pops the item off the bottom of the list
- `linsert`: This function inserts a new item either before or after an element
- `llen`: This function returns the length of the list for a given key
- `lrem`: This function removes an item from the list
- `lrange`: This function returns the elements within the specified range
- `ltrim`: This function trims the list to a specified number of elements

How to do it...

We will create a list by iterating over an array of 2014 car models from the Ford Motor Company and calling `lpush()` with each element in the array:

1. Define our array of vehicle models:

   ```
   fordModels = [ 'C-Max Hybrid', 'E-Series Wagon', 'Edge',
      'Escape', 'Expedition', 'Fiesta', 'Flex', 'Focus',
      'Fusion', 'Mustang', 'Shelby GT500', 'Taurus',
      'Transit Connect Wagon' ]
   ```

2. Use `lpush()` to add each item to a list named **ford**:

   ```
   for model in fordModels
      client.lpush 'ford', model
   ```

How it works...

Once we have our list populated, we can use some of the other list operators.

For example, if we want to get the length of our `ford` list, we can use the `llen()` method in the following way:

```
client.llen 'ford', redis.print
```

This produces the following result:

`Reply: 13`

We can use the `lrange()` method to retrieve items from the array. For example, if we want the first five items, we can do the following:

```
client.lrange 'ford', 0, 4, (err, items) ->
   console.dir items
```

Here, we ask for items 0 to 4 (five items in total). This produces the following output:

```
[ 'Transit Connect Wagon',
  'Taurus',
  'Shelby GT500',
  'Mustang',
  'Fusion' ]
```

 You might notice our list is in the reverse order. This is because lists are in the last-in-first-out order, like a stack.

There's more...

We forgot the Ford Explorer. We can insert the explorer using the `linsert()` method.

When we call this method, we need to indicate the position of the item being inserted by stating that our new element should be `before` or `after` an existing element.

For example, we can insert our explorer in the following way:

```
client.linsert 'ford', 'AFTER', 'Expedition',
  'Explorer', redis.print
```

Once we have inserted Explorer into the list, we can use `lrange()` to view it in its inserted position:

```
client.lrange 'ford', 8, 10, (err, items) ->
  console.dir items
```

This produces the following array:

```
[ 'Expedition', 'Explorer', 'Escape' ]
```

Deleting keys

Keys can be deleted from Redis in two basic fashions. The data can be removed automatically through a cache expiry or by being removed manually using the `del()` method.

How to do it...

Redis can be used very effectively as an application cache. At the heart of this is the idea that some of our data will expire and be invalid.

The Redis client provides the `expire()` and `expireat()` methods that allow us to specify a key and the amount of time in seconds or a Unix timestamp, respectively.

For example, we can cache a configuration object for 5 seconds by doing the following:

```
client.hmset 'config', config, redis.print
client.expire 'config', 5
```

How it works...

We can test this expiry by setting up an interval and testing for the existence of the configuration object as seen in the following code:

```
counter = 0
timerHandle = null
```

```
checkForExpiry = ->
  counter++
  client.hgetall 'config', (err, obj) ->
    unless err?
      if obj?
        console.log "Config is still alive: #{counter} sec"
      else
        console.log "Config is expired: #{counter} sec"
        clearTimeout timerHandle
        client.quit()

timerHandle = setInterval checkForExpiry, 1000
```

In our sample code, we create a method that increments our counter and then checks for the existence of the configuration object and displays the result. If it does not exist, we stop our timer and close our client connection.

We then use `setInterval()` to call our `checkForExpiry()` method every 1,000 milliseconds.

The result can be seen in the following output:

Config is still alive: 1 sec

Config is still alive: 2 sec

Config is still alive: 3 sec

Config is still alive: 4 sec

Config is still alive: 5 sec

Config is expired: 6 sec

There's more...

We can also remove keys immediately by calling the `del()` method. For example, we can manually delete our configuration object by calling `del()` in the following way:

```
client.del 'config', redis.print
```

Working with MongoDB

MongoDB is a no-SQL document database. Instead of saving data as rows within tables with a fixed column structure, a document database offers much more flexibility allowing you to simply store objects, retrieve, update, and delete complex objects.

For example, you might have customer orders, invoices, and payments. In a relational SQL-based database, this data would likely be spread across four or more tables: Customers, Orders, Invoices, Payments, and several other master tables (Addresses, Cities, Order Details, Products, and so on). To determine whether a customer's account has been paid in full, we need to query the data across a number of tables.

In MongoDB, we can store a customer as a document. This document could contain a collection of orders; each order in turn could contain a collection of payment details.

Document databases, in general, greatly facilitate the retrieval of comprehensive information for a given entity.

In this section, we will use CoffeeScript to communicate with a MongoDB database to perform create, read, update, and delete operations.

You can find more information about MongoDB, including information on downloading, installing, and using MongoDB from the project's home page located at `http://www.mongodb.org/`.

Opening a connection

In this section, we will demonstrate how to connect to a Mongo database.

Getting ready...

Once Mongo has been installed, install the Mongo driver for Node. This is available as an NPM module and can be installed using the following command:

```
npm install mongodb --save
```

How to do it...

Once the driver is installed, we can create a client connection:

1. Require the mongodb package and grab MongoClient:

   ```
   MongoClient = require('mongodb').MongoClient
   ```

2. Define the connection URL specifying the host, port, and database name:

```
url = 'mongodb://localhost:27017/test'
```

3. Use the `MongoClient.connect()` function to establish a connection to the `test` database:

```
MongoClient.connect url, (err, db) ->
  unless err?
    console.log 'Connection established'
  else
    console.log err

  db.close()
```

How it works...

In this example, we grab the MongoClient object, which provides access to the Mongo database.

We then define a connection URL. The format of this URL is as follows:

mongodb://[username:password@]host:port/database

In our example, we connect to Mongo's default port of `27017` on `localhost` with no username or password.

We finish by executing the client's `connect()` function with the URL and a callback. Our callback will be called with an error object and an instance of the database object.

If our connection is successful, the error object will be null.

Inserting documents

Mongo stores documents in collections. In this section, we will see how to insert a document object into a collection.

How to do it...

When we save documents to our database, we do so through a collection object as seen in the following example:

1. Open a connection:

```
MongoClient = require('mongodb').MongoClient
url = 'mongodb://localhost:27017/test'
MongoClient.connect url, (err, db) ->
```

2. Grab an instance of the `employees` collection:

    ```
    collection = db.collection 'employees'
    ```

3. Define an array of employee objects:

    ```
    employees =[
        { id: 1, first: 'Tracy', last: 'Ouellette', salesYtd: 22246 }
        { id: 2, first: 'Chris', last: 'Daniel', salesYtd: 3876 }
        { id: 3, first: 'Jason', last: 'Alexander', salesYtd: 4095 }
        { id: 4, first: 'Jennifer', last: 'Hannah', salesYtd: 8070 }
        { id: 5, first: 'Maxx', last: 'Slayde', salesYtd: 2032 }
    ]
    ```

4. Insert the employee object into the `employees` collection:

    ```
    collection.insert employees, (err, result) ->
        unless err?
          console.dir result
        else
          console.log err

    db.close()
    ```

How it works...

In our example, we open a connection and grab the employees collection using the database instance's `collection()` function. Next, we define an employee document and use the collection's `insert()` function.

The `insert()` function takes the document to be added and a callback as arguments. The callback receives the error and result values.

In our example, we display the value of `result` as follows.

We then open a connection to the database, and once opened, we use the `collection()` method to retrieve the employee collection. We then insert our employee object into the employee collection. If successful, the inserted documents are displayed; a portion of this can be seen in the following output:

```
{ result: [Getter],
  connection: [Getter],
  toJSON: [Function],
  toString: [Function],
  ops:
   [ { id: '001',
```

```
      firstName: 'Tracy',
      lastName: 'Ouellette',
      salesYtd: 4503.4,
      _id: 54442757e1fc6d743f84dac7 },

   ...

   ]}
```

Finding documents

Once our documents have been added to the collection, we can use a number of methods provided by the Mongo driver to find them. These include the following:

▸ `find()`: This method finds all documents that match the query

▸ `findOne()`: This method finds the first document that matches the query

How to do it...

The `find()` method has a tremendous amount of flexibility that allows us to specify query parameters, provide sorting instructions, and apply limits perfect to page operations. With no options specified, the `find()` method returns a cursor that includes all records in the collection.

In this example, we return all employees and display each one:

1. Open a connection:

```
MongoClient = require('mongodb').MongoClient
url = 'mongodb://localhost:27017/test'
MongoClient.connect url, (err, db) ->
```

2. Create a helper function to display an employee document:

```
displayEmployee = (emp) ->
  console.log "#{emp.id}\t" +
    "#{emp.first} #{emp.last}\t" +
    "#{emp.salesYtd}"
```

3. Get a handle to the `employees` collection:

```
collection = db.collection 'employees'
```

4. Use `find()` to fetch all employee documents:

```
collection.find().toArray (err, docs) ->
  console.log "ALL"
  (displayEmployee doc) for doc in docs
```

5. Use `findOne()` to fetch a single employee document:

```
collection.findOne {id: 3}, (err, doc) ->
  console.log "\nONE"
  displayEmployee doc if doc?
```

How it works...

In this sample, we created a helper method that will display an employee item. We then open a connection and attach it to the `employees` collection.

The `find()` function takes a number of arguments but when called with none, all records are returned. The return value is a MongoDB cursor instance. We call the `toArray()` method on this cursor and provide a callback that can then operate on the returned records once the `find()` operation is completed. In the preceding sample, we simply display each of the employee items as seen in the following output:

```
ALL

1  Tracy Ouellette   22246

2  Chris Daniel      3876

3  Jason Alexander   4095

4  Jennifer Hannah   8070

5  Maxx Slayde       2032
```

We then retrieved a single document by using the `findOne()` function. This function takes a query object and a callback as arguments. The callback will receive the document that is returned. For example, we can find an employee document that has an ID of 3 using the following code:

```
collection.findOne {id: 3}, (err, doc) ->
  console.log "\nONE"
  displayEmployee doc if doc?
```

In our example, we provide the object literal {id: 3} as our query parameter.

There's more...

By default, Mongo assumes we want a document where the document has a matching property to query a parameter's value. We can specify other types of comparisons as well.

For example, we can call the `find()` method to retrieve all employees whose sales are greater than $5,000.00 as seen in the following code:

```
collection.find({salesYtd: {$gt: 5000}}).toArray (err, docs) ->
  console.log "\nGREATER THAN $5,000"
  (displayEmployee doc) for doc in docs
```

In this sample, we use the $gt compare operator and specify 5,000 as its value.

Mongo supports the following comparison operators:

- $lt: Less than
- $lte: Less than or equal to
- $gt: Greater than
- $gte: Greater than or equal to
- $in: Value is contained in the provided query
- $nin: Value if not contained in the provided query
- $ne: Is not equal to

We can pass an options object to our find() method. There are a number of options that can be used, including skip and limit (for paging operations), and sort.

We can specify a sort order, including a sort: {} property to our options object:

```
collection.find({}, {sort: {firstName: 1}}).toArray \
  (err, docs) ->
    console.log "\nALL SORTED BY FIRST NAME"
    (displayEmployee doc) for doc in docs
```

In the preceding code, we pass an empty query object {}, which will return all records. Then, we specify the sort order by providing an options object with a sort property. In this case, our sort value is {firstName: 1}. This tells Mongo to sort the results by the firstName field in ascending order. The result can be seen in the following output:

```
ALL SORTED BY FIRST NAME
2   Chris Daniel      3876
3   Jason Alexander   4095
4   Jennifer Hannah   8070
5   Maxx Slayde       2032
1   Tracy Ouellette   22246
```

We can change the direction of the sort by using a negative one as follows:

```
collection.find({}, {sort: {firstName: -1}}).toArray \
  (err, docs) ->
    console.log "\nALL SORTED BY FIRST NAME DESCENDING"
    (displayEmployee doc) for doc in docs
```

This produces the following output:

```
ALL SORTED BY FIRST NAME DESCENDING
1   Tracy Ouellette   22246
5   Maxx Slayde       2032
4   Jennifer Hannah   8070
3   Jason Alexander   4095
2   Chris Daniel      3876
```

If we wanted to sort by more than one property, we can do this by including other sorting properties with their sort order. For example, to sort first by `firstName` in ascending order and then by `salesYtd` in descending order, our option object would be `{sort: {firstName: 1, salesYtd: -2}}`.

Updating documents

The Mongo driver provides two functions, `save()` and `update()` to save documents to a collection.

The `save()` function will replace an entire document with the object being persisted, while the `update()` function will update only parts of the selected document.

How to do it...

We will use the `save()` function to update an existing employee document:

1. Open a connection:

    ```
    MongoClient = require('mongodb').MongoClient
    url = 'mongodb://localhost:27017/test'
    MongoClient.connect url, (err, db) ->
    ```

2. Grab an instance of the `employees` collection:

    ```
    collection = db.collection 'employees'
    ```

3. Find an employee document:

    ```
    collection.findOne {id: 3}, (err, employee) ->
    ```

4. If we find the employee, update its year-to-date sales figure and add the employee's department:

    ```
    if employee?
      employee.salesYtd = 6550
      employee.department = 'Sales'
    ```

5. Use the `save()` function to save the updated employee document and display the results:

```
collection.save employee, (err, res) ->
  collection.findOne {id: 3}, (err, employee) ->
    console.dir employee if employee
    db.close()
```

How it works...

In our sample, we open our database and get the employees collection. We then get the employee whose `id` is equal to `3`.

If we get a matching document, we update its `salesYtd` value and add a new department property.

We then save the changed document using `save()`.

If we were to then query the employee object again, we will see that `salesYtd` has been updated and it now has a department property, as seen in the following results:

```
{ id: 3,
  first: 'Jason',
  last: 'Alexander',
  salesYtd: 6550,
  _id: 52e56d3df4b8e76c5770ed4a,
  department: 'Sales' }
```

 You may be wondering what happens if we save a document that does not have an `_id` property. Mongo will add it to the collection as a new document, effectively making treating the call to `save()` as an insert.

Using `save()` can be useful in situations where a document has undergone significant changes but it can be slower for a larger document than using the `update()` function.

There's more...

The `update()` function allows us to save incremental changes to a document. It can be used to change the values of existing properties or add new properties all together.

We could have written our previous example to use an update instead:

```
collection.update {id: 3}, \
  {$set: {salesYtd: 6550, department: 'Sales'}}, \
  (err, result) ->
    collection.findOne {id: 3}, (err, employee) ->
      console.dir employee if employee
      db.close()
```

In this example, we pass a query to the update method to restrict the update to the record with an ID of 3. We also pass an options object that specifies a $set object. Properties associated with the $set object will be updated or added to the documents matching the query.

 Be sure to specify the properties you want to update on $set; otherwise, the entire document will be overwritten effectively deleting all of its content.

By default, updates are limited to a single document. This prevents unintentional updates to an entire collection. We can override this by specifying the {multi: true} option. For example, if we wanted to set the department of all employees to be "sales", we can accomplish this in the following manner:

```
collection.update {}, \
  {$set: {department: 'Sales'}}, \
  {multi: true}, \
  (err, res) ->
    console.log err if err?
    console.dir res if res?
```

In the preceding code, we added the multi flag to inform Mongo we wish to apply this change to all documents matching our query. In this particular case, our query is { }, which matches all documents in the collection.

Deleting documents

Mongo provides a remove() method to delete documents from a collection. We can pass a query object to remove() that specifies the document or documents to be removed.

How to do it...

We will remove the employee document, where the employee's id is 3.

1. Open a connection:

```
MongoClient = require('mongodb').MongoClient
url = 'mongodb://localhost:27017/test'
MongoClient.connect url, (err, db) ->
```

2. Grab an instance of the `employees` collection:

```
collection = db.collection 'employees'
```

3. Use the `remove()` function to remove a document:

```
collection.remove {id: 3}, (err, res) ->
  console.dir res
```

How it works...

In the preceding code, once the database has been opened and the employees collection is selected, we call the `remove()` function with a query object of `{id: 3}` and a callback so that we can view the response.

The result of the callback will contain the number of documents affected. In our case, it is one document. If our query had been something like `{salesYtd: {$lt: 5000}}`, then all documents having a `salesYtd` value less than $5,000.00 would have been deleted.

Using `remove()` is fine if we want to remove entire documents, but what if we want to only remove parts of a document or documents?

We can use the `update()` method for this. Instead of using the `$set` option property, we can specify a `$unset` option property, as seen in the following code:

```
collection.update {}, \
  {$unset: {salesYtd: ''}}, \
  (err, res) ->
    console.log err if err?
    console.dir res if res?
    db.close()
```

In our example, we attempt to update all documents by removing their `salesYtd` property. If we run this, we see that the number of records affected, returned by the `update()` method, is one. We need to specify the `{multi: true}` option to update all documents matching our query as seen in the following revision:

```
collection.update {}, \
  {$unset: {salesYtd: ''}}, \
  {multi: true}, \
  (err, res) ->
    console.log err if err?
    console.dir res if res?
```

Working with CouchDB

CouchDB is an open source Apache project and, like MongoDB, is a no-SQL, document database.

In this section, we will see how to use CoffeeScript to perform create, read, update, and delete actions with a CouchDB database.

You can find more information on CouchDB, including information on downloading, installing, and using CouchDB from the project's home page located at `http://couchdb.apache.org/`.

Opening a connection

We will use the `cradle` NPM package to connect to our CouchDB server. In this example, we will open a connection and verify the existence of a database and, if it does not exist, we will create it.

Getting ready...

Once CouchDB has been installed, install **cradle** with the following command:

```
npm install cradle --save
```

How to do it...

1. Require cradle and create a connection to a database named **test**:

```
cradle = require 'cradle'
db = (new(cradle.Connection)).database 'test'
```

2. Use the `exists()` function to see whether the test database exists:

```
db.exists (err, exists) ->
```

3. If it does not, execute the `create()` function to create it:

```
if exists
  console.log 'test database exists'
else
  console.log 'test database does not exist'
  db.create()
  console.log 'test database has been created'
```

How it works...

Once cradle is installed, you can require it, create a connection, and connect to a database.

Once we have a database object, we can use it to communicate with the database. First, let's verify that the database exists.

The database object has an `exists()` function that takes a callback. Our callback will receive a value of `true` if the database exists or `false` if it does not.

This allows us to create the database if one does not exist. We can do this by calling the `create()` method.

There's more...

In our example, we connect to the default host and port. For CouchDB, this is `127.0.0.1:5984`. We can specify a different host and port using the following syntax:

```
db = (new(cradle.Connection)(hostAsString, portAsInteger).database
'test'
```

We can also pass connection parameters as an object literal. This also allows us to specify SSL and authentication settings:

```
db = (new(cradle.Connection)(host, 443, {
      auth: { username: 'user', password: 'password' }
).database 'test'
```

Creating documents

CouchDB is a document-type database, so our data is in the form of JSON objects. These objects can be as simple or as complex as needed.

In our examples, we will work with our employee database with employees and departments.

Cradle provides a `save()` method to allow us to create new records in our CouchDB database.

How to do it...

We will use the `save()` function:

1. Require cradle and create a connection to a database named **test**:

```
cradle = require 'cradle'
db = (new(cradle.Connection)).database 'test'
```

2. Define an array of employees to be added to the test database:

```
employees =[
  { id: 1, first: 'Tracy', last: 'Ouellette', salesYtd: 22246 }
  { id: 2, first: 'Chris', last: 'Daniel', salesYtd: 3876 }
  { id: 3, first: 'Jason', last: 'Alexander', salesYtd: 4095 }
  { id: 4, first: 'Jennifer', last: 'Hannah', salesYtd: 8070 }
  { id: 5, first: 'Maxx', last: 'Slayde', salesYtd: 2032 }
]
```

3. Execute `save()` for each employee in our array:

```
for employee in employees
  db.save "EMP:#{employee.id}", employee
```

How it works...

The `save()` function takes an optional document key, the object being saved, and an optional callback that provides access to the save's result. Note that if a key is not provided, CouchDB will provide one for you.

 If a key is provided, it must be a string value.

We save an employee object by calling `save()` passing the employee's ID formatted as `EMP:{id}` as the document key, the employee object, and a callback.

When the save operation is completed, the callback is called with an error object and a result object. If the operation is completed without an error, the error object will be null. The result object contains `ok`, `id`, and `rev` properties as seen in the following result:

```
{ ok: true,
  id: 'EMP:1',
  rev: '1-90c3c64a6f2c9d2692fd622f89e06ae7' }
```

 Note that if we did not pass a document key to save, CouchDB would have created one for us. If you need the document's autogenerated key, use the result's ID.

When using the `save()` method, the entire object is replaced. This means in order to update an object using the `save()` method, you must first get the document, make your changes, and save it again.

Updating documents

You can use the `merge()` method to add or update specific attributes.

How to do it...

In this example, we will add `department` and update the year-to-date sales for `EMP:3`:

1. Require cradle and create a connection to a database named `test`:

    ```
    cradle = require 'cradle'
    db = (new(cradle.Connection)).database 'test'
    ```

2. Define an update object with the properties we want to change:

    ```
    update =
      salesYtd: 3405.98
      department:
        id: 1
        description: 'Sales'
    ```

3. Execute the `merge()` function to update employee `EMP:3`:

    ```
    db.merge 'EMP:3', update, (err, result) ->
      unless err?
        console.dir result
      else
        console.log err
    ```

How it works...

In this example, we create an object literal called `update`. We then call the `merge()` method passing our document key and `update` object.

After executing our `merge()` method, the `EMP:3` document is updated and we are provided with a `results` object that looks like the following:

```
{ ok: true,
  id: 'EMP:3',
  rev: '2-89664469ad471a902ef769811c61dbe3' }
```

Reading documents

The cradle module provides a `get()` method to retrieve documents from CouchDB using a key or an array of keys.

How to do it...

We will use `get()` with a single key and then with an array containing two keys to retrieve employee documents.

1. Require cradle and create a connection to a database named `test`:

    ```
    cradle = require 'cradle'
    db = (new(cradle.Connection)).database 'test'
    ```

2. Create a helper function to display an employee:

    ```
    displayEmployee = (emp) ->
      console.log "Employee: #{emp.first} #{emp.last}"
    ```

3. Get a single employee with `get()`:

    ```
    db.get 'EMP:3', (err, doc) ->
      console.log 'Single Document:'
      unless err?
        displayEmployee doc
      else
        console.dir err
    ```

4. Get multiple employees with `get()`:

    ```
    db.get ['EMP:1', 'EMP:5'], (err, docs) ->
      console.log '\nMultiple Documents:'
      unless err?
        (displayEmployee item.doc) for item in docs
    ```

How it works...

When using `get()`, we pass a callback, which will be called once the document(s) have been retrieved. This callback is called with an error object and an object representing the query results.

When reading a single document, the result is the document itself (if the key is found). When reading multiple keys, the result is a collection of objects. Each object has a doc property representing the matching document itself.

When we execute this sample, we get the following output:

```
Single Document:
Employee: Jason Alexander


Multiple Documents:
Employee: Tracy Ouellette
Employee: Maxx Slayde
```

When retrieving a single document, if the key is not found, callback is called with an error object with a `not_found` error value. When retrieving multiple documents using an array of keys, any key that is not found is simply omitted from the results.

Deleting documents

To delete documents from CouchDB, cradle provides a `remove()` function, which takes a document key that identifies the document to be removed, an optional revision number, and a callback function.

How to do it...

We will use the `remove()` function to remove documents:

1. Require cradle and create a connection to a database named **test**.

```
cradle = require 'cradle'
db = (new(cradle.Connection)).database 'test'
```

2. Remove `EMP:3` using `remove()`:

```
db.remove 'EMP:3', (err, res) ->
  unless err?
    console.dir res
  else
    console.dir err
```

3. Let's try getting `EMP:3`, which should be not found:

```
db.get 'EMP:3', (err, res) ->
    console.log err if err?
displayEmployee = (emp) ->
    console.log "Employee: #{emp.first} #{emp.last}"
```

How it works...

In this example, we execute the `remove()` function by passing the document key of `EMP:3` and a callback. Upon the successful deletion, our callback is called with the successful result, as seen in the following result:

```
{ ok: true,
  id: 'EMP:3',
  rev: '4-4d896f03b66e8b88e15ab2c5b852aaff' }
```

When we try to get the document, we receive the following message:

```
{ error: 'not_found', reason: 'deleted' }
```

In CouchDB, documents that are removed are not really deleted, at least not right away. Documents that are removed have a `_deleted: true` value added to them. Documents with this attribute are not returned when performing queries. Documents are not actually deleted until the database has been purged. See the project page for the _purge command at `http://wiki.apache.org/couchdb/Purge_Documents`.

Querying documents using views

CouchDB provides highly indexed and optimized views as a way of searching for documents matching specified criteria.

We can use cradle to create, update, remove, and query views in our database.

Views in CouchDB are simply a wrapper for a function. This function is executed for every document in the database. If the document meets the specific criteria, the function emits a result by passing a result key and result value. This result may be the document itself, but it can be anything you want it to be.

For example, if we had a database of vehicles, we could create a view that provides us with only two-wheeled vehicles using the following function:

```
(doc) ->
  if doc.wheelCount? and doc.wheelCount is 2
    emit doc._id, doc
```

In this example, our method will receive a document. We then verify that the document has a `wheelCount` property and, if `wheelCount` is equal to two. If it is, we simply return the document itself.

How to do it...

To create a view that returns only two-wheeled vehicles in cradle, we will save a document to CouchDB's internal `_design` collection. This document is the view itself.

1. Require cradle and create a connection to a database named test:

```
cradle = require 'cradle'
db = (new(cradle.Connection)).database 'vehicles'
```

2. Create an object literal defining our view:

```
view =
  twoWheels:
    map: (doc) ->
      if doc.wheelCount? and doc.wheelCount is 2
        emit doc._id, doc
```

3. Save the view:

```
db.save '_design/query', view
```

4. Use the `view()` function to execute the new view:

```
db.view 'query/twoWheels', (err, results) ->
  unless err?
    console.dir results
    for doc in results
      console.log doc.value.type
```

How it works...

In this example, we create an object that has a property named `twoWheels`. This property is an object that has a single `map()` method.

We then save our view document with a `_design/query` key.

Next, we use the `view()` method to execute the `query/twoWheels` view. We pass a callback to handle the return value. In this case, the following object is returned:

```
[ { id: 'bicycle',
    key: 'bicycle',
    value:
     { _id: 'bicycle',
       _rev: '1-13ef40d4b48d59d42a9735d3c8ea1e06',
       type: 'Bicycle',
       wheelCount: 2 } },
  { id: 'moped',
    key: 'moped',
    value:
     { _id: 'moped',
       _rev: '1-692f3dd62fc6c7a608157866313e7f03',
       type: 'Moped',
       wheelCount: 2 } },
  { id: 'motorcycle',
    key: 'motorcycle',
    value:
     { _id: 'motorcycle',
       _rev: '1-14b6da9ee717d5f24fb03b91b87a9e9c',
       type: 'Motorcycle',
       wheelCount: 2 } } ]
```

You can see in the object passed to our callback that we have an array of objects. Each object in the array contains a value property that contains the object we emitted from our view's map() function.

There's more...

You can use views to perform mapping and reduction of our data. This allows our views to return aggregate results. For example, we could return the vehicle count by wheelCount using CouchDB's map-reduce functionality for views.

For this, we will create a view that has the map() and reduce() methods:

```
cradle = require 'cradle'
db = (new(cradle.Connection)).database 'vehicles'

view =
  byWheelCount:
    map: (doc) ->
      emit doc.wheelCount, 1
    reduce: (key, values, rereduce) ->
      return (sum values)

db.save '_design/aggregate', view
```

This view is similar to our first view, except we also define a reduce() method as well. Our map() method returns a result with a key of the wheel count and a value of 1.

We then define our reduce function as simply returning the sum of the values for the given key. To visualize what is happening, consider the following result of our mapping function:

```
[ { id: 'unicycle', key: 1, value: 1 },
  { id: 'bicycle', key: 2, value: 1 },
  { id: 'moped', key: 2, value: 1 },
  { id: 'motorcycle', key: 2, value: 1 },
  { id: 'tricycle', key: 3, value: 1 },
  { id: 'car', key: 4, value: 1 },
  { id: 'truck', key: 4, value: 1 },
  { id: 'van', key: 4, value: 1 } ]
```

The result of our mapping call is then passed to our reduce() function as an array of elements grouped by key and an array of values for that key. To help visualize this, consider the following.

```
[ { key: 1, values: [ 1 ] },
  { key: 2, values: [ 1, 1, 1 ] },
  { key: 3, values: [ 1 ] },
  { key: 4, values: [ 1, 1, 1 ] } ]
```

Once our view is created, we can call the view.

```
cradle = require 'cradle'
db = (new(cradle.Connection)).database 'vehicles'

options =
  group: true

db.view 'aggregate/byWheelCount', options, (err, results) ->
  unless err?
    console.log "Wheels\tRecords"
    for result in results
      console.log "#{result.key}\t#{result.value}"
```

We then call the `view()` method as we did previously, but in this example, we include an options object that tells cradle to execute the query to return a grouped result.

 Note that there are other options that can be passed to our view function that allow us to specify a start and end key range, sorting direction, grouping level, limit the number of results, and skip a specified number of results (great for paging). You can see these options in the CouchDB documentation at `http://wiki.apache.org/couchdb/HTTP_view_API`.

Running our aggregate query displays the following results:

Wheels	Records
1	1
2	3
3	1
4	3

You can see that we have one record that has three wheels, three records that have four wheels, and so on.

7
Building Application Services

In this chapter, we will cover the following recipes:

- ▶ Working with base64 encoding
- ▶ Working with domain name services
- ▶ Parsing a URL into its various components
- ▶ Creating RESTful web services

Introduction

Building rich Internet-based applications involves creating client-side application code responsible for rendering views for the user as well as handling user interactions. Requests will be made to the server to load or persist data, and to perform authentication and authorization or other resource-intensive tasks.

In this chapter, we will see how we can use CoffeeScript to perform common Internet-related tasks and create RESTful services to be used by our applications.

Working with base64 encoding

Base64 encoding allows us to transform binary data into text data. The reasons for this are rooted in the history of network protocols, but it is still a widely used form of encoding when shipping binary data.

For example, binary e-mail attachments are first converted to base64 before being sent. It happens to be a handy way to include images within the context of an e-mail body.

In these recipes, we will see how to encode and decode binary and base64-encoded files.

Encoding a string as base64

Node provides a string `Buffer` class that can represent text data in a variety of encodings, including `ASCII`, `UTF-8`, and `Base-64`. This `Buffer` class will be the core of our conversion operations.

Getting ready

Node supports base64 encoding without the need of an external module. We will be using Node's built-in capabilities.

How to do it...

We will create a Node module that exposes a method to convert ASCII `toBase64()` and another Node to convert to ASCII `fromBase64()`:

1. Create a function named toBase64:

    ```
    toBase64 = (text) ->
        return (new Buffer text).toString('base64')
    ```

2. Create a function named fromBase6:

    ```
    fromBase64 = (base64Text) ->
        return (new Buffer base64Text, 'base64').toString 'ascii'
    ```

How it works...

Both the `toBase64()` and `fromBase64()` functions create a new instance of Node's `Buffer` class by providing a text value to the `Buffer` constructor. This text value represents the value the new `Buffer` object will contain.

Node's `Buffer` class can be initialized by providing a buffer size (creates an empty buffer of the specified size), an array of octet (character) values, or a string value with an optional encoding. `Buffer` will default to `UTF-8` for its encoding

Once we have a buffer of values, we use the `Buffer` object's `toString()` method to convert the buffer to a specified encoding and return its result.

We specify the encoding type by passing a string value. These values include `ascii`, `utf8`, `utf16le`, `ucs2`, `base64`, `binary`, and `hex`.

We can use these functions in the following way:

```
original = 'CoffeeScript rocks!'
encoded  = toBase64 original
conole.log "#{original} becomes #{encoded}"
decoded = fromBase64 encoded
console.log "#{encoded} becomes #{decoded}"
```

Executing this example we receive the following output:

```
CoffeeScript rocks! becomes Q29mZmVlU2NyaXB0IHJvY2tzIQ==

Q29mZmVlU2NyaXB0IHJvY2tzIQ== becomes CoffeeScript rocks!
```

Encoding a binary file as base64

Sometimes, we have a need to store or use binary files with systems that were not designed to properly handle binary data. In this section, we will see how to convert binary files to base64 text and vice versa.

Getting ready

We will use the `atob` and `btoa` NPM modules to convert from ASCII to binary and binary to ASCII, respectively.

These can be added to our project by performing the following installation commands:

```
npm install atob
npm install btoa
```

How to do it...

We will create a method to encode a binary file into base64 text file and another to decode a base64 text file back to its binary format:

1. Require the filesystem (`fs`), `btoa`, and `atob` packages:

   ```
   fs = require 'fs'
   btoa = require 'btoa'
   atob = require 'atob'
   ```

2. Create a function to encode a file:

   ```
   encode = (source, destination, callback) ->
     fs.readFile source, (err, data) ->
       base64 = btoa data
       fs.writeFile destination, base64, 'ascii', (err) ->
         callback() if callback?
   ```

3. Create a function to decode a file:

```
decode = (source, destination, callback) ->
  fs.readFile source, 'ascii', (err, data) ->
    binary = atob data
    fs.writeFile destination, binary, 'binary', (err) ->
      callback() if callback?
```

How it works...

The sample code references Node's `fs` library and the `atob` and `btoa` modules.

Both the previous methods accept `source` and `destination` parameters.

The `encode()` method reads the contents of a binary data file and uses the `btoa()` method to convert the binary contents to base64. We then write the base64 text to the file specified by the `destination` parameter.

The `decode()` method performs the opposite operation. It reads the contents of the base64 text file and uses `atob()` to convert this back to binary data. It then writes the binary data to the file specified by the `destination` parameter.

With these methods, we can easily convert binary files to base64 text using the following command in our application:

```
encode 'logo.png', 'logo.encoded', ->
  console.log 'Finished encoding file.'
```

We can also convert a base64 file to binary using the following command in our application:

```
decode 'logo.encoded', 'logo.decoded.png', ->
  console.log 'Finished decoding file'
```

Working with domain name services

Domain names provide convenient and easy-to-remember aliases for IP addresses so that we can navigate to websites and backend servers. Domain name services are responsible for converting domain names such as `http://www.coffeescript.org` or `http://www.google.com` to actual IP addresses.

In the following recipe, we will see how to look up the IP address for a domain name and how to perform a reverse lookup for an IP address.

Retrieving the IP address for a domain name

In this section, we will demonstrate how to look up an IP address for a given domain name.

Getting ready

We will be using Node's built-in DNS module to perform our domain lookups. There is nothing additional to install to perform this task.

How to do it...

We can perform a lookup in the following manner:

1. Import Node's `dns` module:

    ```
    dns = require 'dns'
    ```

2. Create a function to execute the `lookup()` function:

    ```
    lookupIpAddress = (domainName, callback) ->
      dns.lookup domainName, (err, ipAddress) ->
        if err?
          console.log err
        else
          callback ipAddress
    ```

How it works...

In the previous code, we created a reference to Node's DNS module. We then created a method that wraps the `dns.lookup()` method, which returns an error or an object representing the lookup results.

We can use our method in the following way:

```
lookupIpAddress 'coffeescript.org', (result) ->
  console.log "CoffeeScript: #{JSON.stringify result}"

lookupIpAddress 'google.com', (result) ->
  console.log "Google: #{JSON.stringify result}"
```

This will produce the following output:

```
CoffeeScript: "207.97.227.245"
Google: "74.125.226.73"
```

There's more...

The `dns.loopup()` method will return the first IPv4 or IPv6 address that is found. A third, optional parameter will receive either a 4 or 6 to indicate whether the address was indeed an IPv4 or an IPv6, accordingly.

For example, we can modify our code to display this as follows:

```
dns = require 'dns'

lookupIpAddress = (domainName, callback) ->
  dns.lookup domainName, (err, ipAddress, family) ->
    if err?
      console.log err
    else
      callback ipAddress, family

lookupIpAddress 'coffeescript.org', (result, family) ->
  console.log "CoffeeScript: #{JSON.stringify result} IPv#{family}"

lookupIpAddress 'google.com', (result, family) ->
  console.log "Google: #{JSON.stringify result} IPv#{family}"
```

We added the optional `family` parameter to our lookup callback method. We then return it and use it on our output. With this minor change, we can see that both the results are IPv4:

CoffeeScript: "207.97.227.245" IPv4

Google: "74.125.226.6" IPv4

It is possible that a domain lookup may return no data if the domain address is invalid or if there is a network failure of some sort. In this case, the `lookup()` function will pass an error code to the callback method of the lookup.

Common values for a DNS error are as follows:

- ▶ `dns.NOTFOUND`: This error is generated when the `lookup()` function returns no data. Normally, this is because the domain name is invalid.

- ▶ `dns.NODATA`: This error is generated when the server returns an empty response to our `lookup()` call.

- ▶ `dns.SERVFAIL`: This error is generated when the server returns a general error to our `lookup()` call.

Retrieving a hostname for an IP address

Node's DNS module also allows us to perform a reverse domain lookup by providing an IP address and retrieving the domain name, if one is registered.

Getting ready

We will be using Node's built-in DNS module to perform our reverse domain lookups. There is nothing additional to install to perform this task.

How to do it...

We will use the `dns.reverse()` method to perform the reverse lookup. We provide an IP address as a string, and a callback. Once completed, our callback will be called with an array of resulting domain names:

1. Import Node's `dns` module:

    ```
    dns = require 'dns'
    ```

2. Create a function to use the `reverse()` function:

    ```
    reverseLookup = (ipAddress, callback) ->
      dns.reverse ipAddress, (err, result) ->
        if err?
          console.log err
        else
          callback result
    ```

How it works...

In the `reverseLookup()` method, we pass an IP address and a callback method. Once the lookup is completed, our callback method will be called with the lookup result.

We can then call this method in the following way:

```
reverseLookup '74.125.226.73', (domains) ->
  console.log "74.125.226.73: #{JSON.stringify domains}"

reverseLookup '207.97.227.245', (domains) ->
  console.log "207.97.227.245: #{JSON.stringify domains}"
```

The results might not be exactly what you expect. For example, you can see in the following output that the IP address does not return to the domain we originally performed an IP lookup for:

```
74.125.226.73: ["lga15s44-in-f9.1e100.net"]
207.97.227.245: ["pages.github.com"]
```

We can test our results by opening our browser and typing the odd domain name for Google. You will find that it works.

Parsing a URL into its various components

Our modern applications often need to communicate with a backend server. In the server-side code or service code, we may need to analyze the requesting URLs.

In this section, we will investigate ways to parse URLs into their constituent components.

Getting ready

We will be using Node's built-in URL parsing functionality to perform our URL manipulations. There is nothing additional to install to perform this task.

How to do it...

To demonstrate this process, we create a collection of parsed URL properties, execute the `parse()` function, and then iterate over the results:

1. Import Node's `url` module:

    ```
    url = require 'url'
    ```

2. Execute the `parse()` function with a sample URL:

    ```
    address = 'http://coffeescript.org:80/?r=home/#loops'
    urlInfo = url.parse address, true
    ```

3. Display each of the `urlInfo` object's properties:

    ```
    for property of urlInfo
      if urlInfo[property]?
        value = JSON.stringify urlInfo[property]
        if value?
          console.log "#{property.toUpperCase()}: #{value}"
    ```

How it works...

In the preceding code, we used Node's built-in `url.parse()` method to break a sample URL into its constituent parts.

The `parse()` method takes two parameters. The first parameter is the URL to be parsed and is required. The second parameter is an optional Boolean value that tells the `parse()` method to convert any URL query parameters into an actual object literal. By default, this will be false and the query parameters will be returned as a single string.

The `parse()` method will return an object literal with properties representing the various URL pieces. We use CoffeeScript's `for...of` loop to traverse `urlInfo` object's properties and display each to demonstrate the result of `parse()`.

Executing this will produce the following output:

```
PROTOCOL: "http:"
SLASHES: true
HOST: "coffeescript.org:80"
PORT: "80"
HOSTNAME: "coffeescript.org"
HASH: "#loops"
SEARCH: "?r=home/"
QUERY: {"r":"home/"}
PATHNAME: "/"
PATH: "/?r=home/"
HREF: "http://coffeescript.org:80/?r=home/#loops"
```

Notice that our `query` property displays `{"r":"home/"}`. This is because we passed the value of `true` to our `parse()` method. If we omitted this Boolean value, we would have the following output for `query`:

```
QUERY:  "r=home/"
```

There's more...

Along with parsing URLs, the Node URL module also allows us to reassemble URLs based on the various properties we looked at.

For example, if we modified the `urlInfo` object by providing a new object literal for the query parameter, we can use the `url.format()` method as follows:

```
urlInfo.query = { q: 'CoffeeScript Books', p: 4}
urlInfo.search = ''
newAddress = url.format urlInfo
console.log newAddress
```

This produces the following output:

```
http://coffeescript.org:80/?q=CoffeeScript%20Books&p=4#loops
```

Node also provides the `querystring` module to specifically deal with query string data. For example, we can pass an object to the `querystring.stringify()` function to create a string representing the URL query string version of the object. Conversely, we can use the `querystring.parse()` function by passing it in a string and an object will be returned:

```
querystring = require 'querystring'

employee =
  firstName: 'Tracy'
  lastName:  'Ouellette'
  salesYtd: [ 2324.23, 432.34 ]

params = querystring.stringify employee
console.log params

parsed = querystring.parse params
console.log parsed
```

This displays the following output:

```
$ coffee test.coffee
Object to Query String:
  firstName=Tracy&lastName=Ouellette&salesYtd=2324.23&salesYtd=432.34

Query String to Obpject:
  { firstName: 'Tracy',
    lastName: 'Ouellette',
    salesYtd: [ '2324.23', '432.34' ] }
```

Creating RESTful web services

In this collection of recipes, we will create a simple HTTP server using Node and a popular web application called express. Express is a Node package used to create small web applications. It provides support to map HTTP verbs to URL paths, which makes it ideal to set up a quick HTTP server to host an API.

In this section, we will look at managing our application's dependencies as well as building a simple HTTP server and a web API using express.

Managing dependencies with package.json

Nearly all but the extremely simple applications will require one or more external dependencies. Typically, these are NPM modules. In this section, we will look at using a package configuration file. This allows us to configure or project and manage dependencies.

Getting ready

We can create a package.json file by using NPM. Enter the following command in your terminal or command window:

```
npm init
```

How to do it...

The `npm init` command will present you with a series of questions and some with default values. The following table lists the prompts and their default values:

Prompt	Default	Description
`name`	Name of the parent directory	The name of your project
`version`	1.0.0	Your project's version number
`description`	blank	A description of your project
`entry point`	Blank	The main JavaScript file for your project
`test command`	Blank	The command to be executed to run your project's test via the `npm test` command
`git repository`	Blank	The Git repository for your project, if any
`keywords`	Blank	For an NPM package project, the keywords help people find your package
`author`	Blank	Your name `<email address>`
`license`	ISC	Your project's license (ISC is a permissive-free software license functionally equivalent to the simplified BSD and MIT licenses)

When we come to the end, the `package.json` contents are displayed and we are asked whether they are okay. Pressing *Enter* will accept the changes and write them to the file.

 Note that if a package file already exists, running `npm init` will display the prompts with default values. When it writes the package file, it will maintain your custom values.

Once completed, your `package.json` file will look similar to the following:

```
{
  "name": "Sample",
  "version": "1.0.0",
  "description": "A sample package.json file",
  "main": "test.js",
  "scripts": {
    "test": "echo \"Error: no test specified\" && exit 1"
  },
  "author": "Mike Hatfield <mwhatfield@outlook.com>",
  "license": "ISC",
  "keywords": []
}
```

How it works...

A package file also allows us to manage our applications dependencies. For example, because our application requires Express, we can use the following command line to install Express and add it to our package file as a dependency:

```
npm install express@4.9.5 --save
```

The `--save` option will create or add a `dependencies` section to our package file that looks like the following:

```
"dependencies": {
    "express": "^4.9.5"
}
```

Here, we see that express has been added as a dependency to our project, specifically version 4.9.5. The caret (^) tells NPM that our project depends on any version of express matching the major version of 4. This will include 4.0.0, 4.2.3, and so on. We can also use a tilde (~) character to match the minor version. For example, ~4.9.5 would match 4.9.0, 4.9.1, and so on.

Next, we will add CoffeeScript as a development dependency using the following command:

```
npm install coffee-script --save-dev
```

This will add a development dependencies section. This is perfect for NPM modules needed specifically during development such as testing libraries. In the following snippet, we can see the `devDependencies` section that was added to our package file:

```
"devDependencies": {
    "coffee-script": "^1.8.0"
}
```

There's more...

One big advantage of having our dependencies defined in a package file for our project is that when we are configuring a new environment to work on the project, we can simply check out or clone our code repository and install our dependencies with the following command:

```
npm install
```

 If you look inside the `node_modules` folder, you will see a folder for each package that was installed.

Creating a basic express application

In this section, we will create a simple application using CoffeeScript and express.

Getting ready

To begin, we will install express and save it as a dependency for our application with the following command:

```
npm install express --save
```

Next, install CoffeeScript as a development dependency:

```
npm install coffee-script --save-dev
```

How to do it...

In this sample, we will create a simple express application:

1. Create a file named `simple.coffee`.
2. Import the express module and assign it to a variable named `express`:

   ```
   express = require 'express'
   ```

3. Create an express instance and assign it to a variable named `app`:

   ```
   app     = express()
   ```

4. Use the `app.get()` function to register a route mapping:

   ```
   app.get '/', (req, res) ->
   ```

5. Inside the route callback, and send back a familiar message:

   ```
       res.send '<h1>Hello World!</h1>'
   ```

6. Use the `app.listen()` function to listen on port `3000`:

   ```
   console.log 'Ready on port 3000.  Press [Ctrl+C] to stop.'
   app.listen 3000
   ```

How it works...

This is a very simple example, but clearly demonstrates the basic structure of an express application.

First, you require the necessary libraries. In this example, we only need to `require` express itself. We assign it to a variable called `express`.

Next, we create an express application and assign it to the `app` variable.

Using our `app` variable, we then define our routes. Routes are defined by calling a supported HTTP verb and passing a path and callback function. In our example, we create a handler that will listen for `GET` requests on the application's root path:

```
app.get '/', (req, res) ->
```

Express recognizes all of the HTTP verbs, including `GET`, `POST`, `PUT`, and `DELETE`, and these are used in express as `app.get()`, `app.post()`, `app.put()`, and `app.delete()`, respectively.

The path can be defined as a string as it is in our example or as a regular expression, where the URL of the request is matched against the regular expression. The callback is a function that takes a request and a response argument.

From the request argument, we can access the request's form data, query string parameters, route parameters, request headers, and request cookies. The response argument allows us to set response headers and response cookies, and provides methods to return a response in various forms to the client.

In our example, we use the `res.send()` function to send plain text back to the browser.

The last piece of an Express application involves creating a listener to watch for incoming requests. We accomplish this by executing the application's `listen()` function by passing a specific port number.

To execute our little Express sample, use the `coffee` command:

`coffee simple.coffee`

With the application is running, open your web browser and navigate to `http://localhost:3000/`:

Creating a web API

In this section, we will use express to create a web service that will watch for and respond to requests for data.

Getting ready

We will build our web service API using the **Representational State Transfer** (**REST**) architectural style. This is an abstraction that uses a combination of HTTP verbs and a clearly defined URL structure to create an API that will provide access to our resource data.

We will use the widely accepted resource path naming / HTTP verb combinations when we define our API. The following table lists these conventions:

HTTP verb	Path	Description
GET	/api/[items]	Get all items
GET	/api/[items]/:id	Get a single item by ID
GET	/api/[items]/:id/[child-items]	Get all child items for an item
POST	/api/[items]	Create an item
POST	/api/[items]/:id	Update an item
POST	/api/[items]/:id/delete	Delete an item

 Note that REST does not care about the URL structure itself, but this is, instead, a convention that has been popularized by Ruby on Rails. It is a convention that has been adopted by many in the open source community and one that we will follow while defining our API.

We use GET requests to make read-only requests such as requesting all resources or a specific resource, and we use POST for actions that change the state of the resource (creating, updating, or deleting, for example). Adherence to this rule when creating your API will help avoid unintended side effects. For example, users should be able to make GET requests and feel assured that they are not changing or destroying data.

Please note there is nothing that guarantees that a GET request does not change or destroy data, only that the convention recommends against it. It's completely up to the developer to properly implement their GET request handlers.

Our API will be return objects as JSON. Express provides a json() function on the response object, which makes this very easy.

For our example, we will use two helper Node modules, one by CoffeeScript's own Jeremy Ashkenas called underscore that provides a large number of useful functions, and the other is an express helper module that makes working with HTML form data much easier:

```
npm install underscore --save
npm install body-parser --save
```

How to do it...

Our sample comprises three files:

- ▶ server.coffee: This is the main application file that initializes and configures express
- ▶ data.coffee: This is the data module that provides data-related functionality
- ▶ routes.coffee: This is the module that creates the API routes to be used by our application

Follow these steps to create a web API:

1. Create a CoffeeScript file called server.coffee.

2. Import the express, body parser, and our data and route modules, and assign an instance to a variable named app:

```
express     = require 'express'
bodyParser = require 'body-parser'
data       = require './data'
routes     = require './routes'
app        = express()
```

3. Configure express to use the body parser:

```
app.use bodyParser.urlencoded({ extended: true })
```

4. Register our routes:

```
routes.registerRoutes app, data
```

5. Start listening for requests:

```
console.log 'Ready on port 3000.  Press [Ctrl+C] to stop.'
app.listen 3000
```

Next, we will create our data file as follows:

1. Create a file named `data.coffee`.

2. Import the `underscore` module:

```coffee
_ = require 'underscore'
```

3. Create some sample employee and sales data:

```coffee
employeesData = [
  { id: 1, firstName: 'Tracy', lastName: 'Ouellette', \
    sales: [210340.084, 76251.825, 2967.55, 237934.707, \
      333020.396, 222597.24, 322963.891, 38847.682] }
  { id: 2, firstName: 'Chris', lastName: 'Daniel', \
    sales: [104362.4195, 70957.9675, 5490.714, \
      242605.2755, 232524.4215, 100582.983, 320185.112, \
      103374.8915] }
  { id: 3, firstName: 'Jason', lastName: 'Alexander', \
    sales: [226930.102, 72591.8695, 14076.254, \
      229126.6455, 304316.3145, 120713.766, 232629.537, \
      73296.443] }
  { id: 4, firstName: 'Jennifer', lastName: 'Hannah', \
    sales: [133347.813, 27043.249, 3434.7945, \
      324250.3755, 235481.5525, 94006.9505, 343566.8035, \
      55351.8995] }
  { id: 5, firstName: 'Maxx', lastName: 'Slayde', \
    sales: [142030.3425, 52111.8295, 5687.95, 244571.772, \
      242079.538, 103000.685, 271688.082, 99726.1815] }
]
```

4. Create functions to fetch, add, update, and remove employees from the collection. Also, create a helper function that returns the next ID to be assigned to new employees:

```coffee
employeesFetchAll = ->
  employeesData

employeesFetchById = (id) ->
  _.findWhere employeesData, { id: id }

employeesAddToCollection = (employee) ->
  employee =
    id: employeesNextId()
    firstName: employee.firstName || ''
    lastName: employee.lastName || ''
    sales: employee.sales || []
  employeesData.push employee
```

```
    return employee

employeesRemoveFromCollection = (employee) ->
  employeesData = _.reject employeesData, (item) ->
    item.id is employee.id

employeesUpdateExisting = (employee) ->
  employeesRemoveFromCollection employee
  employeesData.push employee

employeesNextId = ->
  _.chain employeesData
    .pluck 'id'
    .max (i) -> i
    .value() + 1
```

5. Export our data functions so that they can be used by our express server:

```
module.exports =
  employees:
    fetchAll: employeesFetchAll
    fetchById: employeesFetchById
    add: employeesAddToCollection
    update: employeesUpdateExisting
    delete: employeesRemoveFromCollection
```

Lastly, we will create a module to register our API routes as follows:

1. Create a file named `routes.coffee`.

2. Export an object with a function named `registerRoutes`:

```
module.exports =
  registerRoutes: (app, data) ->
```

3. Inside the `registerRoutes()` function, create a route to handle GET `/api/employees` to return all employees:

```
app.get '/api/employees', (req, res) ->
  res.json data.employees.fetchAll()
```

4. Create a route to handle GET `/api/employees/:id` to return a specific employee:

```
app.get '/api/employees/:id', (req, res) ->
  employee = data.employees.fetchById Number req.params.id
  if employee
    res.json employee
  else
    res.send(404, 'Resource not found.')
```

5. Create a route to handle GET /api/employees/:id/sales to return the sales for a specific employee:

```
app.get '/api/employees/:id/sales', (req, res) ->
  employee = data.employees.fetchById Number req.params.id
  if employee
    res.json employee.sales || []
  else
    res.send(404, 'Resource not found.')
```

6. Create a route to handle POST /api/employees to create a new employee:

```
app.post '/api/employees', (req, res) ->
  employee = data.employees.add req.body
  res.json employee
```

7. Create a route to handle POST /api/employees/:id to update the information of an existing employee:

```
app.post '/api/employees/:id', (req, res) ->
  employee = data.employees.fetchById Number req.params.id
  if employee
    if req.body.firstName
      employee.firstName = req.body.firstName
    if req.body.lastName
      employee.lastName = req.body.lastName

    data.employees.update employee
    res.json employee
  else
    res.send(404, 'Resource not found.')
```

8. Create a route to handle POST /api/employees/:id/delete to delete an existing employee:

```
app.post '/api/employees/:id/delete', (req, res) ->
  employee = data.employees.fetchById Number req.params.id
  if employee
    data.employees.delete employee
    res.json employee
  else
    res.send(404, 'Resource not found.')
```

How it works...

We separated our application into three files to separate responsibilities.

In server.coffee, we require express, body parser, and our modules, and then create an express instance and assign it to the app variable. We then configure our express instance to use body parser. Body parser is an example of middleware that can be used by express.

Middleware are modules that participate in the request/response pipeline. They allow us to intercept requests and make decisions based on the request or modify the request before our application processes it. In the case of body parser, it will parse URL-encoded, JSON-encoded, or raw form of data being sent by the request and makes this data available as properties in the `request.body` object.

We then call our `registerRoutes()` function from our routes module passing our app and data objects as dependencies.

The `registerRoutes()` function is responsible for registering our API endpoints. We use the `app.get()` and `app.post()` functions to register a callback for each of our API endpoints. Each callback receives a request object and a response object.

We can use the request object to get details about the sender, headers, cookies, and parameters.

In some of our mapping URLs, we specify a token that express will parse for us as a `req.params` property. For example, a request for a specific employee is made to `GET /api/employees/:id`. Express will extract the URL fragment for any tokens in the mapping URL and add a property to the `res.params` object with the token name. In our callback, we access the incoming ID as `req.params.id`.

 Note that the parameter values that are extracted from the URL are extracted as a string. In our case, we want a number, so we force it into a numeric value using the `Number()` function.

The response object allows us to send information back to the client in various formats, return headers, status code, and to set or clear cookie values.

We use the `res.send()` and `res.json()` functions to return the results of each request. The send method can be used to send text back to the client as in `res.send('Hello world!')`.

In our example, we also include a status code of `404` and the text `Resource not found.` when the user requests an employee that does not exist in the collection.

We use the `res.json()` function to return objects to the client in a JSON format. For example, when requesting the employee with the ID of 3 `/api/employees/3`, the client receives the following response:

```
←  →  C  ⌂  |  localhost:3000/api/employees/3
{
  "id": 3,
  "firstName": "Jason",
  "lastName": "Alexander",
  "sales": [
    226930.102,
    72591.8695,
    14076.254,
    229126.6455,
    304316.3145,
    120713.766,
    232629.537,
    73296.443
  ]
}
```

There's more...

To launch the API, use the following command:

```
coffee server.coffee
```

This will display a message stating the application is listening on port 3000 and can be stopped by pressing *Ctrl + C*.

We can use a free Chrome extension called Postman to test our API. Postman allows us to make GET and POST requests to any endpoint and will display the results. It will also keep a history of our requests that allows us to go back to a previous request and modify or resend at any time:

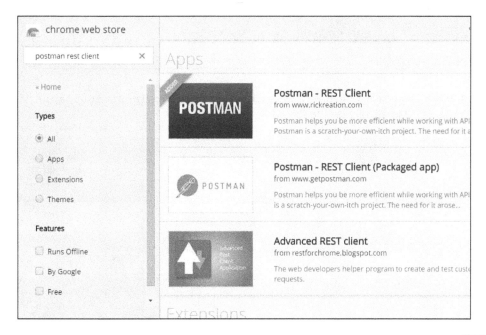

You can install this free Postman REST Client by visiting the Chrome Web Store and searching the extensions catalog for Postman.

Using the Postman extension, you can specify the URL of the API method you want to test, the verb to use and, in some cases, the key value pairs to add and update resources.

Test our API call to retrieve all employees by making `GET` requests to `http://localhost:3000/api/employees` and clicking on the **Send** button. The result can be seen in the following screenshot:

We can request a specific employee by ID such as `http://localhost:3000/api/employees/4`. This will display the following results:

We can update the last name for an employee by submitting form data using Postman's interface to POST /api/employees/4. You can see in the following screenshot that our submission is completed and the employee's last name has indeed been updated:

Be sure to switch the encoding to **x-www-form-urlencoded**, so the API receives the parameters as URL encoded parameters.

As you have seen, the Postman Chrome extension is very useful to test your API endpoints during development and even while troubleshooting APIs that are in production.

Using External Services

8

In this chapter, we will cover the following topics:

- Working with web services
- Sending e-mails
- Sending SMS and MMS messages
- Working with Amazon's S3 storage
- Transferring files via FTP

Introduction

There has been a recent explosion in the number and variety of services targeted to make our lives as software developers easier. Companies, both large and small, provide specialized services that allow us to take advantage of them in our own applications.

In this chapter, we will look at how we can use some popular services in our own applications. We will see how we can use services such as Amazon's **S3** storage to save files to the cloud, services such as **Twilio** to send SMS text messages from our application, and more.

Working with web services

Even though it is likely that our own application exposes some form of JSON API, it may also need to connect with other external services in order to perform its tasks.

It is becoming common for online services to provide web APIs, which allow us to use their services in our own applications.

In this recipe, we will see how to connect to an external service, request information, and process that information.

Getting ready

We will use the REST client for the Node.js `npm` module hosted on GitHub at `github.com/aacerox/node-rest-client`.

This client allows us to call RESTful services and retrieve results.

To get started, we will install the REST client:

```
npm install node-rest-client --save
```

We will use a free RESTful service that provides access to geographic and weather information. You can find out more about this free service from their website at `http://www.geonames.org`.

GeoNames provides a number of web services that expose their geographical database, including country information, weather stations, cities, and capitals.

In this example, we will connect using GeoNames' `countryInfo` web service to query their database for country information by UN country code.

We will also create a configuration file called `service-config.coffee` with the following code:

```
module.exports =
  username: 'beingmikeh'
  rootUrl: 'http://api.geonames.org'
  options:
    mimetypes:
      json: [
        'application/json;charset=UTF-8'
      ]
```

GeoNames allows 2,000 requests per hour, that is, 30,000 requests per day for free. In the previous configuration, I referenced my account. You can create your own account at `http://www.geonames.org/login`.

How to do it...

We will create a module that calls the `countryInfo` method. GeoNames provides an XML and JSON version of this method. We will be using the JSON endpoint located at `api.geonames.org/countryInfoJSON`.

Node-rest-client provides two methods to execute remote methods. Node-rest-client provides methods that mirror HTTP verbs such as `get()`, `post()`, `put()`, `patch()`, and `delete()`. This is helpful for simple one-time requests, but it also allows us to register methods in a way that allows us to build our own library or **domain-specific language (DSL)** to communicate with the web service.

> Creating a domain-specific language is a way to extend a general purpose language such as CoffeeScript to introduce methods, objects, and services that are more specific to a particular domain. For example, when building a banking system, we might create a library that allows us to work with checking and savings accounts, perform transfers, apply interest charges, and so on.
>
> For more information on domain-specific languages, you can reference the Wikipedia article on this topic at `en.wikipedia.org/wiki/Domain-specific_language`.

In this example, we will use node-rest-client's `get()` method to retrieve country information:

1. Load node-rest-client and assign its `Client` object to a `Client` variable:

   ```
   Client = require('node-rest-client').Client
   ```

2. Require our service configuration:

   ```
   config = require './service-config'
   ```

3. Create a new client instance to pass our configuration options:

   ```
   client = new Client config.options
   ```

4. Create a function that receives a country code and a callback as arguments:

   ```
   getCountryInfo = (countryCode, callback) ->
     url = "#{config.rootUrl}/countryInfoJSON"
     args =
       parameters:
         username: config.username
         country: countryCode or ''

     req = client.get url, args, (data, resp) ->
       if data.geonames
         callback null, data.geonames[0]
       else
         callback "No data returned for #{countryCode}"

     req.on 'error', (err) ->
       callback err.request.options
   ```

5. Create an array of country codes, and for each one, call our `getCountryInfo()` function to pass a callback:

```
countries = ['ca', 'us', 'gb']
for countryCode in countries
  getCountryInfo countryCode, (err, result) ->
```

6. Our callback is called when the service call is completed. Display the results of the service call as follows:

```
if err
  console.log 'Error', err
else
  console.log "Country  : #{result.countryName}"
  console.log "Capital  : #{result.capital}"
  console.log "Currency : #{result.currencyCode}"
  console.log "Area     : #{result.areaInSqKm} (sq km)"
  console.log "Continent: #{result.continentName}\n"
```

How it works...

In the preceding code, we begin by requiring the REST client.

We then create an instance of our REST client (`client`) and declare a constant (`BASE`) representing the GeoNames base URL.

Next, we declare a `URL` constant to contain the `countryInfoJSON` endpoint.

We then define a `getCountryInfo()` method that accepts a country code as its only parameter. This method uses node-rest-client's `get()` method to make the call to `countryInfoJSON` for the given country code and display the results.

The `get()` method takes three parameters:

▸ The URL of the method to be called

▸ The arguments to be passed to the method

▸ The callback function that will handle the results

Inside our `getCountryInfo()` method, we define an arguments variable, `args`, as an object literal that has a parameters property. The parameters property in turn is assigned to an object literal that defines the URL parameters to be passed to the `countryInfoJSON` method. In this case, we have the `username` and `country` parameters.

Next, we use the node-rest-client's `get()` method to pass our URL, the arguments, and a callback function.

Node-rest-client will return two parameters to our callback method:

- ▶ The data returned from the web service
- ▶ A response object representing the Node `http.ClientRequest` instance created for the call

 Node-rest-client will try to interpret the format of the data returned by the web service, and if the data is returned with a content-type header matching JSON or XML, node-rest-client will convert the returned data into JSON or XML accordingly.

In our sample, when our call to `countryInfoJSON` returns, `data` contains an array of `geoname` objects, each one representing the country information we queried. We grab the first one, in this example, the only one, and then display some of the data returned.

Lastly, we create an array of country codes we want to query and then call our `getCountryInfo()` method for each one.

The following output is an example of the output of this sample:

```
Country  : United Kingdom
Capital  : London
Currency : GBP
Area     : 244820.0 (sq km)
Continent: Europe

Country  : United States
Capital  : Washington
Currency : USD
Area     : 9629091.0 (sq km)
Continent: North America

Country  : Canada
Capital  : Ottawa
Currency : CAD
Area     : 9984670.0 (sq km)
Continent: North America
```

There's more...

As previously mentioned, we can also register methods with node-rest-client. This gives us the ability to provide our own method aliases. This can be a useful option when dealing with a lot of web service endpoints and allows us to create a DSL.

We could have written the previous example using the `registerMethod()` approach. Follow these steps:

1. Require our node-rest-client and configuration object:

```
Client = require('node-rest-client').Client
config = require './service-config'
```

2. Create a client instance:

```
client = new Client config.options
```

3. Register a GET method to call our JSON endpoint:

```
url = "#{config.rootUrl}/countryInfoJSON"
client.registerMethod 'getCountryInfo', url, 'GET'
```

4. Create a function that receives a country code and callback as arguments and call the JSON endpoint using our registered method:

```
getCountryInfo = (countryCode, callback) ->
  args =
    parameters:
      username: config.username
      country: countryCode or ''

  req = client.methods.getCountryInfo args, (data, resp) ->
    if data.geonames
      callback null, data.geonames[0]
    else
      callback "No data returned for #{countryCode}"

  req.on 'error', (err) ->
    callback err.request.options
```

5. Create an array of country codes, and for each one, call our `getCountryInfo()` function passing a callback that will display the results:

```
countries = ['ca', 'us', 'gb']
for countryCode in countries
  getCountryInfo countryCode, (err, result) ->
    if err
```

```
            console.log 'Error', err
        else
            console.log "Country  : #{result.countryName}"
            console.log "Capital  : #{result.capital}"
            console.log "Currency : #{result.currencyCode}"
            console.log "Area     : #{result.areaInSqKm} (sq km)"
            console.log "Continent: #{result.continentName}\n"
```

In this version of our sample, we register the `countryInfoJSON` endpoint using node-rest-client's `registerMethod()` method:

```
client.registerMethod 'getCountryInfo', url, 'GET'
```

This method takes three parameters:

- ▸ The name of the method we want to register (basically an alias)
- ▸ The URL to call when we execute our method
- ▸ The HTTP verb to use when we execute our method

Then, in our `getCountryInfo()` method, we call the method we registered:

```
client.methods.getCountryInfo args, (data, resp) ->
```

In this version, we pass our arguments and a callback to handle the response from the web server.

Sending e-mail

Sending e-mails is a very common requirement for our applications. Use cases may include system administration alerts, monthly reports for application stakeholders, or even performing bulk mail operations.

In this recipe, we will send e-mails using a popular Node package called **nodemailer**. This will allow us to send text and HTML-based e-mails easily through our applications.

Getting ready

To begin, we must install the `nodemailer` npm package:

npm install nodemailer@0.7.1 --save

> Note that as of this writing, the current version of the nodemailer package has some compatibility issues with using Gmail's SMTP server. For this reason, we install version 0.7.1, a version known to work.

You can view the project documentation for nodemailer on its GitHub home page at `http://www.github.com/andris9/Nodemailer`.

We will also create a configuration file that our examples can use. Create a file named `mailer-config.coffee` with the following content:

```
module.exports =
  service: 'Gmail'
  auth:
    user: '****************'
    pass: '********'
  sender: 'Example Sender <example.sender@gmail.com>'
```

> Replace the asterisk with your Google account's e-mail address, password, and sender information.

How to do it...

Nodemailer allows us to send e-mails using a variety of services, including standard SMTP servers and nearly two dozen online e-mail services such as Gmail, Hotmail, iCloud, and many others.

In our example, we will send an e-mail using Google's Gmail e-mail service:

1. Require `nodemailer` and our configuration object:

   ```
   nodemailer = require 'nodemailer'
   config = require './mailer-config'
   ```

2. Create an SMTP transport object:

   ```
   smtpServer = nodemailer.createTransport 'SMTP', config
   ```

3. Create an `email` object:

   ```
   email =
     from: config.sender
     to: [
   'Mike Hatfield <mwhatfield@outlook.com>'
   config.sender
     ]
     subject: 'Test Email'
     text: 'In plain text, it worked!'
     html: 'In <b>HTML</b>, it worked!'
   ```

4. Use the `sendMail` function passing our e-mail and a callback as arguments:

```
smtpServer.sendMail email, (err, response) ->
  if err
    console.log err
  else
    console.log "Message sent: #{response.message}"

  smtpServer.close()
```

How it works...

In the preceding code, we begin by including the `nodemailer` npm package.

We define a transport configuration object next. This object defines a service and an authentication object.

Nodemailer sends e-mails through a transport. Each transport must specify a service. In our case, we define the service as Gmail. This allows nodemailer to preconfigure a number of settings for us, including the SMTP server, default port number, SSL configuration, and others. The only thing left for us to define is the username and password to be used when connecting to the Gmail service.

We execute `createTransport()` with two parameters: the transport type and a transport configuration object. This will return an instance of a nodemailer transport object.

 In our example, we specify a transport type of **SMTP**, but nodemailer also supports Amazon Web Services' **Simple Email Services** (**SES**), sendmail, pickup, and direct.

Next, we create an object literal that defines our e-mail properties. We specify a from and to e-mail address, subject, and body as both text and HTML.

Lastly, we execute the transport's `sendEmail()` method passing our `email` object and a callback to receive the send results.

Our callback receives an error and a result parameter. In our example, we use the error object to display the error message if an error is returned. Otherwise, we display a confirmation message.

There's more...

The nodemailer e-mail object supports several other parameters, including:

▶ cc, bcc: These are comma-separated lists of addresses as a string or as an array of strings

▶ generateTextFromHTML: If true, the plaintext body will be generated from the HTML body

▶ attachments: This is an array of attachment objects

Apart from these there are many others; see http://www.nodemailer.com/docs/messages for a complete list.

Attachment objects can be defined in a variety of ways:

▶ As a file on disk with a file name specified: { fileName: 'somefile.txt', filePath: '/path/to/somefile.txt' }

▶ As a file on disk with a file name derived: { filePath: '/path/to/somefile.txt }

▶ As a stream instance: { fileName: 'somefile.txt', streamSource: fs.createReadStream('/path/to/somefile.txt') }

▶ As a URL: { fileName: 'somefile.txt', filePath: 'http://www.someplace.com/somefile.txt' }

Sending SMS and MMS messages

In this recipe, we will demonstrate how to send SMS text messages using the very popular Twilio service and the APIs it provides.

To use the Twilio service, you must first have an account. You can sign up for a free trial on their website at http://www.twilio.com. Once you have signed up, you can go to your **Account** page to get **account SID** and **auth token**. These will be used by your application to communicate with the Twilio service.

Short Message Service (**SMS**) messages are text-based messages that are limited to 160 characters. These are messages that can be received by almost all mobile phones whether they are a smart phone or a feature phone.

In this recipe, I will demonstrate how to send an SMS text message from our application.

Getting ready

Once we have a Twilio account, we can use the official npm package to send SMS messages. To begin, install the `twilio` package with the following command:

```
npm install twilio --save
```

Next, create a configuration file called `twilio-config.coffee` with the `sid` and `token` values provided on your Twilio account settings page at `http://www.twilio.com/user/account/settings`:

```coffee
module.exports =
    sid:    '********cd2fc611590b2e91537a8ba5b1'
    token:  '********e619f238f8a9a12bec3d2bb4'
    from:   '+1 777-555-1212'
```

How to do it...

We will create a small console application that demonstrates the basic method to send an SMS message.

To send a message, we must:

1. Require the `twilio` package.
2. Create an instance of the client.
3. Use the client's `message.create()` method to send a message.

The following steps accomplish this:

1. Load the Twilio npm package and our configuration file:

    ```coffee
    TwilioClient = require 'twilio'
    config = require './twilio-config'
    ```

2. Create a client instance to pass our SID and token as arguments:

    ```coffee
    client = new TwilioClient(config.sid, config.token)
    ```

3. Create a `message` object with our SMS details:

    ```coffee
    message =
        body: 'Welcome from CoffeeScript'
        to: '+1 777-440-1212'
        from: config.from
    ```

4. Use our client's `messages.create()` function with our `message` object and a callback as arguments:

```
client.messages.create message, (err, msg) ->
    if err?
        console.log err
    else
        console.log msg.sid
```

How it works...

We begin by requiring the Twilio `npm` package. This returns a constructor object for our Twilio client.

Next, we store our application SID and authentication tokens, and then we use these to create an instance of our Twilio object.

We then create a message object using an object literal. Our message has three properties:

- `body`: This represents the text of the message being sent
- `to`: This represents the telephone number to receive the message
- `from`: This represents the telephone number of the sender

We then execute the `create()` method of our client's messages object. We pass our message object and a callback into this method.

Our callback will be called once the operation has completed either successfully or with an error.

If an error is returned to our callback, it will be displayed on the console window.

If the call is successful, the message identifier will be displayed instead.

There's more...

We can also send **Multimedia Messaging Service** (**MMS**) messages using Twilio.

Using Twilio, we can send MMS messages containing JPEG, GIF, and PNG images. These must be accessible via a web URL and must be returned as an image/jpeg, image/gif, or image/png MIME type, respectively. When sending a compatible image, Twilio will format the image to be compatible with the device.

To send an MMS message with an image, we add a `mediaUrl` property to our `message` object as follows:

```
message =
    mediaUrl: 'http://mwhatfield.com/96910S/cover.jpg'
    to: '+1 777-440-1212'
    from: config.from
```

Twilio supports a number of other formats, including many audio and video formats and even PDF files. For these attachments, however, Twilio sends the content as is without formatting the content to be optimized with the device.

For a full list of supported formats, visit the Twilio API page at `http://www.twilio.com/docs/api/rest/accepted-mime-types`.

Working with Amazon's S3 storage

Amazon provides many cloud services, including their **Simple Storage Service (S3)**, a cloud-based file store.

S3 provides inexpensive storage and retrieval for our digital media, large downloads, and backups.

In this recipe, we will use Amazon's Node-based SDK to add S3 features to our applications.

Getting ready

In S3, a bucket is a storage container where we can keep our files. We can create, list, and remove buckets using CoffeeScript.

In this section, we will demonstrate how to do this.

Before beginning, we need an AWS account. You can create an account by visiting the `http://www.amazon.com` home page and clicking on the **Sign Up** link at the top.

 Even though S3 is a paid service, it allows us to store up to 5GB for free for the first year on new AWS accounts.

Once you have an account, you must create a user account that will be used by your application to authenticate Amazon's web services:

1. To create an account, log on to the `https://aws.amazon.com` website and click on the **Security Credentials** link under the **My Account/Console** menu located at the top.

2. From the **Security Credentials** screen, click on the **Groups** link in the left menu.

    For our example, we will create a new group that has full permissions to add, get, and delete S3 buckets and objects.

3. On the **Groups** screen, click on the **Create New Group** button. In the **Create New Group Wizard** window (seen in the following screenshot), perform the following actions:

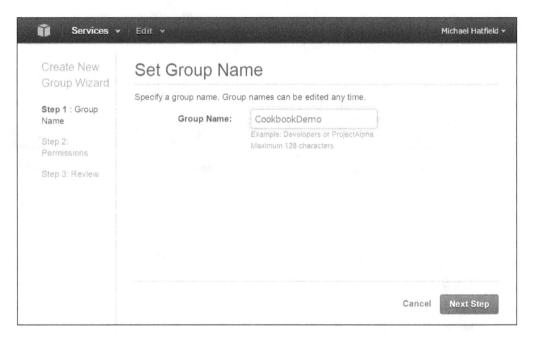

-   Enter our **Group Name** (that is, CookbookDemo) and click on **Next Step**
-   Select the **Amazon S3 Full Access** policy template and click on **Next Step**
-   Review your new group information and click on **Create Group**

    This will create a new group with the permissions we will need for our demonstrations.

4. Next, we need to create our user account. Click on the **Users** link on the left, and then click on the **Create New Users** button.

5. You can create up to five users at the same time. We only need one for our examples. Enter a user name and click on the **Create** button.

6. When we create a new user, a window opens that allows us to download or view the API credentials for the user, as seen in the following screenshot:

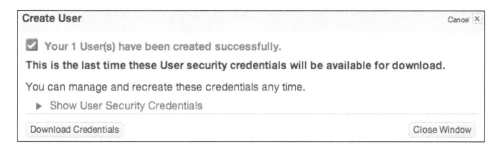

7. The user's security credentials include **Access Key ID** and **Secret Access Key**. We will need both of these to use the Amazon SDK.

8. Lastly, we need to add our new user to the group we created.

9. Click on our newly added user and this will display its associated groups; in our case, there are none:

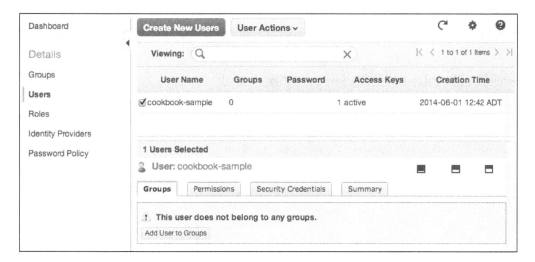

10. Click on the **Add User to Groups** button at the bottom. This will display the **Add User to Groups** window. Select the group we created and click on the **Add to Groups** button.

With our S3 configured, we can now install the AWS tools package for Node using the following command:

```
npm install aws-sdk --save
```

How to do it...

Now that we have a user account and its security credentials, we can have a sample that will create, list, and delete a bucket.

In our sample, we will make several asynchronous calls through the AWS SDK. We want our methods to be called in a specific order and we want to make sure one completes before the next one starts. For example, we want to create a bucket before we delete it. Node allows us to do this via callbacks. This can lead to an unsightly situation known in the community as callback hell. For example, our code would look something like the following:

```
createNamedBucket 'demo.mwhatfield.com', ->
    listAllBuckets ->
        deleteNamedBucket 'demo.mwhatfield.com', ->
            console.log 'Completed.'
```

If we had a few more steps, you can imagine how deeply nested our callbacks could become, and how quickly this could get out of hand. Instead of using callbacks, we will use **promises**.

Promises represent the eventual result of an asynchronous operation.

We will use the Q npm package, which implements the ECMAScript Promises/A+ specification (draft of ES6).

Install the Q package with the following command:

npm install q --save

For security purposes, we will not include our user's security credentials directly in our application code. Instead, we will create a configuration file named config.json with three properties, accessKeyId, secretAccessKey, and region:

```
{
    "accessKeyId": "********QVBRS3G6M2KQ",
    "secretAccessKey": "********pW3oKPhKpUdPbthQr9oaQYH15JQbPtaO",
    "region": "us-west-2"
}
```

With our configuration file (config.json) in place, we can create a CoffeeScript file with the following code:

1. Load the AWS SDK and Q packages:

   ```
   AWS = require 'aws-sdk'
   Q   = require 'q'
   ```

2. Load our configuration file:

   ```
   AWS.config.loadFromPath './config.json'
   ```

3. Create an instance of the S3 object:

```
S3 = new AWS.S3()
```

4. Create a function that will create an S3 named bucket:

```
createNamedBucket = (name) ->
  deferred = Q.defer()

  params = { Bucket: name }

  S3.createBucket params, (err, data) ->
    if err?
      deferred.reject err
    else
      console.log "Created bucket #{name}\n#{JSON.stringify data}"
      deferred.resolve()

  deferred.promise
```

5. Create a function to list all buckets in our S3 account:

```
listAllBuckets = ->
  deferred = Q.defer()

  S3.listBuckets (err, data) ->
    if err?
      deferred.reject err
    else
      console.log 'Listing buckets:'
      for bucket in data.Buckets
        console.log "  Bucket: #{bucket.Name}"

      deferred.resolve()

  deferred.promise
```

6. Create a function to delete an S3 bucket by name:

```
deleteNamedBucket = (name) ->
  deferred = Q.defer()

  params = { Bucket: name }

  S3.deleteBucket params, (err, data) ->
    if err?
      deferred.reject err
    else
```

```
        console.log "Deleted bucket: #{name}"
        deferred.resolve()

    deferred.promise
```

7. Call our `createBucket()` function and chain our calls using the promise's `then()` function:

```
createNamedBucket('demo.mwhatfield.com')
  .then -> listAllBuckets()
  .then -> deleteNamedBucket('demo.mwhatfield.com')
  .catch (error) ->
    console.log "Error: #{error}"
  .done ->
    console.log 'Completed.'
```

How it works...

In our previous example, we begin by requiring the Amazon SDK `npm` package using the SDK's `config.loadFromPath()` method to load the configuration from our `config.json` file.

We then create an instance of the AWS S3 object to handle all of the underlying communications with the S3 service.

We then create three helper methods to create a bucket, list all buckets, and delete a bucket.

Our `createNamedBucket()` helper method relies on the S3 `createBucket()` method. Our helper method takes a name for the bucket to be created and a callback. The S3 `createBucket()` method takes an object that specifies the parameters to be passed to the S3 service and a callback method. In our demo, we create a `params` object literal with a `Bucket` property.

When the operation completes, S3 will execute our `createBucket()` callback method providing an error object and a result object. Our `createBucket()` callback simply displays a success or error message.

Our `listAllBuckets()` helper method calls the `S3.listBuckets()` method with a callback that takes an error and results object. If there is no error, our result object will have a `Buckets[]` array that contains information for each bucket the user has permission to access. In our helper method, we simply iterate through the buckets that are returned by our S3 call and display the buckets' `Name` values.

Similar to our `createNamedBucket()` helper method, our `deleteNamedBucket()` helper method also takes a name and callback as a parameter. This method calls S3's `deleteBucket()` method passing a parameter object that specifies `Bucket` to be deleted.

Lastly, we create a small chain of methods that calls our helper methods, in sequence, to:

1. Create a bucket named `demo.mwhatfield.com`.

2. List all buckets.

3. Delete the bucket named `demo.mwhatfield.com`.

When we execute this sample code, we see the output that follows:

```
Created bucket demo.mwhatfield.com
{"Location":"http://demo.mwhatfield.com.s3.amazonaws.com/"}
Listing buckets:
   Bucket: cookbook-samples.mwhatfield.com
   Bucket: demo.mwhatfield.com
Deleted bucket: demo.mwhatfield.com
Completed.
```

You may have noticed that the result object of the S3 `createBucket()` method includes the location of the newly created bucket. In our sample, this location is `http://demo.mwhatfield.com.s3.amazonaws.com/`. This location can be used as the root URL for the files we store in our bucket. Alternatively, you can also access the resource from the more generally accepted URL of `http://s3.amazonaws.com/bucket/`.

There's more...

In the previous section, we saw how to create and delete buckets hosted with Amazon's S3 cloud storage system.

In this section, we will demonstrate how to create, list, and delete files in our bucket.

We will continue to use the AWS SDK and the user account we created in the previous section.

In this example, we will use the `putObject()`, `listObject()`, and `deleteObject()` methods of S3 to add, list, and delete files in our buckets:

1. Load the AWS SDK and Q packages:

```
fs  = require 'fs'
AWS = require 'aws-sdk'
Q   = require 'q'
```

2. Load our configuration file:

```
AWS.config.loadFromPath './config.json'
```

3. Create an instance of the S3 object:

```
S3 = new AWS.S3()
```

4. Create a function that will upload a file to an existing bucket:

```coffeescript
uploadFile = (bucket, filename, key) ->
  console.log "Uploading #{filename} -> #{key}"

  deferred = Q.defer()
  buffer = fs.readFileSync filename

  params =
    Bucket: bucket
    Key: key
    Body: buffer
    ACL: 'public-read'

  S3.putObject params, (err, data) ->
    if err?
      deferred.reject err
    else
      console.log 'Uploading success:', data
      deferred.resolve()

  deferred.promise
```

5. Create a function that will list all files inside a named bucket:

```coffeescript
listAllFiles = (bucket) ->
  console.log 'Listing all files:'

  deferred = Q.defer()

  params =
    Bucket: bucket

  S3.listObjects params, (err, data) ->
    if err?
      deferred.reject err
    else
      if data.Contents
        for item in data.Contents
          console.log " ETag: #{item.ETag}\n" +
            " Key:  #{item.Key}\n" +
            " Size:  #{item.Size} bytes"
      deferred.resolve()

  deferred.promise
```

6. Create a function that will fetch a remote file by its key contained inside a named bucket:

```coffeescript
fetchFile = (bucket, key, filename) ->
  console.log "Fetching a file #{key} -> #{filename}"

  deferred = Q.defer()

  params =
    Bucket: bucket
    Key: key

  S3.getObject params, (err, data) ->
    if err?
      deferred.reject err
    else
      fs.writeFileSync filename, data.Body
      console.log "Fetching a file success ETag: #{data.ETag}"
      deferred.resolve()

  deferred.promise
```

7. Create a function that will delete a remote file inside a named bucket:

```coffeescript
deleteFile = (bucket, key) ->
  console.log "Deleting remote file #{key}"

  deferred = Q.defer()

  params =
    Bucket: bucket
    Key: key

  S3.deleteObject params, (err, data) ->
    if err?
      deferred.reject err
    else
      console.log 'Deleting success'
      deferred.resolve()

  deferred.promise
```

8. Call our functions in sequential order:

```
bucket = 'demo.mwhatfield.com'

uploadFile bucket, './cover.jpg', 'cover.jpg'
  .then -> listAllFiles bucket
  .then -> fetchFile bucket, 'cover.jpg', './cover-2.jpg'
  .then -> deleteFile bucket, 'cover.jpg'
  .catch (error) ->
    console.log "Error: #{error}"
  .done -> console.log 'Completed.'
```

In this example, you should reference your own bucket. You can create one easily using the S3 Management Console located at `https://console.aws.amazon.com/s3/`.

We are also using a sample image named cover.jpg. You can use your own image and change the filename accordingly or you can download a copy of cover.jpg at `http://mwhatfield.com/96910S/cover.jpg`.

In our previous sample, we begin by requiring the SDK and the Node file system (`fs`) library. The `fs` library will allow us to read our file contents from our local file system.

Next, we load our configuration settings from `config.json` and create an instance of the S3 client as we did in our section to work with buckets.

We then define four helper methods: `uploadFile()`, `listAllFiles()`, `fetchFile()`, and `deleteFile()`. Each helper method wraps the S3 method to put objects into buckets, list objects in a bucket, fetch an object, or delete objects from a bucket.

Our `uploadFile()` method takes a bucket name and the full path name of a file on our local machine as arguments. The key is used by S3 to uniquely identify our object. If the key is new, the object is added. If the key already exists, the object is overwritten.

In our `uploadFile()` method, we use Node's `fs.readFileSync()` method to read our file's contents into a buffer, which is assigned to a `buffer` variable.

Once we have our local file read into our buffer, we prepare a parameter object similar to what we saw previously when calling the S3 methods. This parameter object defines the `Bucket`, `Key`, `Body`, and `ACL` properties:

▶ `Bucket`: This is the name of the bucket in which our object will be placed

▶ `Key`: This is our object's key

▶ `Body`: This is the buffer containing our file's data

▶ `ACL`: This is a string representing the level of permissions to be assigned to this object

The `ACL` value determines the level of access needed to access the file once it has been uploaded. There are several values we can use:

ACL	Scope	Description
`"private"`	Bucket and object	The owner has full control. No one else has access.
`"public-read"`	Bucket and object	The owner has full control. Everyone has read access.
`"public-read-write"`	Bucket and object	The owner has full control. Everyone has read and write access (not recommended).
`"authenticated-read"`	Bucket and object	The owner has full control. Authenticated users have read access.
`"bucket-owner-read"`	Object	The object's owner has full control. The bucket owner gets read access.
`"bucket-owner-full-control"`	Object	The object's owner and bucket's owner have full control.

In our case, we set the ACL to **public-read**. This will permit anyone to download the file via its URL.

Once we have defined our parameters, we execute the `putObject()` S3 client method to upload our file to our S3 bucket.

If the upload completes successfully, the data object will have `ETag`, a string whose value will change if the object's content changes.

Our next helper method, `listAllFiles()`, allows us to view the contents of a bucket. The function takes a string value representing the bucket's name.

We use the S3 client's `listObjects()` method passing a parameters object that specifies the name of the bucket in which our objects are contained and a callback. If the `listObjects()` function completes successfully, the data object has a `Contents` property that is an array of the result object. Each result contains a `Key`, `LastModified`, `ETag`, `Size`, `Owner`, and `StorageClass` property.

Our `fetchFile()` helper accepts a bucket name, key, and a full path filename representing the local file. We create a parameters object containing our `Bucket` and `Key` values. We then call the S3 `getObejct()` client method passing our parameters object and a callback. When this call is completed, our callback method is called with an error and a data object parameter. If successful, the data object contains information about the file requested, which includes the object's `ETag`, `LastModified`, `ContentType`, `Body`, and other properties. The `Body` property contains a buffer of the bytes for our object. In our callback, we use Node's `fs.writeFileSync()` method to write the buffer back to our local machine.

We end our sample with a `deleteFile()` helper method that takes a bucket name and a key. We create a parameters object with `Bucket` and `Key` values just like we did in our previous samples in this section. We then call S3's `deleteObject()` method with our parameters object and a callback.

Lastly, we call our helper methods to store our `cover.jpg` file into the `demo.mwhatfield.com` bucket, list all files, fetch the image from our bucket, and then delete the image from our bucket.

When executed, the following output is displayed:

```
Uploading ./cover.jpg -> cover.jpg
Uploading success: { ETag: '"8f48dd0fb16e36ad22ceecd491dabd2e"' }
Listing all files:
  ETag: "8f48dd0fb16e36ad22ceecd491dabd2e"
  Key:  cover.jpg
  Size:  36997 bytes
Fetching a file cover.jpg -> ./cover-2.jpg
Fetching a file success ETag: "8f48dd0fb16e36ad22ceecd491dabd2e"
Deleting remote file cover.jpg
Deleting success
Completed.
```

Transferring files via FTP

File Transfer Protocol (**FTP**) is nearly as old as the Internet itself, and is still one of the most common methods to transfer files to and from servers.

In this recipe, we will demonstrate how to upload to and download from a remote server using FTP.

Getting ready

We will use the Node-ftp `npm` module. Node-ftp provides a ride implementation of the FTP specification and allows us to connect to FTP servers, transfer files to and from the server, as well as manage files and directories.

You will require access to an FTP server to run the examples in this section.

To begin, we will install the Node-ftp module with the following command:

```
npm install ftp --save
```

We will also use the Q library to help with calling our methods in sequence. Install Q using the following command:

```
npm install q --save
```

We will also create a file that will contain our FTP configuration settings. Create a file called ftp-config.coffee with the following code:

```
module.exports =
  host: 'mwhatfield.com'
  user: 'coffee@mwhatfield.com'
  password: 'c0ffeeScript!'
```

Use your FTP server host address (domain name or IP address), username, and password.

How to do it...

We will create a demo program capable of uploading a file to and downloading a file from an FTP server.

The following steps are a procedure to be followed to accomplish this task:

1. Load Node's fs module, the FTP and Q packages, and our configuration file:

```
fs      = require 'fs'
Client = require 'ftp'
Q      = require 'q'
config = require './ftp-config'
```

2. Define a couple of constants to represent FTP transfer modes (ASCII and binary), and create a variable to hold our active connection once it has been established:

```
FTP_MODE_BIN = 'binary'
FTP_MODE_ASC = 'ascii'
connection = null
```

3. Create a connect() function to establish a connection to the FTP server:

```
connect = ->
  console.log 'Connecting'
  deferred = Q.defer()

  connection = new Client()
  connection.on 'ready', ->
    console.log '   connection established'
    deferred.resolve()
  connection.on 'error', (err) ->
    console.log '   error connecting'
    deferred.reject err
  connection.connect config

  deferred.promise
```

4. Create a `setMode()` function to set our transfer mode:

```
setMode = (mode) ->
  console.log "Setting mode to #{mode}"
  deferred = Q.defer()

  connection[mode] (err) ->
    if err
      console.log '    error setting mode'
      deferred.reject err
    else
      console.log "    mode set to #{mode}"
      deferred.resolve()

  deferred.promise
```

5. Create an `upload()` function to perform the file upload:

```
upload = (local, remote) ->
  console.log "Uploading #{local} to #{remote}"
  deferred = Q.defer()

  connection.put local, remote, (err) ->
    if err
      console.log '    error uploading'
      deferred.reject err
    else
      console.log '    upload complete'
      deferred.resolve()

  deferred.promise
```

6. Create a `download()` function to perform the file download:

```
download = (remote, local) ->
  console.log "Downloading #{remote} to #{local}"
  deferred = Q.defer()

  connection.get remote, (err, stream) ->
    if err?
      deferred.reject err
    else
      stream.once 'close', ->
        console.log '    download complete'
        deferred.resolve()

      stream.pipe fs.createWriteStream(local)

  deferred.promise
```

How it works...

In this example, we begin by requiring Node's file system module `fs` and the `node-ftp` module, as well as Q and our FTP configuration settings.

Next, we declare two constants to represent the **ASCII** and **binary** modes for FTP and a connection variable to hold our active connection. This will be used by our `connect()`, `setMode()`, and `upload()` functions.

In each of the `connect()`, `setMode()`, and `upload()` functions, we create a new deferred object and return its promise. If the function's outcome is successful, we resolve our promise with `deferred.resolve()`. If the function's outcome fails, we reject our promise with an error using `deferred.reject err`.

Next, we define the `connect()` function. This function establishes a connection to the remote FTP server using the `config` object. Inside `connect()`, we assign a new instance of Node-ftp's client object. We then assign two event listeners, `ready` and `error`. If the connection is successful, the `ready` event will be triggered and our event handler simply resolves our `deferred` promise. If a connection error occurs, the `error` event will be raised and we simply reject our `deferred` promise.

We then create a `setMode()` function. The FTP protocol can transfer files using ASCII or binary modes. ASCII mode is used to send text data such as source code files (HTML, CSS, JavaScript, and so on), while binary is used for non-text files such as images or file archives (zip, tar.gz, and so on). Our `setMode()` function receives a single argument representing the mode to use. Our `FTP_MODE_ASC` and `FTP_MODE_BIN` values represent the `binary()` and `ascii()` functions provided by the FTP client.

We then define our `upload()` function. This function takes two arguments to represent the local and remote file paths. We call the FTP client's `put()` function passing the local and remote file paths as well as a callback to be called once the file transfer has finished. Inside our callback, we check to see whether there was an error. If there was, we reject our promise passing the error. If there was no error, we resolve our promise.

Lastly, we define the `download()` function. This function receives the remote and local file paths as arguments. Inside the `download()` function, we call the FTP client's `get()` function with two arguments: the remote file path and a callback. This callback will be called with an error object if the `get()` attempt fails or with a stream object if it succeeds.

If there is an error, we `reject()` our promise passing the error as an argument.

If the `get()` request has succeeded, we do two things:

▶ Pipe our stream into a new write stream created by a call to `fs.createWriteStream()`, which will send the incoming file buffer to a local file.

▶ Register an event listener on the returned stream object for the stream's `close` event.

When the `close` event is triggered, we will simply `resolve()` our promise.

To upload a file to the FTP server, we can execute the following code:

```
connect()
  .then -> setMode FTP_MODE_BIN
  .then -> upload 'cover.jpg', '/cover.jpg'
  .catch (err) ->
    console.log "Error:", err
  .fin ->
    connection.end() if connection?
    console.log 'Connection closed'
```

Executing this script produces the following output:

```
Connecting
    connection established
Setting mode to binary
    mode set to binary
Uploading cover.jpg to /cover.jpg
    upload complete
Connection closed
```

To download a file from the FTP server, we can execute the following code:

```
connect()
  .then -> setMode FTP_MODE_BIN
  .then -> download '/cover.jpg', 'cover-downloaded.jpg'
  .catch (err) ->
    console.log "Error:", err
  .fin ->
    connection.end() if connection?
    console.log 'Connection closed'
```

This produces the following results:

```
Connecting
    connection established
Setting mode to binary
    mode set to binary
Downloading /cover.jpg to cover-downloaded.jpg
    download complete
Connection closed
```

There's more...

We saw how to upload and download files using FTP. In this section, we will see how to perform some other common FTP actions, including listing FTP files, creating and removing directories, and deleting files.

We will continue to use the `Node-ftp` and `ftp-config.coffee` configuration files that we used in our previous sections.

We can use the following FTP client functions to perform other common FTP tasks including the following:

- `list()`: This returns a list of files and directories at the desired path
- `mkdir()`: This creates a new directory for the path provided
- `rmdir()`: This deletes the directory specified by the path provided
- `delete()`: This deletes the file specified by the file path provided

We can wrap each of these with simple functions that return promises similar to our `connection()`, `setMode()`, and other functions earlier in this recipe.

Let's create a `getDirectoryList()` function that wraps the FTP client's `list()` function:

```
getDirectoryList = (rootPath) ->
  console.log "Getting list: #{rootPath}"
  deferred = Q.defer()

  connection.list rootPath, (err, data) ->
    if err?
      deferred.reject err
    else
      console.dir data
      console.log '  listing complete'
      deferred.resolve()

  deferred.promise
```

When executing this function, `list()` calls a callback that passes the results as an array of file and directory objects. The following is a sample of a directory and file object:

```
[ { type: 'd',
    name: '.',
    target: undefined,
    rights: { user: 'rwx', group: 'rx', other: 'rx' },
    owner: 'oakra3',
    group: 'oakra3',
```

```
        size: 4096,
        date: Thu Jan 01 2015 14:22:00 GMT-0400 (Atlantic Standard Time)
    },
      { type: '-',
        name: 'cover.jpg',
        target: undefined,
        rights: { user: 'rw', group: 'r', other: 'r' },
        owner: 'oakra3',
        group: 'oakra3',
        size: 36997,
        date: Sun Jan 04 2015 11:32:00 GMT-0400 (Atlantic Standard Time) }
    ]
```

The results include the type, name, permissions, owner, group, size, and create date for each item.

The `mkdir()`, `rmdir()`, and `delete()` functions can be wrapped in a similar way as in the following code:

```
createDirectory = (directoryName) ->
  console.log "Creating directory: #{directoryName}"
  deferred = Q.defer()

  connection.mkdir directoryName, (err) ->
    if err?
      deferred.reject err
    else
      console.log '   create directory completed'
      deferred.resolve()

  deferred.promise

deleteDirectory = (directoryName) ->
  console.log "Deleting directory: #{directoryName}"
  deferred = Q.defer()

  connection.rmdir directoryName, (err) ->
    if err?
      deferred.reject err
    else
      console.log '   delete directory completed'
      deferred.resolve()

  deferred.promise
```

```
deleteFile = (filePath) ->
  console.log "Deleting file: #{filePath}"
  deferred = Q.defer()

  connection.delete filePath, (err) ->
    if err?
      deferred.reject err
    else
      console.log '   delete file completed'
      deferred.resolve()

  deferred.promise
```

Let's execute these functions to demonstrate their use:

```
connect()
  .then -> getDirectoryList '/'
  .then -> createDirectory '/temp'
  .then -> deleteDirectory '/temp'
  .then -> deleteFile '/cover.jpg'
  .catch (err) ->
    console.log "Error:", err
  .fin ->
    connection.end() if connection?
    console.log 'Connection closed'
```

This produces the following output (abridged for brevity):

```
Connecting
   connection established
Getting list: /
[ { type: 'd',
    name: '.',
    target: undefined,
    rights: { user: 'rwx', group: 'rx', other: 'rx' },
    owner: 'oakra3',
    group: 'oakra3',
    size: 4096,
    date: Sun Jan 04 2015 11:32:00 GMT-0400 (Atlantic Standard Time) } ]
   listing complete
Creating directory: /temp
   create directory completed
Deleting directory: /temp
   delete directory completed
Deleting file: /cover.jpg
   delete file completed
Connection closed
```

In this recipe, we only scratched the surface of using Node-ftp. For more information on this library and its available features, please visit the project's home page on GitHub at https://github.com/mscdex/node-ftp/.

9
Testing Our Applications

In this chapter, we will cover the following recipes:

- ▶ Unit testing with QUnit
- ▶ End-to-end testing with Mocha and Zombie.js
- ▶ Stubbing and mocking with Sinon

Introduction

In this chapter, we will look at various methods of testing our CoffeeScript applications using a variety of techniques and libraries.

For our recipes in this chapter, we will require a lightweight web server. I recommend that you use `live-server`, a Node-based web service that exposes the local directory as a website.

You can install `live-server` via NPM using the following command:

```
npm install -g live-server
```

Once installed, we can launch the web server using the following command:

```
live-server
```

Unit testing with QUnit

QUnit is a popular testing framework for JavaScript that supports a **Test Driven Design** (**TDD**) approach to writing tests.

When using QUnit, we write our tests in the form of CoffeeScript functions that describe our desired functionality. When these tests are run, the QUnit test runner will execute our tests against our application's code and display the test results.

In this recipe, we will demonstrate how to configure QUnit and write a variety of tests to verify that our CoffeeScript code is working as expected.

Getting ready

We will begin by downloading the QUnit package and configuring the test runner.

QUnit can be installed in a variety of ways. We will be using Node's bower package installer to grab the QUnit files we need.

Bower is a package manager similar to NPM, but where NPM specializes in server-side packages, bower specializes in frontend packages. To install bower, use the following command:

```
npm install -g bower
```

With bower installed, we can install QUnit using bower with the following command:

```
bower install qunit --save-dev
```

We will also be using the CoffeeScript compiler within our browser to compile our source and test files. We can install this with bower using the following command:

```
bower install coffee-script --save-dev
```

With QUnit and CoffeeScript installed, create a new HTML file called `index.html`; this will be our test runner. Inside this file, add the following code:

```
<!DOCTYPE html>
<html>

<head>
  <meta charset="UTF-8" />
  <title>QUnit Test Suite</title>
  <link rel="stylesheet" href="bower_components/qunit/qunit/qunit.css"
type="text/css" media="screen">
</head>
```

```
<body>
  <h1 id="qunit-header">QUnit Tests</h1>
  <h2 id="qunit-banner"></h2>
  <div id="qunit-testrunner-toolbar"></div>
  <h2 id="qunit-userAgent"></h2>
  <ol id="qunit-tests"></ol>
  <div id="qunit-fixture">
  </div>

  <script type="text/javascript"
    src="bower_components/qunit/qunit/qunit.js"></script>

  <!-- source files -->

  <!-- tests -->

  <script type="text/javascript"
    src="bower_components/coffee-script/extras/coffee-script.js"></
script>

</body>

</html>
```

If we launch `live-server`, our browser should open automatically with our test runner loaded. You should see the following output:

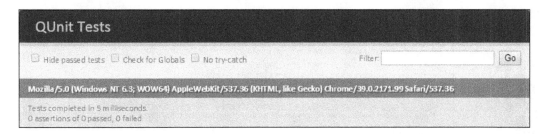

As you can see, the runner has executed zero tests. Next, we will look at adding our first test.

How to do it...

Now that we have our spec runner in place, we will write some tests for a simple calculator module that can add, subtract, multiply, and divide numbers:

1. Create a directory named `test` to contain our QUnit tests.

2. Inside the `test` directory, create a new CoffeeScript file named `CalculatorTests.coffee`.

3. Inside our new test file, add the following code:

```coffeescript
QUnit.module 'Calculator',
  beforeEach: ->
    @calculator = new Calculator()

QUnit.test 'should add two numbers', (assert) ->
  assert.equal @calculator.add(4, 5), 9
```

4. Update `index.html` to include our new test file:

```html
<!-- tests -->
  <script type="text/coffeescript"
  src="test/CalculatorTests.coffee"></script>
```

When we save our test and revised `index.html` files, `live-server` will detect the files that have changed and automatically reload our test runner. When this happens, we should see the following output:

You can see that we have two failures, both related to the fact that we have not yet defined our `Calculator` object. Let's create a new `Calculator` class. Follow these steps:

1. Create a new directory to hold our source files named `src`.

2. Create a new file called `Calculator.coffee` inside the `src` directory.

3. Add the following code to our new `Calculator` file:

   ```
   class window.Calculator
     add: (a, b) ->
       a + b
   ```

4. Add our new `Calculator` source file to `index.html`:

   ```html
   <!-- source files -->
     <script type="text/coffeescript"
       src="src/Calculator.coffee"></script>
   ```

After saving our test and test runner files, `live-server` reloads the test runner and should display the following results:

As you can see, we have our first passing test.

Next, we will add a test to validate our subtraction feature. Add the following test to our `CalculatorTests.coffee` file:

```
QUnit.test 'should subtract two numbers', (assert) ->
  assert.equal @calculator.subtract(9, 5), 4
```

When saved, `live-server` will run our tests. We can see that our new test failed in the following screenshot:

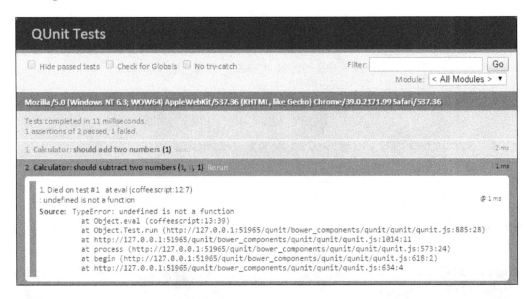

Next, we will implement the `subtract` function so that our test passes. Add the following highlighted code to our `Calculator.coffee` file:

```coffeescript
class window.Calculator
  add: (values...) ->
    sum = 0
    sum += value for value in values
    return sum

  subtract: (a, b) ->
    a - b
```

When we save `Calculator.coffee` with these changes, our test runner will execute and we see that all of our tests now pass, as shown in the following image:

The process we followed here, one of writing our tests first and then writing the code we need to make the tests pass, is known as **Test First Development** or **Test Driven Development (TDD)**. This helps us to write only the code we need in order for our tests to pass. This approach also helps to shape and evolve our code by providing a suite of tests that we can run in the future when we add or change features.

<h2 style="background:#888;color:#fff;display:inline-block;padding:4px 8px">How it works...</h2>

Our test file is a collection of QUnit modules and tests.

The `QUnit.module()` function allows us to group related tests and provides a mechanism to execute code before and after each test. This function takes a string argument representing the name of the module and an optional hooks object that provide a `beforeEach()` and `afterEach()` function.

We defined our addition module in the following manner:

```coffee
QUnit.module 'Adding',
  beforeEach: ->
    @calculator = new Calculator()
```

After defining our addition module, we define the tests responsible for verifying our calculator's addition feature using a series of `QUnit.test()` functions, each representing a single test.

The `QUnit.test()` function receives a string representing the title of the test as well as a callback function representing the body of our test. When the test executes, this callback will be called with an instance of QUnit's `assert` object. This `assert` instance provides access to QUnit's assertion functions.

Our first addition test looks like the following:

```
QUnit.test 'should add two numbers', (assert) ->
  assert.equal @calculator.add(4, 5), 9
```

In this example, we use assert's `equal()` function to compare the result of our calculator's `add(4, 5)` function to the expected value of 9. If the results are equal, the test will pass, otherwise it will fail.

The `assert` object provides a number of assertion functions including the following:

- `assert.equal()`: This is a non-strict comparison between two values. The test passes if the values are the same or if the two values are equal by type coercion such as 9 and `"9"`.

- `assert.strictEqual()`: This is a strict comparison between two values. The test passes if the values are the same by type and value.

- `assert.notEqual()`: This is a non-strict comparison between values. The test passes if values are not the same and cannot be coerced into the same value.

- `assert.notStrictEqual()`: This is a strict comparison between two values. The test passes if the values are not the same by type and value.

- `assert.deepEqual()`: This is a non-strict recursive comparison between two objects. The test passes if both objects contain the same properties/values and were created using the same constructor function. Note that this function does not compare object identities.

- `assert.propEqual()`: This is a strict recursive comparison between two objects. The test passes if both objects contain the same properties/values. This assertion is similar to `deepEqual()` but does not require both objects to be created using the same constructor function.

- `assert.notDeepEqual()`: This is a non-strict recursive comparison between two objects. The test passes if objects differ by at least one property/value or if the objects were not created by the same constructor function.

- `assert.notPropEqual()`: This is a strict recursive comparison between two objects. The test passes if the objects contain at least one different property/value regardless of the method of construction.

There's more...

Out of the box, QUnit provides a great set of built-in assertions. There may be times, however, when you need more than what is provided out of the box. For example, what would happen if we test our `Calculator` object's `add()` method with decimal values? Here is an example:

```
QUnit.test 'should add decimal numbers', (assert) ->
    assert.equal @calculator.add(285.72, 142.86), 428.58
```

When we rerun our tests, we see that it fails, as shown in the following screenshot:

```
3. Adding: should add decimal numbers (1, 0, 1) Rerun                                              2 ms

  1. failed                                                                                       @ 0 ms
  Expected:  428.58
    Result:  428.58000000000004
      Diff:  428.58 428.58000000000004
    Source:    at Object.eval (coffeescript:17:17)
               at Object.Test.run
            (http://127.0.0.1:62784/qunit/bower_components/qunit/qunit/qunit.js:885:28)
               at http://127.0.0.1:62784/qunit/bower_components/qunit/qunit/qunit.js:1014:11
               at process (http://127.0.0.1:62784/qunit/bower_components/qunit/qunit/qunit.js:573:24)
               at begin (http://127.0.0.1:62784/qunit/bower_components/qunit/qunit/qunit.js:618:2)
               at http://127.0.0.1:62784/qunit/bower_components/qunit/qunit/qunit.js:634:4
```

Because of the way JavaScript handles numbers, adding `285.72` and `142.86` does not exactly equal `428.58`, like it should.

> It turns out that this is not a problem limited to JavaScript. Most other languages have this problem. It is due to the fact that computers use a format known as **binary format** and some numbers cannot be exactly expressed as binary formatted decimals. You can learn more about this interesting and sometimes confusing problem at `http://floating-point-gui.de/`.

In this case, it would be handy to have an assertion that verifies the result is close to the expected value within an acceptable tolerance.

Let's define a new assertion to handle this. We will create a new `CoffeeScript` file inside our test folder called `TestHelper.coffee` that will contain our new assertion.

We will then use QUnit's `extend()` function to extend its `QUnit.assert` instance with an object instance that has our custom assertion.

Begin by defining a function to perform the required validation by adding the following code to a file named `test/TestHelper.coffee`:

```coffee
closeTo = (expected, actual, tolerance) ->
  difference = if expected is actual then 0 else \
    Math.abs(expected - actual)

  result = difference <= tolerance

  message = if result
    "#{expected} is close to #{actual}"
  else
    "#{expected} is not close to #{actual}"

  QUnit.push result, expected, actual, message
```

In the preceding code, we create a function named `closeTo()` that receives the expected value, the actual value, and the acceptable tolerance as its arguments.

In our function, we use the `QUnit.push()` function to add the result of our comparison. The `push()` function takes four arguments:

- `test result`: This returns true (pass) or false (fail)
- `expected value`: This is the value we expected
- `actual value`: This is the actual value we received
- `message`: This is the string to be displayed as the test result in the test runner

Lastly, we use the `QUnit.extend()` function to add our assertion to QUnit's `assert` object:

```coffee
QUnit.extend QUnit.assert,
  closeTo: closeTo
```

With our `TestHelper.coffee` file complete, save the file and add a reference to our test runner:

```html
<!-- tests -->
<script type="text/coffeescript"
  src="test/TestHelper.coffee"></script>
<script type="text/coffeescript"
  src="test/CalculatorTests.coffee"></script>
```

Now that our custom assertion is being loaded by our test runner, we will finish up by updating
`CalculatorTests.coffee` to use our new `closeTo()` assertion by replacing our `should`
`add decimal numbers` test:

```
QUnit.test 'should add decimal numbers', (assert) ->
  assert.closeTo @calculator.add(285.72, 142.86), 428.58, \
    0.000000001
```

When we save this and our tests are run, we should see a passing test because `285.72` plus
`142.86` is indeed `428.58` within the acceptable tolerance of `0.000000001`. We can see this
passing test in the following screenshot:

Mozilla/5.0 (Windows NT 6.3; WOW64) AppleWebKit/537.36 (KHTML, like Gecko) Chrome/40.0.2214.93 Safari/537.36	
Tests completed in 16 milliseconds. 4 assertions of 4 passed, 0 failed.	
1. Adding: should add two numbers (1)	0 ms
2. Adding: should add many numbers (1)	0 ms
3. Adding: should add decimal numbers (1)	2 ms
4. Subtracting: should subtract two numbers (1)	0 ms

For the sake of completeness, if we edit our test to have an acceptable tolerance of 0, we see
that the test fails with the following error:

```
3. Adding: should add decimal numbers (1, 0, 1)  Rerun                                    1 ms

     1. 428.58000000000004 is not close to 428.58                                        @ 0 ms
   Expected:  428.58
     Result:  428.58000000000004
       Diff:  428.58 428.58000000000004
     Source:    at Object.closeTo (coffeescript:9:16)
                at Object.eval (coffeescript:17:17)
                at Object.Test.run
          (http://127.0.0.1:62784/qunit/bower_components/qunit/qunit/qunit.js:885:28)
                at http://127.0.0.1:62784/qunit/bower_components/qunit/qunit/qunit.js:1014:11
                at process (http://127.0.0.1:62784/qunit/bower_components/qunit/qunit/qunit.js:573:24)
                at begin (http://127.0.0.1:62784/qunit/bower_components/qunit/qunit/qunit.js:618:2)
                at http://127.0.0.1:62784/qunit/bower_components/qunit/qunit/qunit.js:634:4
```

You can find more information in the QUnit documentation on the project's website at
`http://qunitjs.com`.

End-to-end testing with Mocha and Zombie.js

Mocha is a testing framework similar to QUnit but more suited for console-based testing, as opposed to browser-based testing. It has familiar `describe()` and `it()` blocks.

Zombie.js is a headless testing tool that allows us to test our application end-to-end. Using Zombie, we can open our application within a simulated browser environment and interact with the server layer of our application to verify both the backend and frontend functions as expected.

In this recipe, we will use Mocha and Zombie together as an effective tool to test our application end-to-end.

Getting ready

In our example, we will create a test that will launch our simple Calculator app and verify that it can add two numbers. We will have a simple HTML form with two input boxes, a button to trigger the calculation, and then verify the answer that is displayed.

We will need to install Mocha and Zombie. These are both available as NPM packages.

Mocha has a test runner executable, so we will install this as a global NPM package using the following command:

```
npm install -g mocha
```

Next, we will install Zombie with the following command:

```
npm install zombie --save
```

We will also need jQuery and the `CoffeeScript.js` compiler. We can install these with bower using the following command:

```
bower install coffeescript jquery#1.11 --save-dev
```

Next, we will create our `index.html` file with the following contents:

```
<!DOCTYPE html>
<html>
<head>
  <title>Calculator</title>
</head>
<body>
  <h1>Calculator App</h1>
```

```
<div>
  <label for="firstValue">First value:</label><br />
  <input type="text" id="firstValue">
</div>

<div>
  <label for="secondValue">Second value:</label><br />
  <input type="text" id="secondValue">
</div>
<button id="calculateButton">Calculate</button>

<div id="answer"></div>

<script src="bower_components/jquery/dist/jquery.min.js"></script>
<script type="text/coffeescript" src="src/Calculator.coffee"></
script>
<script type="text/coffeescript" src="src/App.coffee"></script>
<script src="bower_components/coffee-script/extras/coffee-script.
js"></script>
</body>
</html>
```

This is the user interface for our application.

Next, we will create our source files, one to define our Calculator app and another to represent our application.

Create an `src` folder and inside it a `Calculator.coffee` file with the following code:

```
class window.Calculator
  add: (a, b) ->
    return a + b
```

Next, create our application source file as `App.coffee` with the following code:

```
class window.App
  constructor: ->
    @calculator = new Calculator()

    $('button#calculateButton').click =>
      @calculate()
```

```
firstValue: ->
  parseInt $('input#firstValue').val()

secondValue: ->
  parseInt $('input#secondValue').val()

displayResult: (result) ->
  $('div#answer').text "Answer: #{result}"

calculate: ->
  result = @calculator.add @firstValue(), @secondValue()
  @displayResult result
```

When you open `index.html`, you should see the following form:

With the app open, you can enter the values `11` and `22` and click on the **Calculate** button, and **Answer: 33** will be displayed:

Once Mocha and Zombie have been installed and the sample application is ready, we can write a test.

How to do it...

We will create a new folder called e2e (end-to-end) to contain our Mocha tests. Inside the new e2e folder, create a file named calculateTest.coffee. This will be our end-to-end test to ensure our calculator can add two numbers.

Inside calculateTest.coffee, add the following code:

```
Browser = require 'zombie'
assert = require 'assert'

describe 'calculator page', ->
  before ->
    @browser = new Browser site: 'http://localhost:8080/'

  before ->
    @browser.visit '/index.html'

  it 'should load the calculator page', ->
    assert.equal @browser.text('h1'), 'Calculator App'

  it 'should add two numbers', ->
    @browser.fill '#firstValue', '4'
    @browser.fill '#secondValue', '5'
    @browser.pressButton '#calculateButton', =>
      assert.equal @browser.text('div#answer'), 'Answer: 9'
```

In order for the test to run, index.html must be available via the Web. I use live-server, a lightweight static file web server available as an NPM package.

You can install live-server with the following command:

npm install -g live-server

Once installed, we can launch the server with the following command:

live-server

You can now access index.html from the browser by visiting http://localhost:8080/.

Let's try running our tests. Simply type the following command at the root of your project:

mocha --compilers coffee:coffee-script/register e2e

If everything is hooked up correctly, you should see the following output:

```
[18:20:19] mike:zombie $ mocha --compilers coffee:coffee-script/register e2e

calculator page
  ✓ should load the calculator page
  ✓ should add two numbers


2 passing (262ms)
```

How it works...

Our `calcualteTest.coffee` test begins by loading Zombie and Node's `assert` package, a package that comes with Node.

Next, we describe our test using Mocha's `describe()` function. This is similar to the `module()` function we saw in QUnit and serves the same purpose.

Inside our `describe()` block, we define two `before()` methods. These are methods that are executed before each test is run.

In the first `before()` method, we instantiate a new instance of Zombie's browser object. In Zombie, the browser object represents the web browser. It allows us to navigate URLs and fetch DOM elements by text, ID, or CSS selector. It also allows us to interact with our application. We do each of these in our tests.

We initialize our browser instance by passing a default value for the browser's site property. This property is used as the default root URL for Zombie's navigation functions. In this case, all of our navigation will be to the base URL of `http://localhost:8000/`.

In the second `before()` method, we use Zombie's browser instance to visit the `/index.html` page. This ensures that for every test we run, the app will be on the correct page.

Next, we define two tests using Mocha's `it()` syntax. This is similar to the `test()` function we saw in our QUnit section.

Our first test checks to make sure the correct page is loaded by checking an `H1` tag's text content. We do this by using the browser's `text()` function passing our Node selector, `'H1'` in this case. We use `assert.equal()` to make sure our `H1` contains the text we expect.

Zombie uses the sizzle selector engine, which is the same engine used by jQuery. This means that our selectors can be tags, classes, IDs, and even pseudo-selectors. You can view Zombie's CSS selector documentation for a full list of selectors at `http://zombie.labnotes.org/selectors`.

Our next test is a bit more interesting. It automatically populates the `INPUT` boxes of **First value** and **Second value** with test values and then simulates a click of the **Calculate** button. The test then evaluates the contents of the answer `DIV` element to ensure the correct answer is displayed.

We use the browser's `fill()` method to populate our two input boxes with our numbers to be added for the test. This method takes a selector and a value as parameters. We have given our two text boxes the IDs `firstValue` and `secondValue`, respectively. We can therefore fill `'#firstValue'` and `'#secondValue'` with our desired values.

Once our first and second input boxes have been populated, we use the browser's `clickButton()` function to trigger a click event on our button. The `clickButton()` function takes two parameters, a selector to specify the element on our page to be clicked on and a callback that will be called once the click event has been handled by the browser.

In our test, our `clickButton()` callback uses the browser's `text()` function again to verify that our application correctly updates the `#answer` DIV with the proper answer.

There's more...

Zombie supports a number of browser automation commands we can use in our tests. Here are some of the common functions:

- `back()`: This function navigates to the previous page in history.
- `clickLink(selector, [callback])`: This function clicks on a link identified by a selector and receives a callback.
- `link(selector)`: This function returns a link element identified by a selector or text value.
- `location()`: This function returns the browser's location.
- `visit(selector, [callback])`: This function opens a document from the specified URL and receives an optional callback to be executed once the navigation is completed.
- `check(selector)`: This function checks a checkbox DOM element identified by a selector or label's text value.
- `choose(selector)`: This function selects a radio button identified by a selector or label's text value and receives an optional callback.
- `select(selector)`: This function selects an option element identified by a selector or text value.

- ▶ `field(selector)`: This function returns the form field identified by a selector or label's text value.

- ▶ `fill(selector)`: This function fills a form field (`INPUT` or `TEXTAREA`) identified by a selector or label's text value.

- ▶ `button(selector)`: This function returns the button DOM element identified by a selector or button's text value.

- ▶ `pressButton(selector, callback)`: This function triggers a button's click event identified by a selector or button's text value and receives a callback to be executed once the click event has been handled.

- ▶ `onalert(callback)`: This function receives a callback that will be called if an alert is called.

- ▶ `onconfirm(question, response)`: This function is used to specify a response to a specific question.

- ▶ `onconfirm(callback)`: This function executes a callback if the browser's `confirm()` function is called.

- ▶ `onprompt(message, response)`: This function is used to specify a response to a specific message.

- ▶ `onprompt(callback)`: This function executes a callback if the browser's `prompt()` function is called.

- ▶ `wait(duration, [callback])`: This function waits in seconds before proceeding with the following statement. An optional callback will be executed once the duration has timed out.

 For full documentation on these automation functions and the others supported by Zombie, you can view their website and downloadable documentation at `http://zombie.labnotes.org/`.

Stubbing and mocking with Sinon

In this recipe, we will use a JavaScript library called Sinon to create test doubles to help improve our tests.

Test doubles are fake objects that replace actual dependencies in our tests. Why would you want to use a mocking library? Some of the benefits of using a library such as Sinon include the following:

- ▶ They allow us to focus on our code under test without having to worry that its dependencies are working correctly, or even exist

- ▶ They allow us to speed up our tests by faking out network calls, database access, and other tasks that slow our tests down

Getting ready

In this section, we create and use stubs in our tests.

A stub is a fake object that provides stand-in functionality of an external dependency of our object under test.

For our example, we want to test an `Employee Manager` class that is responsible for managing collections of employees. `Employee Manager` uses a data service that retrieves employee information from an API.

Since our tests are concerned with the functionality of `Employee Manager`, we will create a fake data service and use a stub to provide our `Employee Manager` with a predictable collection of `Employees` that we can build our tests around.

Specifically, our `Employee Manager` will provide access to a collection of `Employees` and a method called `topEmployee()`, which will return the `Employee` with the largest year-to-date sales.

We will use Sinon to create our stub. The easiest way to get Sinon is from its website at `http://sinonjs.org/`. Download the most recent version, version **1.10.3** at the time of this writing, and save a copy in our project's `lib` folder.

 Note that you can install Sinon using bower, but this version installs a Node/AMD version that is more difficult to get running in a web browser. Downloading directly from the website downloads all of Sinon's modules in one file.

We will write our tests using a QUnit test runner. Please refer to the *Unit testing with QUnit* recipe earlier for help with configuring QUnit.

Add a reference to our Sinon library and its various components to our QUnit `index.html` test runner:

```
<script src="lib/sinon-1.10.3.js"></script>
```

How to do it...

We will first write our test in a file called `test/EmployeeManagerTest.coffee`. Inside this test, add the following code:

```
QUnit.module 'Employee Manager',
  beforeEach: ->
    dataService = new DataManager()
    @manager = new EmployeeManager(dataService)
    @manager.fetch()

QUnit.test 'should load Employee information', (assert) ->
  assert.equal @manager.employees.length, 4

QUnit.test 'should return the top employee with the best YTD sales',
(assert) ->
  assert.equal @manager.topEmployee().name, 'Tracy Ouellette'
```

If we run this, both specs fail because neither Employee Manager nor Data Manager exists.

Let's create these now. Create our `src/EmployeeManager.coffee` file with the following code:

```
class window.EmployeeManager
  constructor: (@dataService) ->
    @employees = []

    fetch: ->
    @employees = @dataService.fetchEmployees()

  topEmployee: ->
    comparer = (a, b) ->
      if a.ytdSales >= b.ytdSales
        return a
      else
        return b

    employee = @employees.reduce comparer, { ytdSales: -Infinity }
```

We will also create a bare bones data manager class named `src/DataManager.coffee` with the following code:

```coffee
class window.DataManager
  constructor: ->

  fetchEmployees: ->
    # this method performs a network call to retrieve employee
    # records.  When stubbed out, this version should not be
    # called
    console.log 'This should not be called'
    return []
```

We must update our QUnit `index.html` test runner with references to our new `EmployeeManager.coffee` and `DataManager.coffee` files:

```html
<script type="text/coffeescript"
  src="src/DataManager.coffee"></script>
<script type="text/coffeescript"
  src="src/EmployeeManager.coffee"></script>
```

When we run our tests, they still fail because we do not have any data to work with yet. Our production system has a `Data Manager` object that makes a network call to retrieve data via a backend API:

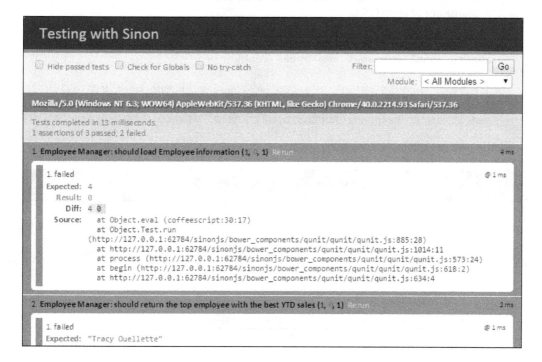

Because we do not want to make a network call each time we run this test and also ensure we have predictable results when running our tests, we will create a stub for the `fetchEmployees()` method in our data manager that always returns the same data when called.

We will update our `Employee Manager` test to stub out our data manager's `fetchEmployees()` method. Update our `test/EmployeeManagerTest.coffee` file to match the following:

```coffee
testData =      [
  {name: 'Mike Hatfield', ytdSales: 1000}
  {name: 'Tracy Ouellette', ytdSales: 2000}
  {name: 'Chris Daniels', ytdSales: 1800}
  {name: 'Jason Alexander', ytdSales: 1570}
]

QUnit.module 'Employee Manager',
  beforeEach: ->
    dataService = new DataManager()
    stub = sinon.stub dataService, 'fetchEmployees'
    stub.returns testData

    @manager = new EmployeeManager(dataService)
    @manager.fetch()

QUnit.test 'should load Employee information', (assert) ->
  assert.equal @manager.employees.length, 4

QUnit.test 'should return the top employee with the best YTD sales',
(assert) ->
  assert.equal @manager.topEmployee().name, 'Tracy Ouellette'
```

Now, when we run our tests, they both pass:

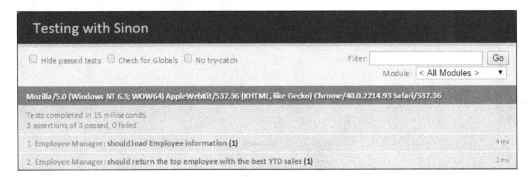

How it works...

In our `Employee Manager Spec`, we create a Sinon stub by calling `sinon.stub()` with the object we want to create the stub on and the name of the function we want to call. In this case, we pass our data manager `instance`, `dm`, and the `fetchEmployees` string.

We then use the stub's `returns()` method to specify the return value when `dm.fetchEmployees()` is called. In our case, it will return a static array of four employee records.

We wire this up in the `beforeEach()` method to make sure it is properly configured before each test is executed.

There's more...

Sinon provides a lot of flexibility when it comes to creating stubs. You can create stubs in a variety of ways and have a degree of control on how the stubbed method behaves.

For example, you can easily create a stub for a callback in the following way:

```
trueStub = sinon.stub().returns true
```

In this case, `trueStub` will always return true when executed. So the following code will always confirm that these roses are indeed red:

```
rosesAreRed = (predicate) ->
  if predicate()
    console.log 'Yes, these roses are red.'
  else
    console.log 'No, these roses are not red.'

rosesAreRed trueStub
```

We can also control how the stub will behave. The following list contains some of the common behavior-related methods supported by `stub()`:

- `onFirstCall().returns(value)`: This method defines the value to be returned the first time the stub is executed
- `onSecondCall().returns(value)`: This method defines the value to be returned the second time the stub is executed
- `onThirdCall().returns(value)`: This method defines the value to be returned the third time the stub is executed
- `onCall(n).returns(value)`: This method defines the value to be returned the *n*th time the stub is executed (0 = first, 1 = second, and so on)

- ▸ `throws()`: This method causes the stub to throw an exception when executed
- ▸ `throws("ErrorType")`: This method causes the stub to throw an exception of the type provided

 You can see the full documentation on the Sinon.js website at `http://sinonjs.org/docs/#stubs`.

We can also use Sinon to create mock objects. Mocks are very similar to stubs in that they can provide stand-in functionality for external dependencies, but they also allow us to assert that methods were called in these fake objects. In other words, they allow us to ensure our code executes the functions within our faked objects that we expect them to.

For our example, we will extend our test from the previous section that had an `Employee Manager` class to deal with `Employee` objects and a data manager that is responsible for retrieving data from an external API.

We want to make sure that when we fetch employees from the `Employee Manager` that it, in turn, fetches employees from the data service. We can use a Sinon mock for this.

Create a new test in `test/EmployeeManagerTest.coffee` using the following code:

```coffee
QUnit.test "should call Data Manager's fetchEmployees method",
(assert) ->
  dataService = new DataManager()
  mock = sinon.mock(dataService)\
    .expects('fetchEmployees').once()

  manager = new EmployeeManager(dataService)
  manager.fetch()

  assert.ok mock.verify()
```

With this new test in place, when we run the new specs, we see that they pass:

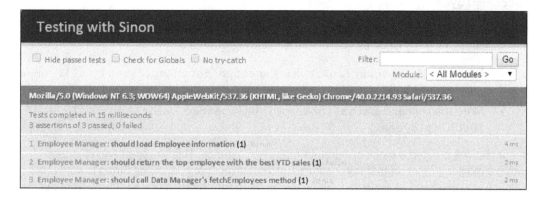

When we create a Sinon mock, it creates a wrapper around the function we are interested in being called. As such, we created a new `DataManager` instance within the test itself instead of using the one created in the `beforeEach()` function.

We create a mock using the `sinon.mock()` function passing our `DataManager` instance as its only parameter. This returns an object that allows us to define our expectations describing how we expect the data manager to be used.

In our example, we expect the data manager's `fetchEmployees()` function to be called exactly one time.

We describe this using Sinon's `expects()` and `once()` functions as follows:

```
mock = sinon.mock(dataService).expects('fetchEmployees').once()
```

Sinon's fluid API makes our expectations read very much like English.

We then pass our mocked data manager instance to the new `Employee Manager` instance.

We then call the `fetch()` function of `Employee Manager`.

Lastly, we use our mock's `verify()` function to determine whether our data manager's `fetchEmployees()` method was called exactly once.

If `fetchEmployees()` was not called exactly once, `verify()` will throw an error with a message indicating the issue as shown in the following examples:

- Never called: `ExpectationError: Expected fetchEmployees([...]) once (never called)`
- More than once: `ExpectationError: Unexpected call: fetchEmployees()`

In our test, we created a mock of our data manager instance. This wrapped each function within a mocking function that can capture function invocations, allowing Sinon to verify the function was executed as expected. Sinon allows us to remove its mock wrappers from our instance by using the `mock.restore()` function.

Sinon also provides a number of expectations to help us mock our expected behaviors, including the following:

- `expectation.atLeast(n)`: This ensures the method is called at least the specified number of times
- `expectation.atMost(n)`: This ensures the method is called no more than the specified number of times
- `expectation.never()`: This ensures the method is never called
- `expectation.once()`: This ensures the method is called exactly one time
- `expectation.twice()`: This ensures the method is called exactly two times
- `expectation.exactly(n)`: This ensures the method is called exactly *n* times

As mentioned earlier, each of these expectations returns an expectation object, which means the expectations can be chained. So, for example, we can specify that a method should be called at least twice but no more than five times using the following syntax:

```
sinon.mock(dataService)\
      .expects('fetchEmployees').atLeast(2).atMost(5)
```

 For more information on Sinon mocks and its other features, please see Sinon's website for its full documentation at `http://sinonjs.org/`.

10
Hosting Our Web Applications

In this chapter, we will cover the following recipes:

- ► Compiling our source with Grunt
- ► Preparing deployments for staging and production
- ► Deploying our application to Heroku
- ► Deploying our application to Microsoft Azure

Introduction

In this chapter, we will look at preparing our application for deployment using a JavaScript task runner named Grunt to compile our source, copy files, clean build folders, and much more.

Once our application files are ready for deployment, we will demonstrate how to deploy our application to both the Heroku and Microsoft Azure cloud platforms.

Compiling our source with Grunt

In our development environment, we can get away with having our browser compile our CoffeeScript. In production, however, this introduces an unwelcomed decrease in performance. In this section, we will use a tool called **Grunt** to prepare our source for production by compiling the CoffeeScript into JavaScript as well as combining and minifying our code into a single source file.

Grunt is a task runner similar to Rake for Ruby developers, Ant for Java developers, or NAnt for .NET developers.

In this section, we will use Grunt to compile our CoffeeScript and concatenate it into a single JavaScript file better suited to be used by our application in production.

Getting ready

The first step is to install Grunt. Grunt comes as two NPM packages.

First is the Grunt library. This can be installed locally in our project's folder using the following command:

```
> npm install grunt
```

Next, we need to install the Grunt command-line client tool into our global NPM package repository:

```
> npm install -g grunt-cli
```

This will install `grunt`. Before we can use it, however, we must create a file that represents the tasks we want Grunt to perform for us. This file can be in either JavaScript or CoffeeScript and it is called `gruntfile.js` or `gruntfile.coffee`, respectively.

How to do it...

Let's create a minimal Grunt file using CoffeeScript called `gruntfile.coffee`. The basic structure is as follows:

```coffee
module.exports = (grunt) ->

  grunt.registerTask 'default', ->
    grunt.log.writeln 'This from the default grunt task'
```

Save this file, and from the command prompt, execute `grunt`:

```
> grunt
```

This will display the following output:

```
Running "default" task
This from the default grunt task

Done, without errors.
```

By itself, this is not very exciting, but what happened exactly?

Inside our Grunt file, we register tasks by using the `grunt.registerTask()` function passing a task name and either a function to be executed when we run the task, or an array of dependent task names.

If we run the `grunt` command without any arguments, it will try to execute a task named `default`.

In our sample, we registered a task named `default` and provided a simple function to be executed when the default task is run.

Let's register another task called `greeting` by adding the following to our `gruntfile.coffee` file:

```
grunt.registerTask 'greeting', ->
    grunt.log.writeln 'This from the greeting grunt task'
```

Now, we can execute our new `greeting` tab by passing the task name to `grunt` as a command-line parameter:

> **grunt greeting**

This produces the following output:

```
Running "greeting" task
This from the greeting grunt task

Done, without errors.
```

Let's look at a slightly more complex example by adding two tasks to be called either individually or together.

We do this by registering two tasks called `first` and `second`, as well as a third task called `firstNsecond` that will run them both:

```
grunt.registerTask 'first', ->
  grunt.log.writeln 'This from the [first] grunt task'

grunt.registerTask 'second', ->
  grunt.log.writeln 'This from the [second] grunt task'

grunt.registerTask 'firstNsecond', ['first', 'second']
```

You can see in our last task that we passed an array of tasks. Grunt will execute these tasks in the order they are provided in the array. So, if we execute the `firstNsecond` task, we will get the following screen:

```
Running "first" task
This from the [first] grunt task

Running "second" task
This from the [second] grunt task


Done, without errors.
```

We can issue the execution of the `grunt --help` command for guidance on the command-line parameters we can use for Grunt and also see the list of available tasks. If we run that now, we see the following:

```
Available tasks
        default  Custom task.
          first  Custom task.
         second  Custom task.
   firstNsecond  Alias for "first", "second" tasks.
       greeting  Custom task.
```

So far, we have seen how to register tasks that can execute functions for us. How do we write a function to compile, concatenate, and minify our CoffeeScript code for production?

Thankfully, there is an entire ecosystem of Grunt packages out there that allows us to register Grunt tasks to do just this.

First, we will look at the `grunt-contrib-coffee` NPM module. This package provides CoffeeScript compile functions for our Grunt file. Let's install it:

```
> npm install grunt-contrib-coffee
```

Once installed, we can use Grunt's `grunt.loadNpmTasks()` function to pass the name of the NPM package that contains Grunt tasks. Add the following to our Grunt file:

```
grunt.loadNpmTasks 'grunt-contrib-coffee'
```

Once that has been added, we can use the `--help` command-line parameter again and see that we now have a new `coffee` task:

```
Available tasks
         coffee  Compile CoffeeScript files into JavaScript *
        default  Custom task.
```

Before we can use our new `coffee` task, we need to configure it so it knows where to find our source files. We do this within the `grunt.initConfig()` function.

The `coffee` task expects a `coffee` property to be there for our `grunt` configuration object that provides the necessary configuration. Let's add that now to our `initConfig()` function:

```
grunt.initConfig

  coffee:
    compile:
      files:
          'public/js/app.js': 'src/app/app.coffee'
          'public/js/all.js': 'src/app/*.coffee'
          'public/js/two.js': [
            'src/app/csmain.coffee', 'src/app/data.coffee'
          ]
```

In our configuration, we assign an object literal to the expected `coffee` property. This object has a `compile` property that contains a `files` property. This `files` property contains three entries.

These file entries specify a key-value pair, where the key represents the name of the output file and the value represents the CoffeeScript file(s) we want to compile.

In the first case, we compile a single CoffeeScript file, `app.coffee`, into a single JavaScript file, `app.js`, located in the `public/js` directory.

In the second case, we use a wildcard (`*`) to compile all `.coffee` files found in the `src/app` directory into a single file called `all.js` in the `public/js` directory. Each file matching the pattern is compiled and concatenated together.

The last case is an example of using an array of source files to be compiled and concatenated into a single output file.

How it works...

Using Grunt and Grunt plugins allows us to create tasks that can greatly simplify our common build tasks, but it can also do much more.

For example, we have our CoffeeScript files compiled and concatenated into a single JavaScript file, but we should also minify this JavaScript file before we push it to our production server.

Minifying our JavaScript file is a way to compress our source code in a way that maintains the same functionality. The process will strip out unnecessary white space, and typically rename functions and variables. The end result can be a much smaller file that your application will need to download from the server.

Again, the vast expanse of the NPM module ecosystem comes to our aid through the `grunt-contrib-uglify` package. Let's install it:

```
> npm install grunt-contrib-uglify
```

Once installed, we can load its Grunt tasks by adding the following to our Grunt file:

```
grunt.loadNpmTasks 'grunt-contrib-uglify'
```

If we get a list of tasks now, we see a new `uglify` task as follows:

```
Available tasks
        coffee  Compile CoffeeScript files into JavaScript *
        uglify  Minify files with UglifyJS. *
       default  Custom task.
```

Now, let's configure this new `uglify` task by updating the `grunt.initConfig()` function again with the following code:

```
uglify:
  target:
    files:
      'public/js/all.min.js': 'public/js/all.js'
```

This is similar to our `coffee` configuration in that we specify a collection of file key-value pairs that specify the key (destination) and value (source files).

In this case, we will take our large `all.js` file and create a minified version called `all.min.js` in the same directory.

When we use this minification library, we will typically see compression rates between 40 percent and 60 percent, though your mileage may vary.

You may have noticed a dependency our `uglify` task has to the `coffee` task. More specifically, we cannot minify a file that has not yet been created. Let's add a new build task to our Grunt file that will compile using `coffee` and minify the result using `uglify`. Add the following to our Grunt file:

```
grunt.registerTask 'build', ['coffee', 'uglify']
```

Now, when we want to build our source files, we can issue the following command:

```
> grunt build
```

> Are you using Less or Sass in your project? If yes, then you can use the `grunt-contrib-less` and `grunt-contrib-sass` packages to compile your Less and Sass into CSS much in the same way we did with `grunt-contrib-coffee`, and then use `grunt-contrib-cssmin` to minify your CSS as well.

Preparing deployments for staging and production

In the previous section, we created and configured a Grunt file to compile our source files. In this section, we will look at extending our Grunt file to include options to prepare files for deployments to staging and production environments.

Getting ready

In this section, we will use a few Grunt NPM packages to help us prepare our deployments, including the following:

- `grunt-contrib-clean`: This removes files and directories
- `grunt-contrib-copy`: - This copies files and directories
- `grunt-text-replace`: This replaces text found within files

Install these NPM modules with the following commands:

```
> npm install grunt-contrib-clean --save-dev
> npm install grunt-contrib-copy --save-dev
> npm install grunt-text-replace --save-dev
```

How to do it...

Let's load the copy and replace tasks in our Grunt file by adding the following lines to `gruntfile.coffee`:

```
grunt.loadNpmTasks 'grunt-contrib-clean'
grunt.loadNpmTasks 'grunt-contrib-copy'
grunt.loadNpmTasks 'grunt-text-replace'
```

If we run `grunt -help`, we see that there are three new tasks available to us named `clean`, `copy`, and `replace`.

In our scenario, our project has the following structure:

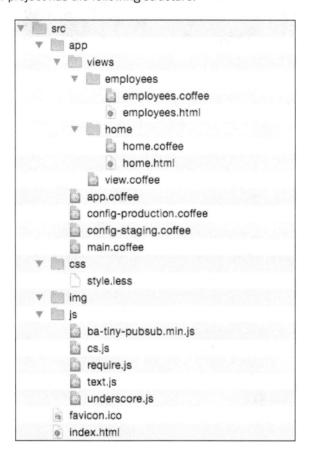

Our application uses `RequireJS` with the `Require-CS` library to load and compile our CoffeeScript code as needed, and the `Require-Text` library to load our HTML views as needed.

When we deploy our application to staging or production, we want to accomplish the following tasks:

- Remove the existing `staging` or `release` directories
- Compile our source including our CoffeeScript and Less style sheets
- Minify our style sheets
- Copy our files
- Update `index.html` to reference our newly versioned compiled assets

With our `clean`, `copy`, and `replace` tasks in place, we can configure each task in the `grunt.initConifg()` function.

First, let's look at our configuration for the `clean` task:

```
clean:
  staging: ['build', 'staging']
  release: ['build', 'release']
```

Next, let's review our compile configuration settings to compile our Less style sheets and our application code via `require.js`:

```
less:
  development:
    files: [
      concat: true
      src: [ 'src/css/*.less' ]
      dest: 'build/css/styles.css'
    ]
```

```
requirejs:
  compile:
    options:
      out: "build/js/v#{versionNumber}.min.js"
      baseUrl: 'src/app'
      mainConfigFile: 'src/app/main.js'
      paths:
        text: '../js/text'
        app: 'app'
        underscore: '../js/underscore'
      shim:
        underscore:
          exports: '_'
      include: [ '../js/require' ]
      insertRequire: [ 'main' ]
      name: 'main'
      removeCombined: true
```

> We did not discuss `require.js`, but I have found it to be very useful to build modern CoffeeScript applications, and it helps me keep my code modular and more maintainable by following a simple view and view-model pattern. We can then use Grunt's `grunt-contrib-requirejs` NPM module to compile, combine, and minify our CoffeeScript and templates for us.

Then, we add our CSS minification settings as follows:

```
cssmin:
  staging:
    src: 'build/css/styles.css'
    dest: 'build/css/staging.min.css'

  release:
    src: 'build/css/styles.css'
    dest: 'build/css/release.min.css'
```

Next, we add our copy settings:

```
copy:
  staging:
    files: [{
      expand: true
      cwd: 'src'
      src: [ 'img/**', 'js/ba-tiny-pubsub.min.js' ]
      dest: 'staging/' }
    {
      expand: true
      cwd: 'build'
      src: "js/v#{versionNumber}.min.js"
      dest: 'staging/' }
    {
      src: 'build/css/styles.min.css'
      dest: "staging/css/styles.#{versionNumber}.min.css" }]
  release:
    files: [{
      expand: true
      cwd: 'src'
      src: [ 'img/**', 'js/ba-tiny-pubsub.min.js' ]
      dest: 'release/'
      filter: 'isFile' }
    {
      expand: true
      cwd: 'build'
      src: "js/v#{versionNumber}.min.js"
      dest: 'release/'
      filter: 'isFile' }
    {
      src: 'build/css/styles.min.css'
      dest: "staging/css/styles.#{versionNumber}.min.css" }]
```

Lastly, we finish up by configuring our text `replace` task:

```
replace:
  staging:
    src: 'src/index-release.html'
    dest: 'staging/index.html'
    replacements: [
      from: '[BUILDNUMBER]'
      to: "#{versionNumber}"
    ]

  release:
    src: 'src/index-release.html'
    dest: 'release/index.html'
    replacements: [
      from: '[BUILDNUMBER]'
      to: "#{versionNumber}"
    ]
```

How it works...

The previous configuration was pretty lengthy, but once you become familiar with the Grunt task configuration pattern, even working with new Grunt plugins will become easier.

Most Grunt tasks support what is known as a multi-task. A multi-task allows us to have specific configurations depending on our intent. For example, the `clean` task is a multi-task that has two targets: staging and release. Grunt allows us to call a target using the `task:target` syntax. So, for example, we can call the `staging` target for the `clean` task by executing the `clean:staging` task.

 Note that executing a task without specifying a target will execute the task for each target. For example, calling `grunt clean` will execute the `clean` task for both staging and release.

The `clean` task configuration defines a target for staging and release. It takes an array of file paths and, when run, each path is removed, including all files and directories contained within that path. In our example, if we ran `grunt clean:staging`, it would delete the `build` and `staging` directories.

The `less` task is configured to compile all Less files in the `src/css` folder and contact all compiled CSS into a single file called `styles.css` in the `build/css` folder.

The `cssmin` task will minify the `build/css/styles.css` file into a `build/css/styles.min.css` file.

Our `copy` task is larger, but it is not too complicated. There are two targets: `staging` and `release`. Each target will copy an array of file objects from `src` to `dest`.

The `copy:staging` target will copy `index.html`, everything under the `img/` folder, and a library needed by our application under the `js/` folder. Then, our compiled and minified application code will be copied from the `build/js` folder into the `staging/js` folder. Lastly, we copy our compiled and minified CSS into the `staging/css` folder. Notice that the CSS and JS application code has been versioned with the current system date/time stamp. This will ensure the browser loads the freshly compiled files instead of using any cached versions.

With our compiled and versioned source files, we need to update our `index.html` file to reference the proper version. We use the `replace` task to do a textual find and replace within the `index.html` file.

Inside the `index.html` file, we have the following HTML:

```
<link href="css/styles.v[BUILDNUMBER].min.css" rel="stylesheet" />
<script src="js/v[BUILDNUMBER].min.js"></script>
```

Our `replace:staging` and `replace:release` targets define a `src` and `dest` path and an array of replacements to be made. Each replacement has a `from` and `to` value. In our case, we are replacing the `[BUILDNUMBER]` text with our version number.

With these tasks defined, we can create compound tasks to perform our preparation for deployment to staging or production:

```
grunt.registerTask 'build:staging', [ 'clean:staging', 'less', \
  'cssmin', 'requirejs', 'copy:staging', 'replace:staging' ]
grunt.registerTask 'build:release', [ 'clean:release', 'less', \
  'cssmin', 'requirejs', 'copy:release', 'replace:release' ]
```

Here, we declared a `build:staging` and a `build:release` task. Each will call the various subtasks with their appropriate targets to prepare our deployment for staging and release accordingly.

There's more...

There are other tasks that can be helpful during development. For example, there is a Grunt module called `grunt-contrib-connect` that will provide an express web server to host our development code.

You can install this with the following:

```
> npm install grunt-contrib-connect --save-dev
```

Once installed, we can add a `connect` task to our Grunt file with the following:

```
grunt.loadNpmTasks 'grunt-contrib-connect'
```

Let's configure a target to host our development code. Inside the `grunt.configInit()` function, add the following:

```
connect:
  dev:
    options:
      keepalive: true
      hostname: 'localhost'
      port: 8080
      base: './src'
      open: true
```

We will register a task called `server` to execute the `connect` task:

```
grunt.registerTask 'server', [ 'connect' ]
```

Now, we can run `grunt server` in our command window and the express server will start and your default browser will open your application at `http://[hostname]:[port]`:

```
Running "connect:dev" (connect) task
Waiting forever...
Started connect web server on http://localhost:8080
```

Deploying our application to Heroku

Heroku is a popular cloud-hosting platform that is particularly suited for open source platforms, including Node, Ruby on Rails, and PHP. In this section, we will look at deploying our application to Heroku.

If you do not have a Heroku account, you can create a free account and follow along at the Heroku website at `https://signup.heroku.com`.

Getting ready

Heroku provides powerful command-line tools for Mac, Windows, and Debian/Ubuntu that allow us to easily work with our hosted application, any necessary add-ons, log files, and other tools.

To begin, install the Heroku toolbelt for your operating system. You can download the toolbelt from the Heroku website at `https://toolbelt.heroku.com`.

Our sample application is a very simple express website. We have an `src` folder with an `app.coffee` file with the following code:

```coffee
express = require 'express'
cool = require 'cool-ascii-faces'

app = express()

app.set 'port', (process.env.PORT or 5000)
app.set 'views', __dirname + '/views'
app.set 'view engine', 'jade'

app.use express.static(__dirname + '/public')

app.get '/', (req, res) ->
  faces = []
  times = process.env.TIMES || 5
  faces.push cool() for [0...times]
  res.render 'index', { title: 'Home', faces: faces }

app.listen app.get('port'), ->
  console.log "Node app is running at localhost:" + \
    app.get 'port'
```

This sample provides access to files under `/public` as static files and uses Jade templates found under the `/views` folder. It also provides a root route that renders the `index.jade` view and passes to it an array of funny ASCII faces thanks to the `cool-ascii-faces` Node module.

We use Grunt to compile our CoffeeScript and Less style sheets and prepare them for deployment.

How to do it...

Once the Heroku toolbelt is installed, we will use its `heroku` command-line utility to provision a new application on Heroku.

Deployments to Heroku are performed using the Git source control system. Let's create a new local Git repository for our application. Open a command window and navigate to the project's root directory and enter the following command:

```
> git init
```

Once our Git repository has been created, you can provision a new Heroku application:

```
> heroku create
```

This will display something similar to the following screenshot:

```
[15:41:04] mike:sample2 $ heroku create
Creating boiling-meadow-8438... done, stack is cedar
http://boiling-meadow-8438.herokuapp.com/ | git@heroku.com:boiling-meadow-8438.git
```

When we create a new application on Heroku, we receive the Git endpoint for our new application. In the preceding screenshot, the endpoint is `git@heroku.com:[application-id].git`.

Once we have the Git endpoint, we can add it as a remote repository for our application by typing in the following command:

```
> git remote add heroku git@heroku.com:[application-id].git
```

Now, when we commit changes to our local repository and push them to the `heroku` remote repository, Heroku will perform a deployment for you.

Before we can deploy, we need to let Heroku know how to start our application. We do this by creating a new file called `Procfile`. In this file, add the following line:

```
web: node target/index.js
```

We now have everything in place for our deployment. Let's compile and commit our local changes:

```
> grunt build
```

```
> git add .
```

```
> git commit -m 'Prepped for deployment.'
```

With our changes committed to our local repository, let's push that to Heroku:

```
> git push heroku
```

When we push to Heroku, we see the following output:

```
Fetching repository, done.
Counting objects: 5, done.
Delta compression using up to 4 threads.
Compressing objects: 100% (3/3), done.
Writing objects: 100% (3/3), 299 bytes | 0 bytes/s, done.
Total 3 (delta 2), reused 0 (delta 0)

-----> Node.js app detected
-----> Requested node range:  0.10.x
-----> Resolved node version: 0.10.31
-----> Downloading and installing node
-----> Restoring node_modules directory from cache
-----> Pruning cached dependencies not specified in package.json
       npm WARN package.json cs-book-heroku@0.1.0 No repository field.
       npm WARN package.json cs-book-heroku@0.1.0 No README data
-----> Exporting config vars to environment
-----> Installing dependencies
       npm WARN package.json cs-book-heroku@0.1.0 No repository field.
       npm WARN package.json cs-book-heroku@0.1.0 No README data
-----> Caching node_modules directory for future builds
-----> Cleaning up node-gyp and npm artifacts
-----> Building runtime environment
-----> Discovering process types
       Procfile declares types -> web

-----> Compressing... done, 9.7MB
-----> Launching... done, v5
       http://dry-coast-8382.herokuapp.com/ deployed to Heroku

To git@heroku.com:dry-coast-8382.git
   356a10d..b63a5c5  master -> master
```

With our application deployed, we can open our application with the following command:

```
> heroku open
```

How it works...

Heroku's toolbelt provides some very powerful commands for us to use. Some common commands include the following:

- `addons`: This allows us to manage add-ons available to our application
- `apps`: This allows us to create and destroy applications
- `config`: This allows us to manage our application's configuration variables
- `logs`: This displays logs for an app
- `ps`: This allows us to manage the number of worker processes assigned to our application

Our application displays ASCII art faces in a sidebar. It uses a configuration variable called TIMES to determine how many faces are to be displayed (five by default).

When we run it with the default value, we see an output similar to the following:

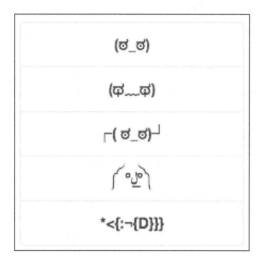

Let's set it to display three faces. In the command window, enter the following:

```
> heroku config:set TIMES=3
```

This produces the following output:

```
[16:44:10] mike:sample git:(master) $ heroku config:set TIMES=3
Setting config vars and restarting dry-coast-8382... done, v11
TIMES: 3
```

Note that updating our application's configuration also causes it to restart.

Without TIMES set to 3, we can refresh our application and see the following:

Deploying our application to Microsoft Azure

Azure is a cloud-hosting platform from Microsoft with support for Node and .NET applications. In this section, we will look at deploying our application to Azure.

If you do not have an Azure account, you can create a free trial and follow along at the Azure website at `https://account.windowsazure.com/signup`.

Azure also allows up to ten free websites to be hosted on their cloud and is accessible to anyone via the World Wide Web. It is a perfect solution to learn the platform and available services.

Getting ready

Like Heroku, Azure offers an easy deployment through Git. Unlike Heroku, we manage applications using the Azure management portal. Let's create a website.

Visit the Azure management portal at `https://manage.windowsazure.com`.

Click on the **New** button at the bottom of the screen, as shown in the following screenshot:

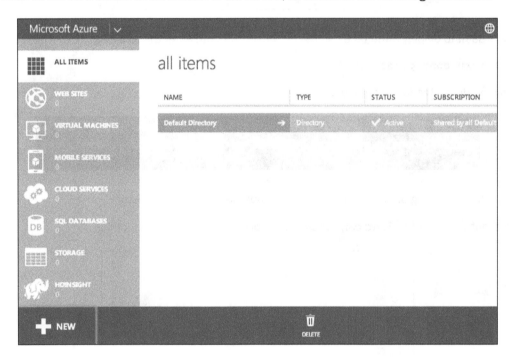

In the **New** dialog, click on **WEB SITES** and then **QUICK CREATE**. This should display the quick create form, as follows:

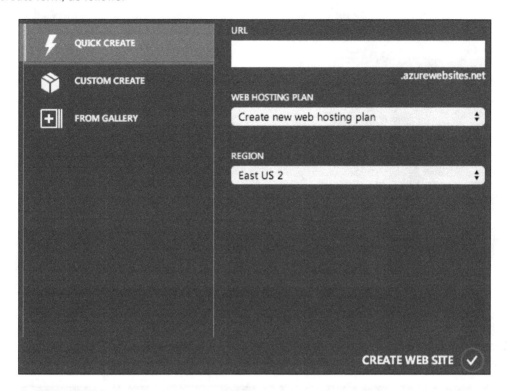

Enter a name for our new website and choose a region. Click on the **CREATE WEB SITE** button at the bottom to continue.

How to do it...

The new website dialog will close and we will see that our website is being created. Once that is completed, click on the website to view its settings.

Here we can view the application's dashboard, configure monitoring, change the configuration, link resources, and manage backups:

Once the website is created, click on the application name (**cs-book** in the previous image). This will display the application dashboard seen in the following screenshot:

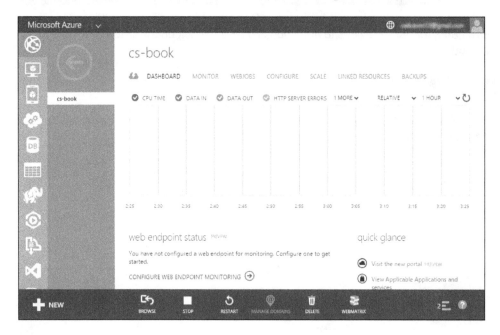

Next, we will configure the ability to deploy our application via pushing our code updates, much in the same we do in the *Deploying our application to Heroku* recipe.

At the bottom-left corner of the dashboard, we see a quick-glance menu. Scroll down and click on the **Set up deployment from source control** link. This will display the following window:

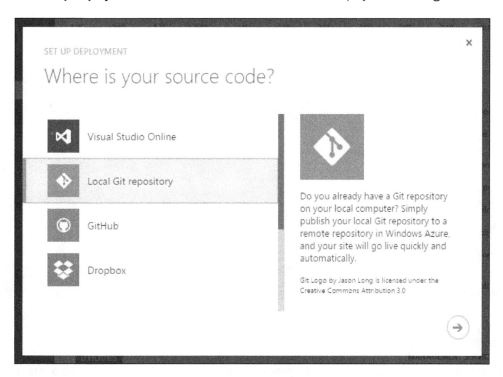

On the next screen, choose **Local Git repository** as our source control location. Click on the next button.

After a few moments, you will see a message that the local repository has been created successfully, as seen in the following screenshot:

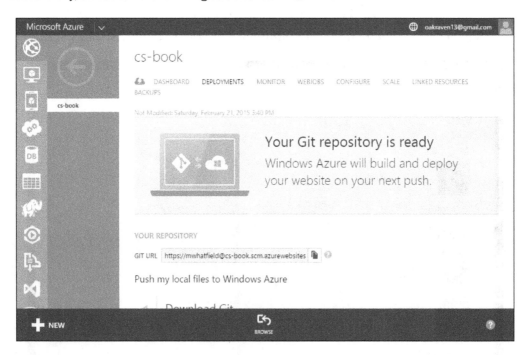

Lastly, we are prompted to create the credentials we want to use when pushing our local repository to Azure.

The last screen has instructions to configure our local repository. Step three is of particular importance, **Add remote Windows Azure repository and push your stuff**, seen in the following screenshot:

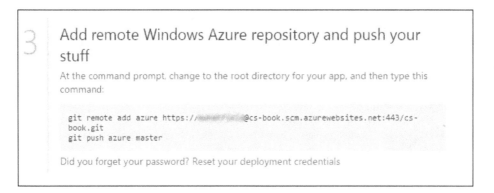

Using these instructions, create a remote branch for the application source.

How it works...

We now have our website created on Azure and the information to configure a `git` remote branch that will allow us to push our application to Azure. Next, we will configure the application for deployment.

Like our Heroku sample, we are going to deploy a simple express application using Jade views and Less style sheets.

We have a Grunt file that will compile our CoffeeScript source files into JavaScript files and our Less style sheets into CSS.

We need to tell Azure how our application is to be launched. We do this in our `package.json` file. Add the following to our `package.json` file:

```
"main": "target/server.js",
"scripts": {
  "start": "node target/server.js"
}
```

This instructs Azure to use the compiled JavaScript file to launch our application.

Next, we can check our changes and push them to Azure:

```
> git push azure master
```

When we push to Azure, we see something similar to the following:

```
Counting objects: 19, done.
Delta compression using up to 4 threads.
Compressing objects: 100% (13/13), done.
Writing objects: 100% (19/19), 3.74 KiB | 0 bytes/s, done.
Total 19 (delta 0), reused 0 (delta 0)
remote: Updating branch 'master'.
remote: Updating submodules.
remote: Preparing deployment for commit id '194f50e106'.
remote: Generating deployment script.
remote: Generating deployment script for node.js Web Site
remote: Generated deployment script files
remote: Running deployment command...
remote: Handling node.js deployment.
remote: KuduSync.NET from: 'D:\home\site\repository' to: 'D:\home\site\
wwwroot'
```

```
remote: Deleting file: 'hostingstart.html'
remote: Copying file: '.gitignore'
remote: Copying file: 'gruntfile.coffee'
remote: Copying file: 'gruntfile.js'
remote: Copying file: 'package.json'
remote: Copying file: 'public\css\style.css'
remote: Copying file: 'src\server.coffee'
remote: Copying file: 'src\css\style.less'
remote: Copying file: 'target\server.js'
remote: Copying file: 'views\index.jade'
remote: Copying file: 'views\layout.jade'
remote: Using start-up script target/server.js from package.json.
remote: Generated web.config.
remote: Node.js versions available on the platform are: 0.6.17, 0.6.20,
0.8.2, 0.8.19, 0.8.26, 0.8.27, 0.8.28, 0.10.5, 0.10.18, 0.10.21, 0.10.24,
0.10.26, 0.10.28, 0.10.29, 0.10.31.
remote: Selected node.js version 0.10.31. Use package.json file to choose
a different version.
remote: Updating iisnode.yml at D:\home\site\wwwroot\target\iisnode.yml
remote: npm WARN package.json cs-book-heroku@0.1.0 No repository field.
remote: npm WARN package.json cs-book-heroku@0.1.0 No README data
remote: ..........
remote: cool-ascii-faces@1.3.3 node_modules\cool-ascii-faces
remote: +-- stream-spigot@3.0.4 (xtend@3.0.0, readable-stream@1.0.31)
remote:
remote: jade@1.6.0 node_modules\jade
remote: +-- character-parser@1.2.0
remote: +-- commander@2.1.0
remote: +-- void-elements@1.0.0
remote: +-- mkdirp@0.5.0 (minimist@0.0.8)
remote: +-- transformers@2.1.0 (promise@2.0.0, css@1.0.8, uglify-
js@2.2.5)
remote: +-- with@3.0.1 (uglify-js@2.4.15)
remote: +-- monocle@1.1.51 (readdirp@0.2.5)
remote: +-- constantinople@2.0.1 (uglify-js@2.4.15)
remote:
```

```
remote: express@3.4.8 node_modules\express
remote: +-- methods@0.1.0
remote: +-- merge-descriptors@0.0.1
remote: +-- range-parser@0.0.4
remote: +-- fresh@0.2.0
remote: +-- cookie-signature@1.0.1
remote: +-- debug@0.8.1
remote: +-- buffer-crc32@0.2.1
remote: +-- cookie@0.1.0
remote: +-- mkdirp@0.3.5
remote: +-- commander@1.3.2 (keypress@0.1.0)
remote: +-- send@0.1.4 (mime@1.2.11)
remote: +-- connect@2.12.0 (uid2@0.0.3, pause@0.0.1, qs@0.6.6, raw-
body@1.1.2, batch@0.5.0, bytes@0.2.1, negotiator@0.3.0, multiparty@2.2.0)
remote: Finished successfully.
remote: Deployment successful.
To https://[username]@cs-book.scm.azurewebsites.net:443/cs-book.git
 * [new branch]      master -> master
```

When we open our browser and navigate to our application, we see it's running as expected, and we see our cool little ASCII art faces:

There's more...

Azure has a number of services, including the following:

- **Cloud services**: Perfect to create highly scalable web APIs
- **SQL databases**: Relational databases built on MS SQL Server
- **Table storage**: Non-relational data store for blob, table, and queue storage
- **Media services**: Cloud-based media service to host on-demand, live streaming, and content protection services
- **Redis cache**: Redis database that is accessible from any application within Microsoft Azure
- **CDN**: Content delivery network service to host static content with high bandwidth and low latency

You can learn about all of these and more from the Microsoft Azure Services site at `http://azure.microsoft.com/en-us/services`.

11
Scripting for DevOps

In this chapter, we will cover the following recipes:

- ▸ Executing shell commands with exec
- ▸ Executing shell commands with spawn
- ▸ Copying, moving, and deleting files and directories
- ▸ Archiving files and directories
- ▸ Parsing CSV files
- ▸ Parsing fixed-width files
- ▸ Padding and aligning output
- ▸ Formatting dates with moment.js
- ▸ Formatting numbers with accounting.js

Introduction

In recent years, IT operations staff has turned to software development to help simplify their day-to-day tasks through scripting and automation. In this chapter, we will look at ways that DevOps can use CoffeeScript to perform some common tasks.

We will begin by demonstrating how we can execute shell commands from our CoffeeScript files using Node's `child_process` library.

We will then see how we can manage our filesystem with our scripts, including copying, moving, deleting, and archiving files and directories.

Next, we will see how we can load and parse **Comma-separated Values** (**CSV**) and fixed-width files.

We will end the chapter by looking at ways we can format date and numeric data that is better suited for human interpretation.

Executing shell commands with exec

Node has a built-in library called `child_process` that allows us to execute shell commands using either the `child_process.exec()` function or the `child_process.spawn()` function.

In this section, you will learn how to execute shell commands using the `exec()` function in Node's `child_process` library.

Getting ready

We will be using the native Node library for this example.

How to do it...

In this example, we will execute the `coffee` command with the `--help` parameter to get the help text displayed by the CoffeeScript executable:

1. Load the `child_process` library and grab its `exec()` function:

   ```
   exec = require('child_process').exec
   ```

2. Execute CoffeeScript's `coffee --help` command, which will display the help text for CoffeeScript:

   ```
   exec 'coffee -help', (error, stdout, stderr) ->
   ```

3. The following result will be displayed:

   ```
   if stdout
     console.log "Received #{stdout.length} bytes."
     console.log stdout

   if stderr
     console.error stderr
   ```

How it works...

The `exec()` function takes a string representing the shell command we wish to execute, including parameters and a callback. The callback receives an error object, a standard output buffer, and a standard error buffer.

If the command fails, for example if the command is not found, the error object will contain information regarding this.

If the command succeeds, `exec` will capture both the output to standard out and to standard error. Both are returned to the callback as buffer instances.

In our example, when we execute this script, we display the length of the output buffer. It tells us that the `coffee --help` command will return 1,193 characters:

```
Usage: coffee [options] path/to/script.coffee -- [args]


If called without options, `coffee` will run your script.


  -b, --bare          compile without a top-level function wrapper
  -c, --compile       compile to JavaScript and save as .js files
  -e, --eval          pass a string from the command line as input
  -h, --help          display this help message
  -i, --interactive   run an interactive CoffeeScript REPL
```

There's more...

We can pass an optional configuration object into the `exec()` function. This configuration object can specify the encoding, timeout period, maximum buffer size, kill signal, current working directory, and environment.

By default, the following options are used:

- `encoding` : 'utf8'
- `timeout` : 0 milliseconds,
- `maxBuffer` : 204,800 bytes (200 KB)
- `killSignal` : 'SIGTERM'
- `cwd` : null
- `env` : null

If a timeout is provided or if the maximum buffer size is reached, the process will be terminated. For example, if we wanted to make sure our CoffeeScript command returns in 5 milliseconds or less, we could call `exec` in the following manner:

```
exec 'coffee --help', { timeout: 5 }, (error, stdout, stderr) ->
```

If you are curious, CoffeeScript did not execute this command in 5 milliseconds or less. Instead, the following error was returned indicating the command was terminated:

```
{ [Error: Command failed: ] killed: true, code: null, signal:
'SIGTERM' }
```

Executing shell commands with spawn

The `spawn()` function of the `child_process` library is very similar to the `exec()` function, except that instead of returning buffers, it returns a stream. Streams are extremely handy for certain circumstances. For example, what if we wanted to take the output of one command and send that as the input for a second command? The `spawn()` function can help with this.

Getting ready

In our example, we will use `spawn` to execute a simple CoffeeScript statement and retrieve the results.

We will be using the native Node library for this example.

How to do it...

In this example, we will demonstrate the use of `spawn()` to execute a CoffeeScript statement:

1. Begin by loading the `child_process` library and grabbing its `spawn()` function:

    ```
    spawn = require('child_process').spawn
    ```

2. Define our CoffeeScript statement:

    ```
    coffeeCode = 'console.log "The answer to life is #{6 * 7}"'
    ```

3. In our example, we want two processes: `echo` and `coffee`. The `echo` process will place our CoffeeScript statement into the `standard out` stream that we will then write to the `coffee` process's `standard in` stream:

    ```
    echo    = spawn 'echo', [coffeeCode]
    coffee  = spawn 'coffee', ['-s']
    ```

4. Add event listeners for the `data` and `close` events:

```
echo.stdout.on 'data', (data) ->
  coffee.stdin.write data

echo.on 'close', (code) ->
  coffee.stdin.end()

coffee.stdout.on 'data', (data) ->
  displayResult data.toString()
```

5. Create a helper function to display the result of the executed CoffeeScript statement:

```
displayResult = (answer) ->
  console.log answer
```

Note that because `stdin.write` is an output stream, we can shorten our `echo.stdout.on 'data'` handler to the following:
`echo.stdout.on 'data', coffee.stdin.write`

How it works...

The `spawn()` function takes two required parameters: the first is the name of the command we want to execute and the second is an array of arguments to be supplied to the command. For example, if we wanted to get a full file listing on Mac or Linux, we can execute the following:

```
spawn 'ls', ['-a', '-1']
```

On Windows, we can run a similar command:

```
spawn 'cmd', ['/C', 'dir /L']
```

Notice however that the `spawn()` function does not take a callback function. This is because the `spawn()` function returns an input, output, and error stream (`stdin`, `stdout`, and `stderr`, respectively).

When working with Node streams, we use events to know when key actions take place.

In our example, we use the `data` event on both the `echo.stdout` and `coffee.stdout` streams.

Our `data` event listeners provide a callback that receives a data value. For the `echo` process, we are interested in the output value, our CoffeeScript statement. When our `echo.stdout` stream receives its data, we write it to the `coffee.stdin` stream using the `stream.write()` function passing out data.

We also add an event listener for the `echo.stdout` event handler's `close` event. This allows us to end the `coffee.stdin` event handler's stream, which will flush any remaining bytes from its stream.

Executing our script, we get the following result on our screen:

The answer to life is 42

However, you may ask, what was the question?

There's more...

Node's streams are very powerful and help us to load and manipulate data from even very large files because we do not need to read the entire buffer into memory.

It turns out that reading from one stream and writing to another as we did in our `echo.stdout` data event handler is a very common stream-related task. Node provides a shortcut for doing just this.

The `stream.pipe()` function will pass bytes being read into a stream into a write stream. To better clarify this, here is our earlier `spawn()` example using pipes:

```coffeescript
spawn = require('child_process').spawn

coffeeCode = 'console.log "The answer to life is #{6 * 7}"'

echo    = spawn 'echo', [coffeeCode]
coffee  = spawn 'coffee', ['-s']

echo.stdout.pipe(coffee.stdin)

coffee.stdout.on 'data', (data) ->
  displayResult data.toString()

displayResult = (answer) ->
  console.log answer
```

Here, we pipe the data from the `echo.stdout` event handler into the `coffee.stdin` event handler. When using the `pipe()` function, we do not need to worry about the `read` or `close` events as the `pipe()` function handles this for us. We continue to use a data event on the `coffee.stdout` function so that we can get its output data and display the results. If we execute this modified script, we achieve the same result.

Copying, moving, and deleting files and directories

Working with files and directories is a very common task. In this recipe, we will see how we can do this using CoffeeScript and Node.

Getting ready

In this recipe, we have a file named `chinook.sqlite` and a directory named `src`. Both are part of the source code from *Chapter 9, Testing Our Applications*, but you can use any file and directory renamed to match this setup.

How to do it...

Node provides the filesystem module to work with files and directories. It allows us to create, open, close, read, write, and rename files and directories. To see how we can perform these tasks, follow these steps:

1. Using Node's filesystem module, we can copy a file by creating read and write streams and piping file contents from one to the other:

   ```
   fs = require 'fs'

   src = 'chinook.sqlite'
   dest = 'chinook2.sqlite'

   # copy from a read stream into a write stream
   fs.createReadStream(src).pipe  fs.createWriteStream(dest)
   ```

2. We can also use the filesystem's `rename()` function to effectively move a file or directory:

   ```
   # rename a file
   fs.rename 'chinook.sqlite', 'chinook2.sqlite', (err) ->
     return console.error(err) if err
   ```

```
      console.log 'success'


  # rename a folder
  fs.rename 'src', 'src2', (err) ->
    return console.error(err) if err
    console.log 'success'
```

3. We can use the `mkdir()` and `rmdir()` functions to create and remove directories, respectively:

```
  # create a folder
  fs.mkdir 'new-dir', (err) ->
    return console.error(err) if err
    console.log 'success'


  # remove a folder
  fs.rmdir 'new-dir', (err) ->
    return console.error(err) if err
    console.log 'success'
```

4. We can use the `unlink()` function to remove a file:

```
  fs.unlink 'chinook3.sqlite', (err) ->
    return console.error(err) if err
    console.log 'unlink: success'
```

How it works...

Though the filesystem functions are helpful, they have their limitations. For example, if we try to remove a non-empty directory, we get a filesystem error as follows:

```
# remove non-empty directory
fs.rmdir 'src', (err) ->
  return console.error(err) if err
  console.log 'rmdir non-empty directory: success'
```

Executing this code produces the following error:

```
{ [Error: ENOTEMPTY, rmdir 'src'] errno: 53, code: 'ENOTEMPTY', path:
'src' }
```

We could create a recursive function that will delete all files and directories inside the directory we wish to remove by doing something like the following:

```
deleteFolderAndContents = (path) ->
  if fs.existsSync path
    fs.readdirSync(path).forEach (file) ->
      currentPath = "#{path}/#{file}"
      if fs.statSync(currentPath).isDirectory()
        deleteFolderAndContents currentPath
      else
        fs.unlinkSync currentPath

  fs.rmdirSync path
```

> Note that by default all of Node's functions are asynchronous. That is usually the desirable behavior. In this case, however, we use the `fs` module's synchronous versions to make sure an action does not proceed until the previous action has completed.

There's more...

This is a lot of work to be able to delete a folder and you might expect there to be an NPM module to make things easier for us. You would be right.

Let's look at the `fs-extra` module. It provides all of the features of Node's `fs` module, but adds a number of very convenient methods to make our file management tasks easier.

Install it with the following command:

```
npm install fs-extra --save
```

What can we do with the `fs-extra` module?

We can copy all files to a path that does not exist as follows:

```
fs = require 'fs-extra'


# copy only js files
fs.copy 'src/js', 'src2/js', '*.js', (err) ->
  return console.error(err) if err
  console.log 'copy: success'
```

In the previous example, we copy only JavaScript files from the `src/js` folder to a `src2/js` directory that does not yet exist. The `fs-extra` module will try to create the necessary directory structure if it does not exist. This is extremely helpful.

We can move files and directories:

```
fs.move 'src2', 'tmp/src3', (err) ->
  return console.error(err) if err
  console.log 'move: success'
```

Here we move the `src2` directory and its contents into a nested directory that does not exist. The `fs-extra` module will create any missing directories if necessary.

We can also remove a folder and all of its contents:

```
fs.remove 'tmp', (err) ->
  return console.error(err) if err
  console.log 'remove: success'
```

In the previous snippet, we simply call the `remove()` function and pass the file or directory we want to remove. In the case of a directory with contents, the directory and contents will be removed.

One last note, you do not need to load both the `fs` and `fs-extra` modules into your script. The `fs-extra` module builds upon the standard `fs` module, giving us the best of both worlds.

Archiving files and directories

In this recipe, we will look at creating archives of our files and directories.

Getting ready

We will be using the `archiver` NPM module. Install it with the following command:

```
npm install archiver --save
```

How to do it...

With the `archiver` module installed, we can use it to create a backup file of our entire workspace tree by following these steps:

1. Load the `fs` and `archiver` modules:

   ```
   fs = require 'fs'
   archiver = require 'archiver'
   ```

2. Create a write stream:

```
output = fs.createWriteStream 'backup.zip'
```

3. Create an instance of a ZIP archive:

```
archive = archiver 'zip'
```

4. Add event handlers to the stream and archive:

```
output.on 'close', ->
  console.log "Total bytes: #{archive.pointer()}"


archive.on 'error', (err) ->
  console.error err
```

5. Set the archive's output pipe to our stream writer:

```
archive.pipe output
```

6. Perform the compression:

```
archive.bulk
  expand: yes
  cwd: 'workspace'
  src: ['**']
  dest: 'src'
archive.finalize()
```

How it works...

We start by requiring the `fs` and `archiver` modules.

We then create a write stream to a file named `backup.zip` using the `createWriteStream()` function of the `fs` module passing in the name of the file we want our output to be written to; `backup.zip` in this case. We assign our new write stream to the variable output.

We then create an instance of the `archiver` module specifying the `zip` compression algorithm. Out of the box, the `archiver` module supports the `zip` compression and `tar` but other compression modules can be used and referenced with the archive's `registerFormat()` function.

On the output stream, we add an event listener for the stream's close event. When the stream closes, we use the archive's `pointer()` function to display the size of the bytes written.

We also add an event listener archive to handle any error events, which we simply display on the console.

We then use the archive's `pipe()` function to set the archive's output stream.

Next, we use the archive's `bulk()` function to specify what file, files, and/or directories we wish to add to our archive.

We pass an object literal to the `bulk()` function. This object represents our file mapping. This is very similar to what we saw in the *Grunt* section of *Chapter 10, Hosting Our Web Applications*. In this example, our mapping contains the following options:

- `expand` : This enables dynamic expansion
- `cwd` : This sets the base path for the files to be included
- `src` : In this option, an array of files and / or paths to be added to our archive based on the `cwd` value
- `dest` : This sets the destination path prefix

Lastly, we call the archive's `finalize()` function. This will lock the queue and finish processing the files. We must call `finalize()` to ensure the archive is fully written and closed.

Parsing CSV files

One of the common tasks we face is the processing of textual data files.

In this recipe, we will parse a CSV-formatted file by using an NPM library that supports reading from an input stream. In our example, we want to parse a contact database collecting customer counts by state. Our goal is to see which states have the most customers.

Getting ready

We will be using the node-csv NPM module. We will begin by installing the module:

```
npm install csv --save
```

If we inspect our sample CSV file, we see the first three lines that follow:

```
"first_name","last_name","company_name","address","city","county","sta
te","zip","phone1","phone2","email","web"
"James","Butt","Benton, John B Jr","6649 N Blue Gum St","New Orlean
s","Orleans","LA",70116,"504-621-8927","504-845-1427","jbutt@gmail.
com","http://www.bentonjohnbjr.com"
"Josephine","Darakjy","Chanay, Jeffrey A Esq","4 B Blue Ridge
Blvd","Brighton","Livingston","MI",48116,"810-292-9388","810-374-
9840","josephine_darakjy@darakjy.org","http://www.chanayjeffreyaes
q.com"
```

As you can see, the first line contains the names for our columns. This will come in handy later.

How to do it...

In this example, we load the contents of a CSV file as a stream and parse the file to perform some calculations and then display the results:

1. Load the `fs` and `csv` modules:

```
fs = require 'fs'
csv = require('csv')
```

2. Declare an array to hold our `countsByState` values and get a CSV parser instance:

```
countsByState = []
parser = csv.parse columns: true
```

3. Add handlers for the parser's `readable` and `end` events:

```
parser.on 'readable', ->
  while record = parser.read()
    addOrIncrement record, countsByState


parser.on 'end', ->
  displayTopResults countsByState
```

4. Define helper methods to add or increment our state counters, calculate the sum of our counts, and display the results:

```
addOrIncrement = (record, countsByState) ->
  items = countsByState.filter (item) -> item.state is
record.state
  if items.length is 1
    items[0].count += 1
  else
    countsByState.push state: record.state, count: 1


sumOfCounts = (array) ->
  sum = 0
  sum += item.count for item in array
  return sum


displayTopResults = (countsByState, n = 5) ->
```

```
sortByDescComparer = (a, b) ->
  if b.count > a.count then return 1
  if a.count > b.count then return -1
  return 0


sorted = countsByState.sort sortByDescComparer


topN = sorted[0...n]


console.log '\nTop Results\n-----------'
for item in topN
  console.log "#{item.state}: #{item.count}"


sumOfTopNCount = sumOfCounts topN
sumOfAll = sumOfCounts countsByState


console.log "\nTop #{n} of #{countsByState.length} states " + \
    "account for #{(sumOfTopNCount / sumOfAll) * 100} %\n"
```

5. Create a read stream to process our CSV file and use the stream's `pipe()` method to send the stream to our parser:

```
# kick off our processing
fs.createReadStream('us-500.csv').pipe(parser)
```

How it works...

In our script, we create an instance of the CSV parser by using the `parse()` method to which we pass an object literal representing our configuration options. Some of the common configuration options include the following:

▶ `delimiter` : This specifies the field delimiter (defaults to comma).

▶ `rowDelimiter` : This specifies the row delimiter. By default, it will inspect the source file to try and determine Unix, Mac, or Windows line endings. It can be one of the following values: `auto`, `unix`, `mac`, `windows`, or `unicode` (defaults to `auto`).

▶ `quote` : This specifies the character used to surround a field (defaults to a double quote).

- columns : This allows us to specify an array of column names or the value of true for auto discovery of fields from the first line of the file. A null value will parse each line as an array of fields; otherwise, each line will be parsed as an object (null by default).

- auto_parse : If set to true, each field will be parsed into their native types (defaults to false).

In our case, we want to automatically parse the columns by name using the first row as the column name. As the file stream is being processed, the node-csv module will raise two events that we are interested in:

- readable : This indicates that a chunk of data is ready to be read from the stream

- end : This indicates that there is no more data to be read and the stream is empty

Our readable event listener executes the parser's read() function that will return one line at a time. When the end of the stream is reached, read() returns null.

Inside our readable handler, each record that is read is parsed automatically by the node-csv parser and is passed to our helper function that aggregates the data.

Our end event listener simply calls our helper function to display the results.

We create three helper methods:

- addOrIncrement() : This method extracts the aggregate information by adding a state if it does not already exist or by incrementing the count if the state has already been added

- sumOfCounts() : This method returns a sum over a collection of aggregates

- displayTopResults() : This method displays the top *N* results

We finish our script by creating a read stream using Node's fs.createReadStream() function with the name of the file we wish to process and then use the stream's pipe() function to send the data into our parser instance. Our readable and end event listeners take it from there.

When we execute this script, we see the following output:

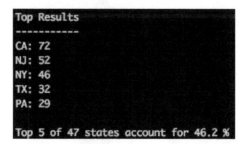

There's more...

The node-csv module is a powerful library to parse CSV data but it does more and includes the following modules:

- ▸ `generate` : This module creates a CSV generator for random CSV data
- ▸ `parse` : This module creates a CSV parser as we saw in our example
- ▸ `transform` : This module creates a process that can be used like a parser but where records can be manipulated and returned as a stream
- ▸ `stringify` : This module creates a process that converts a record or collection back into CSV strings suitable for the output

All four of these modules can work with streams, pipes, or a simple callback mechanism depending on your need.

We may have a scenario in which we have a CSV file and we may need to manipulate a particular field or fields, but we still want a CSV file as a result.

The node-csv package allows us to handle this very eloquently, using pipes:

```
fs = require 'fs'
csv = require 'csv'

parser = csv.parse columns: yes

transformer = csv.transform (data) ->
  data.first_name = data.first_name.toUpperCase()
  data.last_name = data.last_name.toUpperCase()
  return data

stringifier = csv.stringify { header: true, quoted: true }

input = fs.createReadStream 'us-500.csv'
output = fs.createWriteStream 'us-500-upper.csv'

input
  .pipe(parser)
  .pipe(transformer)
  .pipe(stringifier)
  .pipe(output)
```

Here, we create an instance of node-csv's `parse`, `transform`, and `stringify` objects. We use streams for each of these which allow us to pipe the output of one process into the next process in the chain. Effectively, this allows us to:

1. Send our `input` to the `parser` function.

2. Send our parsed values to the `transformer` function.

3. Send our transformed values to the `stringifier` function.

4. Send our stringified values to the `output` stream.

Our `transformer` function receives a data record. It then converts the record's first and last name values to uppercase. The modified record is then returned.

Our `stringifier` function takes an object literal similar to our `parser` function. Here we set two options; we set the header option to `true`, which will output a header row, and set the quoted option to `true`, which will wrap each field in double quotes.

After running this simple script, we have a version of our CSV file with the first and last names in uppercase.

For more information on the node-csv module, you can check out the project home page at `http://csv.adaltas.com`.

Parsing fixed-width files

In this recipe, we will parse a fixed-width file by creating a simple streaming parser. Our sample file will contain fixed-width columns of strings, numbers, dates, and Boolean values of accounting data. Our goal is to count the records and get a total credit and debit amount for all records that have been posted.

Our sample file looks like the following:

```
244   278405  03  02/15/2013  2552213911  WVU ROH ZSVQ            S1   No   ZCVM   Yes        70,435.49               Yes
245   261026  03  02/08/2013  5960631180  PMF ISF                 S1   No          Yes           271.01               Yes
246   261028  03  02/08/2013  1030628918  YPP ALC                 S1   Yes         No                       6,558.82  Yes
247   261022  03  02/08/2013  5906656552  NBV AMY                 S1   Yes         Yes                         66.86  No
248   261030  03  02/08/2013  5343641388  LRX YNR                 S1   Yes         Yes                     12,756.60  Yes
249   271830  03  02/13/2013  1925205129  PXRUSCQJ WE BPYVSZCW    S1   Yes  GNBQ   Yes                     37,721.25  Yes
250   284323  03  02/19/2013  3604245175                          S1   Yes  UFTK   Yes                      2,129.71  Yes
251   278418  03  02/15/2013  3981558828  NFT EWM INZB            S1   Yes  BIHZ   Yes        4,211.50               Yes
252   294648  03  02/25/2013  4248670489  KNRS MW IX JZ           S1   No   GBUW   No                      47,273.40  Yes
253   261032  03  02/08/2013  5970510360  ZXY LEY                 S1   Yes         Yes            15.54               Yes
254   261034  03  02/08/2013  1526941717  JNZ YBA                 S1   No          Yes         4,335.46               No
255   271829  03  02/13/2013  5725612637  FIRNPCBT ZW AEFDXZPP    S1   No   DOVZ   Yes                     51,319.63  Yes
256   284322  03  02/19/2013  5588443229                          S1   Yes  UQBD   Yes                    407,947.96  Yes
```

Getting ready

In this section, we will create our own parser for fixed-width files. When considering the features we would like for our basic parser, it should:

▸   Work with a stream reader to allow parsing very large data files

▸   Use a schema to define our column names, positions, sizes, and data types

▸   Parse data to native types

We will use Node's built-in stream reader to read our data files.

We will create our schema as an array of column objects. Each column has a `name`, starting position (`start`), `size`, and `type`. Supported type values include `string`, `float`, `date`, and `Boolean`.

Because of the variety of date and number formats, we will use two NPM modules to help us process these effectively. We will use moment.js to parse date values and accounting.js to parse floating point numbers, including currencies.

We can install both of these NPM modules using the following commands:

```
npm install moment --save
npm install accounting --save
```

How to do it...

In this example, we will load a fixed-width text file as a stream, parse each line, and calculate some running totals:

1. Load Node's `fs`, `readline`, and `stream` modules along with the `accounting` and `moment` modules we added:

    ```
    fs =         require 'fs'
    readline =   require 'readline'
    stream =     require 'stream'
    accounting = require 'accounting'
    moment =     require 'moment'
    ```

2. Define our column specification. This is an array of object literals that provide the name, starting position, size, and type for each column in our file:

    ```
    spec = [
      { name: 'entry', start: 0, size: 8, type: 'string' }
      { name: 'period', start: 8, size: 4, type: 'string' }
    ```

```
    { name: 'post_date', start: 12, size: 12, type: 'date' }
    { name: 'gl_account', start: 24, size: 13, type: 'string'}
    { name: 'description', start: 37, size: 27, type: 'string' }
    { name: 'source', start: 64, size: 5, type: 'string' }
    { name: 'cash_flow', start: 69, size: 4, type: 'boolean' }
    { name: 'reference', start: 73, size: 10, type: 'string' }
    { name: 'posted', start: 83, size: 5, type: 'boolean' }
    { name: 'debit', start: 88, size: 20, type: 'float' }
    { name: 'credit', start: 108, size: 20, type: 'float' }
    { name: 'allocated', start: 128, size: 4, type: 'boolean' }
]
```

3. Define a configuration object. At this time, we will define the date format found in our file. This will be used by moment.js when parsing any date values:

```
config =
    dateFormat: 'MM/DD/YYYY'
```

4. Define four helper functions responsible to extract field data from a record and handle the conversion to the native types:

```
parseLine = (line) ->
  item = {}

  extractSegment = (field) ->
    value = line.substr(field.start, field.size).trim()
    switch field.type
      when 'float', 'integer' then value = parseNumber value
      when 'date' then value = parseDate value
      when 'boolean' then value = parseBoolean value

    item[field.name] = value

  extractSegment(field) for field in spec

  return item


parseNumber = (value) ->
```

```
        return accounting.parse value


    parseDate = (value) ->
        return moment(value, config.dateFormat).toDate()


    parseBoolean = (value) ->
        return ['true', 'yes', 'on'].indexOf(value.toLowerCase()) >= 0
```

5. Create the counter values. We want to process our data file and do the following:

   ❏ Count the number of records

   ❏ Calculate the total debit and credit amount across all records

   ❏ Determine the earliest and latest posting dates in our dataset:

```
recordCount = 0
totalCredit = 0.00
totalDebit  = 0.00
minPostDate = moment('2100-01-01').toDate()
maxPostDate = moment('1900-01-01').toDate()
```

> Note that we will use the `minPostDate` option to hold the minimum value read from our file. We set it to a very large value so that even the first record we read will be less than our initial value, therefore setting it to the first value.
>
> This is true for the `maxPostDate` option. We set it to a very small value so that the first record read will set the initial value.

6. Create the read stream and use Node's `readline` module. This module allows us to read from an input stream, one line of data at a time:

```
input = fs.createReadStream 'transactions.txt'
rl = readline.createInterface input: input, terminal: no
```

7. Add event listeners for readline's `line` event and the read stream's `end` event. We use the `line` event to parse our line into a record object and accumulate our desired statistics. We use the `end` event as our trigger to display our result summary:

```
rl.on 'line', (line) ->
    record = parseLine line
```

```
    recordCount += 1
    totalDebit += record.debit
    totalCredit += record.credit
    minPostDate = record.post_date if record.post_date <
minPostDate
    maxPostDate = record.post_date if record.post_date >
maxPostDate


  input.on 'end', ->
    console.log "\nBetween " +
      "#{moment(minPostDate).format(config.dateFormat)} and " +
      "#{moment(maxPostDate).format(config.dateFormat)}, " +
      "#{recordCount} records were processed.\n"


    console.log "Total DB:
#{accounting.formatMoney(totalDebit)}"
    console.log "Total CR:
#{accounting.formatMoney(totalCredit)}\n"
```

How it works...

The `parseLine()` function is responsible for converting a line from our file into an object representing the parsed data. This function receives a full record in the form of a string from the file being processed. For each field in the column specification, a helper function named `extractSegment()` is used to extract and parse the data for that field from the line. The `extractSegment()` function takes a field and uses the string's `substr()` method with the field's start and size values to extract the proper sub string from the line. This value is passed to the appropriate type parsing function.

In our `parseNumber()` helper function, we call the `accounting` module's `parse()` method. This is a super flexible method that will parse numbers as the currency, with or without commas, and even localized values.

In our `parseDate()` helper function, we call the `moment` module's constructor function with our date-formatted string and our `dateFormat` string from our `config` object. This tells the `moment` module whether it's month/day/year, day/month/year, and so on. For a date like `02/04/2014`, the order is important.

We create our read stream using the `fs.createReadStream()` function in the same manner we did in the CSV section.

Once we have a read stream, we configure our `readline` instance. We do this by calling the `createInterface()` function. This takes an object with the required `input` and `output` properties, both of which are stream instances. In our case, we do not have an output stream, so we set the output to null. We also set the optional `terminal` property to false. This prevents the output from being written to the terminal screen. By default, the `readline` instance will read from the standard input stream `process.stdin` (a keyboard, for example) and write to the standard output stream `process.stdout` (a terminal window, for example). This is not the behavior we want for our script, so we set `terminal` to no.

Once we have a `readline` instance, we add a listener for the `line` event. The `line` event is raised when the `readline` instance detects an end of line character (\n) and it provides the line to the event handler. In our handler, we parse the line using our `parseLine()` function and use the returned record object then accumulate our summary information.

On our read stream object, we add a listener for the `end` event. This signals us that the read stream is empty and complete. In our handler, we display the results.

When we execute our script, we see the following results:

```
Between 01/02/2013 and 02/26/2013, 382 records were processed.

Total DB: $21,739,353.22
Total CR: $12,740,550.84
```

Padding and aligning output

It is a common requirement to pad our display values to a specified size. This may involve padding to the left, right, or even center values. This is especially useful when generating fixed-width output. In this recipe, we will see how to pad our values by creating a useful, multipurpose padding function.

Getting ready

We will be using the basic tools provided by Node.

We want to create a function that will accept a string value, which will pad it to a specified size (number of characters) with a padding character. It should be able to pad our values to the left or right.

Padding can also provide some alignment functionality. For example, if we pad a value to the right, it will be left aligned, while padding to the left will right align our value.

Let's look at how we can accomplish this.

How to do it...

In this example, we will create a function called `pad()` to perform padding and alignment:

1. Create the function signature. This function will accept a value, a desired size, a padding character, and a padding direction:

   ```
   pad = (size, value, char = ' ', direction = 'left') ->
   ```

   For convenience, we default our padding character to a blank space and our direction to be padded `right` or `left` aligned.

2. Create a string of our padding character equal to the desired length:

   ```
   padding = ''
   padding += char for i in [0...size]
   ```

3. Examine the direction to determine whether we are to pad to the left, right, or both sides (centered):

   ```
   switch direction
     when 'left' then return (value + padding).substr 0, size
     when 'right' then return (padding + value).substr -1 *
   size
     when 'center'
       if value.length > size
         return value.substr(0, size)

       halfPadding = padding.substr(0, (size - value.length) /
   2)
       return (halfPadding + value + padding).substr(0, size)
   ```

4. Define some helper functions that will allow us to perform padding and alignment more easily in our code:

   ```
   padRight = (size, value, char = ' ') ->
     pad size, value, char, 'right'


   padLeft = (size, value, char = ' ') ->
     pad size, value, char, 'left'


   alignCenter = (size, value, char = ' ') ->
     pad size, value, char, 'center'
   ```

5. Export the functions to be used by our programs:

```
module.exports =
  pad: pad
  padRight: padRight
  padLeft: padLeft
  alignLeft: padLeft
  alignRight: padRight
  center: alignCenter
```

Note that we export the padRight() and padLeft() functions twice, effectively giving them each an alignment-related alias.

How it works...

Our pad() function is pretty straightforward. There are still a few interesting areas to be pointed out.

First, we use a comprehension to create a string of our padding character of the size we need. Our comprehension uses the exclusive range syntax [0...size]. This will iterate from 0 up to the number before the size but not include the size. For example, [0...5] will contain the set [0, 1, 2, 3, 4] and won't contain 5.

Next, the string.substr() method can be used with a negative integer. This instructs substr() to return n number of characters from the end. For example, 'CoffeeScript Rocks'.substr(-5) will return 'Rocks'.

Lastly, since we exported our function, we can easily use our padding functions from other scripts.

The following is a small example of how to use our padding / alignment functions:

```
padding = require './padding'


console.log padding.alignLeft('CoffeeScript Rocks', 30, '.')
console.log padding.alignRight('CoffeeScript Rocks', 30, '.')
console.log padding.center('CoffeeScript Rocks', 30, '.')
```

Executing this code will display the following output:

```
CoffeeScript Rocks............

............CoffeeScript Rocks

......CoffeeScript Rocks......
```

Here we can see the phrase `CoffeeScript Rocks` padded to the right (left aligned), padded to the left (right aligned), and center all producing strings that are 30 characters in size.

Formatting dates with moment.js

In this recipe, we will look at how we can format our dates and times for display. There are a number of options to accomplish this, such as using Node's `util.format()` function but we will use a popular date processing library called moment.js.

Getting ready

We will begin by making sure the `moment` NPM module is installed:

```
npm install moment --save
```

How to do it...

In this example, we will demonstrate ways to use moment.js to format dates:

1. Load the moment.js library:

   ```
   moment = require 'moment'
   ```

2. For the sake of our examples, create an object literal to represent a date value:

   ```
   date = year: 2014, month: 11, day: 15, hour: 15
   ```

3. Format dates as strings by using the `format()` function.

   The `format()` function takes a string containing several formatting tokens.

   For example, if we use the string `YYYY-MM-DD HH:mm`:

   ```
   # date as 2014-12-15 15:00

   console.log moment(date).format('YYYY-MM-DD HH:mm')
   ```

   The following will be displayed:

   ```
   2014-12-15 15:00
   ```

Likewise, let's use the string `dddd, MMMM Do [at] h A`:

```
console.log moment(date).format('dddd, MMMM Do [at] h A')
```

This will display the date and time as follows:

```
Monday, December 15th at 3 PM
```

How it works...

The moment.js library supports a very large number of formatting options. The following table lists some of the more common options:

Date / time component	Token	Output
Month	M	1 2 ... 11 12
	MM	01 02 ... 11 12
	MMM	Jan Feb ... Nov Dec
	MMMM	January February ... November December
Day of month	D	1 2 ... 30 31
	DD	01 02 ... 30 31
Day of week	ddd	Sun Mon ... Fri Sat
	dddd	Sunday Monday ... Friday Saturday
Year	YY	70 71 ... 29 30
	YYYY	1970 1971 ... 2029 2030
AM/PM	A	AM PM
	a	am pm
Hour	H	0 1 ... 22 23
	HH	00 01 ... 22 23
	h	1 2 ... 11 12
	hh	01 02 ... 11 12
Minute	m	0 1 ... 58 59
	mm	00 01 ... 58 59
Second	s	0 1 ... 58 59
	ss	00 01 ... 58 59

There's more...

The moment.js library is a very thorough library to parse and display formatted dates and times, and provides a very flexible API.

One aspect that is particularly interesting is moment.js's ability to display localized dates and times.

For example, you can use the localized shortcut of LL to display a date formatted as December 15 2014 for English, 15 décembre 2014 for French, 15 de diciembre de 2014 for Spanish, and 2014年12月15日 for Mandarin.

By default, moment.js picks up the locale of the machine on which it executes. We can easily override the locale by using the `moment.locale()` function passing a string or an array of strings for the locale we desire.

The moment.js library supports more than 80 locales out of the box and allows you to easily define your own locales as well.

For more information on moment.js, check out the project's website at `http://momentjs.com`.

Formatting numbers with accounting.js

The accounting.js module can be used to parse strings into numeric values as we saw earlier in this chapter. It is also very good at preparing numbers for display and provides a number of functions to help with this.

In this recipe, we will look at various methods to display numbers using accounting.js.

Getting ready

Before we begin, let's make sure the accounting.js NPM module is installed:

```
npm install accounting --save
```

How to do it...

In this example, we will demonstrate ways to use accounting.js to format numbers:

1. Load the `accounting` module:

   ```
   accounting = require 'accounting'
   ```

2. Use the `formatMoney()` function:

```
# formatting as currency (default formatting)
console.log accounting.formatMoney 31415.9535
console.log accounting.formatMoney([100, 200, 300])
```

This will produce the following output:

```
$31,415.95
[ '$100.00', '$200.00', '$300.00' ]
```

3. Use the `formatNumber()` function in a similar way:

```
# format as number
console.log accounting.formatNumber 31415.9535
console.log accounting.formatNumber([100, 200, 300])
```

This will produce the following results:

```
31,416
[ '100', '200', '300' ]
```

4. Use the `toFixed()` function to properly round a decimal value to a specified number of digits:

```
# toFixed
console.log accounting.toFixed 31415.9535, 3
```

It will produce the following:

```
31415.954
```

How it works...

The accounting.js library has three general methods to format numbers for display:

- `formatMoney()` : This method formats a number as a currency with a dollar sign, a thousand's separator using a comma, and a precision of two decimal places
- `formatNumber()` : This method formats a number with a thousands separator using a comma and a precision of zero
- `toFixed()` : This method displays a number without a thousands separator and a precision of zero, unless otherwise provided

Both the `formatMoney()` and `formatNumber()` methods accept a single number or an array of numbers. If a single number is used, a single formatted result will be provided. If an array is used, the result, as we can see, is an array of formatted values.

These two functions also accept an optional configuration object. For `formatMoney()`, this object contains the following:

▸ `symbol` : The symbol to be used as the currency symbol (defaults to $)

▸ `decimal` : The character to be used as the decimal point (defaults to .)

▸ `thousand` : This character is to be used as the thousands separator (defaults to ,)

▸ `precision` : This option specifies number of digits to be included after the decimal point (defaults to 2)

▸ `format` : This option specifies a string with `%s` (symbol) and `%v` (value) (defaults to `%s%v`)

For example, the following the `formatMoney()` function calls different configuration options:

```
# format as money with British pound
console.log accounting.formatMoney 31415.9535, { symbol: '£' }


# format as money precision of 3
console.log accounting.formatMoney 31415.9535, { precision: 3 }
```

After running these two `formatMoney()` methods, we see the following:

```
£31,415.95
$31,415.954
```

Similarly, the `formatNumber()` function can take an optional configuration object with one or more of the following properties:

▸ `decimal` : The character to be used as the decimal point (defaults to .)

▸ `thousand` : The character to be used as the thousands separator (defaults to ,)

▸ `precision` : This option specifies number of digits to be included after the decimal point (defaults to 0)

Lastly, let's look at the `toFixed()` function. This function has the default precision of 0, but we can pass our desired precision with our value.

You may wonder why not simply use the `toFixed()` function that is built on top of the numeric prototype.

It turns out that numbers, or more specifically precision, is one of JavaScript's weak areas. The accounting.js `toFixed()` function addresses these precision issues by treating the floating point numbers more like decimal values.

As a case in point, what happens if we use the native `toFixed()` function with the value of 0.615? If we round it to two digits, we should receive 0.62:

```
console.log (0.615).toFixed(2)
```

When we execute this, we receive the following:

```
0.61
```

This is incorrect. With accounting.js, we can do the following:

```
console.log accounting.toFixed 0.615, 2
```

This in fact does produce the expected result as seen here:

```
0.62
```

There's more...

The accounting.js library has another nice formatting function called `formatColumn()`. The format column takes an array of numbers and formats each of them as money with the same length making them ideal to be displayed in a column.

We can see how to do this in the following snippet:

```
# format as money column

console.log accounting.formatColumn([1025, 2500, 300])
```

When this runs, we receive an array of formatted strings:

```
[ '$1,025.00', '$2,500.00', '$  300.00' ]
```

If we were to display these values, we would see them align nicely as shown in the following code:

```
$1,025.00
$2,500.00
$  300.00
```

We can also format these using the same configuration object as the `formatMoney()` function. Let's change the currency symbol to the Euro and add some spacing between the currency symbol and value:

```
options =

  symbol: '€'

  format: '%s %v'
```

```
console.log accounting.formatColumn([1025, 2500, 300], options)
```

This will return an array of the following formatted values:

```
€ 1,025.00
€ 2,500.00
€    300.00
```

For more information on the accounting.js library, you can check out the project's website at `http://openexchangerates.github.io/accounting.js/`.

Index

C

camera, Cordova application
 using 147-151
character casing
 converting 27-29
classes
 defining 55-57
 inheritance, dealing with 57-59
 methods 59-61
 properties 59-61
 working with 55
coffee command-line utility 14
CoffeeScript
 about 10-12
 debugging, Node Inspector used 18, 19
 debugging, source maps used 16-18
 features 2
 REPL 14-16
 style guide, URL 13
collections, Backbone
 creating 87, 88
commands
 about 5
 Coffee: Check Syntax 6
 Coffee: Compile File 6
 Coffee: Run Script 6
Comma-separated Values (CSV) 310
connection
 opening, for CouchDB 191, 192
 opening, for MongoDB 181, 182
contacts, Cordova application
 using 155-158
controllers, Angular
 creating 98-104
Cordova application
 camera, using 147-150
 contacts, using 155-158
 creating 146
 device information, getting 159, 160
 geolocation, using 151-154
CouchDB
 connection, opening 191, 192
 documentation, URL 200
 documents, creating 192, 193
 documents, deleting 196, 197
 documents querying, views used 197-200

 documents, reading 194, 195
 documents, updating 194
 URL 191
 working with 191
counters, Redis
 using 174, 175
credit card checksum
 checking 37-39
CSV files
 auto_parse 323
 columns 323
 delimiter 322
 helper methods 323
 parsing 320-325
 quote 322
 rowDelimiter 322
 URL 325

D

dates
 calculations, performing 40-42
 formatting, moment.js used 333-335
 working with 39
degrees
 and radians, converting between 35, 36
deployments
 preparing, for production 289-295
 preparing, for staging 289-295
device information, Cordova
 getting 159, 160
directives, Angular
 creating 108-110
directories
 archiving 318-320
 copying 315-317
 deleting 315-317
 moving 315-317
documents, CouchDB
 creating 192, 193
 deleting 196, 197
 querying, views used 197-200
 reading 194-196
 updating 194
documents, MongoDB
 deleting 190
 finding 184-187

N

node-csv module
parse 324
stringify 324
transform 324
Node Inspector
used, for debugging CoffeeScript 18, 19
Node.js
URL 3
nodemailer
about 231
e-mail object, parameters 234
URL 232, 234
Node Package Manager (NPM) 2
numbers
bases, converting between 32, 33
credit card checksum, checking 37-39
degrees and radians, converting
between 35, 36
formatting, accounting.js used 335-339
random numbers, generating 34, 35
working with 32

O

output
aligning 330-332
padding 330-333

P

package.json
used, for managing dependencies 210-212
providers, Angular
creating 104-107
purge command
URL 197

Q

queries, SQLite
executing, in parallel versus serial 169, 170
QUnit
URL 267
used, for unit testing 258-267

R

radians
and degrees, converting between 35, 36
random numbers
generating 34, 35
Read Evaluate Print Loop (REPL) 3, 14-16
records, SQLite
inserting 162-164
reading 165-168
updating 162-164
Redis
counters, using 174, 175
hashes, retrieving 175-177
hashes, storing 175, 176
keys, deleting 179, 180
lists, retrieving 177
lists, storing 177
server, connecting to 171, 172
single values, retrieving 172, 173
single values, storing 172, 173
URL 171
working with 171
regular expression
about 23
tester, URL 32
URL 32
using 30-32
visualization tool, URL 32
REST client
URL 226
RESTful web services
creating 210
dependencies managing, package.json
used 210-212
express application, creating 213, 214
web API, creating 215-224
routers
for Angular, creating 110-112
for Backbone, creating 94, 95
rpop function 177
rpush function 177

S

selectors
URL 273

Thank you for buying
CoffeeScript Application Development Cookbook

About Packt Publishing

Packt, pronounced 'packed', published its first book, *Mastering phpMyAdmin for Effective MySQL Management*, in April 2004, and subsequently continued to specialize in publishing highly focused books on specific technologies and solutions.

Our books and publications share the experiences of your fellow IT professionals in adapting and customizing today's systems, applications, and frameworks. Our solution-based books give you the knowledge and power to customize the software and technologies you're using to get the job done. Packt books are more specific and less general than the IT books you have seen in the past. Our unique business model allows us to bring you more focused information, giving you more of what you need to know, and less of what you don't.

Packt is a modern yet unique publishing company that focuses on producing quality, cutting-edge books for communities of developers, administrators, and newbies alike. For more information, please visit our website at www.packtpub.com.

About Packt Open Source

In 2010, Packt launched two new brands, Packt Open Source and Packt Enterprise, in order to continue its focus on specialization. This book is part of the Packt open source brand, home to books published on software built around open source licenses, and offering information to anybody from advanced developers to budding web designers. The Open Source brand also runs Packt's open source Royalty Scheme, by which Packt gives a royalty to each open source project about whose software a book is sold.

Writing for Packt

We welcome all inquiries from people who are interested in authoring. Book proposals should be sent to author@packtpub.com. If your book idea is still at an early stage and you would like to discuss it first before writing a formal book proposal, then please contact us; one of our commissioning editors will get in touch with you.

We're not just looking for published authors; if you have strong technical skills but no writing experience, our experienced editors can help you develop a writing career, or simply get some additional reward for your expertise.

CoffeeScript Programming with jQuery, Rails, and Node.js

ISBN: 978-1-84951-958-8   Paperback: 140 pages

Learn CoffeeScript programming with the three most popular web technologies around

1. Learn CoffeeScript, a small and elegant language that compiles to JavaScript and will make your life as a web developer better.

2. Explore the syntax of the language and see how it improves and enhances JavaScript.

3. Build three example applications in CoffeeScript step by step.

CoffeeScript Application Development

ISBN: 978-1-78216-266-7   Paperback: 258 pages

Write code that is easy to read, effortless to maintain, and even more powerful than JavaScript

1. Learn the ins and outs of the CoffeeScript language, and understand how the transformation happens behind the scenes.

2. Use practical examples to put your new skills to work towards building a functional web application, written entirely in CoffeeScript.

3. Understand the language concepts from short, easy-to-understand examples which can be practised by applying them to your ongoing project.

Please check **www.PacktPub.com** for information on our titles

*   9   7   8   1   7   8   3   2   8   9   6   9   1   *